MW00813450

SOCIAL IDENTITY AND CONFLICT

Social Identity and Conflict
Structures, Dynamics, and Implications

Karina V. Korostelina

SOCIAL IDENTITY AND CONFLICT
Copyright © Karina V. Korostelina, 2007
All rights reserved. No part of this book may be used or reproduced in any
manner whatsoever without written permission except in the case of brief
quotations embodied in critical articles or reviews.

First published in 2007 by
PALGRAVE MACMILLAN™
175 Fifth Avenue, New York, N.Y. 10010 and
Houndmills, Basingstoke, Hampshire, England RG21 6XS.
Companies and representatives throughout the world.

PALGRAVE MACMILLAN is the global academic imprint of the
Palgrave Macmillan division of St. Martin's Press, LLC and of
Palgrave Macmillan Ltd. Macmillan® is a registered trademark in
the United States, United Kingdom and other countries. Palgrave is a
registered trademark in the European Union and other countries.

ISBN-13: 978-1-4039-8375-6
ISBN-10: 1-4039-8375-5

Library of Congress Cataloging-in-Publication Data

Korostelina, K. V. (Karina Valentinovna)
   Social identity and conflict : structures, dynamics, and implications
/ Karina V. Korostelina.
       p. cm.
   Includes bibliographical references and index.
   ISBN 1-4039-8375-5 (alk. paper)
       1. Group identity. 2. Social conflict. 3. Intergroup relations.
4. Conflict management. I. Title.

HM753.K67 2007
303.601—dc22   2006100982

A catalogue record for this book is available from the British Library.

Design by Macmillan India Ltd.

First edition: August 2007

10 9 8 7 6 5 4 3 2 1

Printed in the United States of America.

Transferred to digital printing in 2008.

CONTENTS

LIST OF TABLES

LIST OF FIGURES

ACKNOWLEDGMENTS

Many people have influenced and supported me in my study of the dynamics and structure of the social identity system. Several studies in this book were conducted in collaboration with my colleagues Louk Hagendoorn, Edwin Poppe, and Daniel Druckman. Together with my colleague Daniel Rothbart, we have developed the theory of collective axiology that is partly presented in this book. I am very grateful to them for the dynamic and prolific discussions and inspiring collaboration.

I want to express my gratitude to Samuel Gaertner, Herbert Kelman, Joseph Montville, and my co-fellows of the Fulbright New Century Scholars Program, especially David Brown, James Peacock, Thomas Pettigrew, and Edward Tiryakian, for sharing their ideas about social identity and intergroup conflict, for fruitful suggestions, and for stimulating comments. Several of my Ukrainian colleagues supported and encouraged me during my work: Vladimir Berjanski, Ludmila Karamuska, and Igor Petrov.

This book was also inspired by colleagues at my home institution—the Institute for Conflict Analysis and Resolution (ICAR) at George Mason University. The productive discussions during in-house meetings, academic conferences, and casual conversations have provided a lot of insights into the writing of this book. I am very grateful to my ICAR colleagues and especially to the institute director, Sara Cobb, for encouraging and supporting me in this project. Three ICAR graduate students deserve special thanks for helping me to finalize the manuscript: Kim Toogood, Adam Nester, and Martha Mutisi.

I offer special thanks to the editors of Palgrave Macmillan for their support, professionalism, and efficiency at various stages of this work.

One person in particular has supported and encouraged me through the years of our inspiring friendship, so I would like to express my gratitude to Leila Dane for her professionalism and wonderful personality.

Finally, I would like to thank my family—husband Andrei, daughter Olga, and my parents—for their patience, intellectual and emotional support, encouragement, and belief in my work. I am also grateful to Olga for her design of the book cover.

INTRODUCTION

The idea of this book came to me during consultations for students at the Institute for Conflict Analysis and Resolution. Each of them was planning to study identity conflicts on different levels—community, national, or international—and had diverse research interests. But all of them had exactly the same question: "How I can study social identity?"

I spent hours describing social identity as a complex systemic phenomenon that is characterized by different forms, types, and relationships; I encouraged students to concentrate on one or several aspects of it. As I talked with them, a second question came: "Where I can read about it?"

It was obvious: I had to write a book—a book that would serve as a theoretical and methodological handbook on social identity and identity-based conflicts, a book that brought various conceptions of identity together in one source to act as a guide for those wishing to study social identity.

This book integrates ideas from the fields of philosophy, social psychology, sociology, political, and cultural studies and provides conceptual frameworks and methodological tools for understanding, analyzing, and examining social identities. Using both systemic and synergetic approaches, it presents the conception of a system of social identities, including its structure, development, and dynamics. It does this by describing different types, forms, modes, and levels of social identities, functions, and patterns of group inclusiveness, as well as sources and stages of the identity formation process. It explores the influence of cultural dimensions on the interrelations between personal and social identity and the impact of identity salience on attitudes, stereotypes, and the structures of consciousness. The "Four C" model of identity-based conflicts provides a novel analysis of the patterns through which social identities become salient and dominant. This model offers insight into the development and prevention of violent conflicts.

This book includes examples of social identities and conflicts in several countries, including Argentina, Bosnia, Burma, China, Germany, Hungary, Italy, Japan, Mexico, Pakistan, Russia, Senegal, Thailand, Ukraine, and the

United States. In every chapter, theory is followed by examples of research and methodological tools, including methods of collecting and analyzing data on social identities and identity-based conflicts. Studies were conducted in Crimea, Ukraine, during 1998–2005 using different qualitative and quantitative methods as well as advanced methods of data analysis. This book presents the results of research supported by the MacArthur Foundation, Soros Foundation, United States Institute of Peace, Fulbright program, INTAS, and IREX.

The book consists of four parts. Chapter 1 explores liberal, humanistic, and postmodernist approaches to understanding identity, stressing that social identity provides people with a sense of social protection from the risk of interpersonal opposition and saves them from solitude by establishing boundaries and a common space for a group. The main problem for people in the new millennium is not how to develop an identity and making it accepted by others, but which identity to choose and how to be ready for changes.

Identification is described as an open, evolving process of socialization. This process prompts a person to actively search for one's own personality and strengthens the subjective component in the formation of a self-concept and identity. The chapter describes the functions of this process as well as the different parameters that characterize identity: actuality, salience, and valence.

In this chapter, existing theories of identity are organized into several classes: identity is analyzed as interrelations among individual, group, and society, in the frameworks of intergroup relations and psychodynamic approach, in its interrelation to culture, and as a function of a border between groups.

In approaching identity in this way, one can analyze the merits of these different approaches and methodologies. The systemic approach characterizes identity as a structure with complex interrelations among different subidentities. According to this approach, social identity is understood through the following components: (1) as a part of its class or type, which defines the regularities of its development and functioning; (2) as a system that has specific characteristics; (3) as a set of subsystems that influences its functioning; and (4) by its external interactions in the processes of developing and resolving social conflicts.

The second part of this book describes the system of social identities. In Chapter 2, I outline a new approach to the problem of the relationship between social and personal identity on the basis of an analysis of various cultural dimensions. The dimensions of individualism and collectivism influences the degree of people's dependence on their group, their orientation toward personal or group values and goals, and their readiness for interaction with representatives of other cultures. In individualistic cultures, personal identity is developed as initial and basic. Collectivistic cultures, to a significantly greater extent than individualistic cultures, contribute to the development of group identity and encourage greater possibilities for the manifestation of this identity among members of the society.

Insight into the impact of this cultural dimension on the structure of the identity system requires one to distinguish between belonging to a category and the internalization of this category's meaning. I argue that the prevalence of categorical groups characterizes individualistic culture and the prevalence of membership groups depicts collectivistic cultures. This prevalence is one of the most important factors in the process of identity formation.

Theoretical analysis is followed by empirical studies. Study I identifies the main themes in the narratives of representatives from collectivistic and individualistic cultures. It shows that in collectivistic cultures with predominant social identities, topics such as a close relationship with family, ethnic group, and social recognition along with group support play important roles in the perception, understanding, and interpretation of one's social reality. In individualistic cultures, the most important topics reflect personal growth, personal achievement, and close relationships with partners.

Study II shows that for representatives of collectivistic cultures, strong attachment to an ingroup determines the readiness for conflict behavior, whereas for representatives of individualistic cultures, individual perception of a situation has the strongest impact on the readiness for conflict behavior.

In Chapter 3 several models of social identity are discussed, including the traditional "onion" model, the Four-Component model, the comparative identity model, the crossed categorization model, as well as several models concerning the multiplicity of identity. I present the concept of social identity as an open, unstable system where all identities are interrelated and thus the correlations within the subsystem of core identities are stronger. The progressive development of an identity system is a contradictory process, in which two factors play an important role: (1) asymmetry and (2) feedback. Changes in social environment, the relationship between groups, status, and power, and the supremacy of both ingroups and outgroups can lead to the reorganization of one's identity system, different contradictions, and even an identity crisis. However, core identities can remain even in situations of the destruction or disappearance of respective social groups. Thus, this memory of the identity system potentially leads to a contradiction in the system of personal identities.

Chapter 3 presents the various factors that have an impact on the development of and changes in the salience and meaning of social identities. Two approaches to the study of the functions of social identity are presented: (1) the emphasis on general functions including the motives underlying one's acceptance of social identity (theory of optimal distinctiveness, concept of reduction of uncertainty, theory of perceived interdependence) and (2) the functions that certain social identities fulfill. I describe the following social identity functions in relation to the aforementioned approaches: (1) increasing self-esteem, (2) increasing social status, (3) personal safety, (4) group support and protection, and (5) recognition by ingroup.

Study I, "The Functions of Social Identity," examines the impact of the functions of social identity on its salience. It also puts forth a system for predicting the outbreak of violent identity-based conflicts.

Chapter 4 maintains that identity salience is the most important dimension of identity and that various identities exist for the individual in a hierarchy of salience. It discusses functional and "practice" approaches to salience. To understand the nature of identity salience and its impact on conflict behavior, I analyze identity formation during socialization and acculturation and then propose three factors that determine the salience of various social identities: the level of differences among groups, prevalence of the intergroup or interpersonal contact, and the level of competition among groups. The chapter stresses that the salience of social identity is connected to the *primacy of the ingroup,* which is the extent to which ingroup goals and values are given supremacy over personal ones. The primacy of the ingroup has several components: (1) predominance of ingroup aims over personal aims, (2) the readiness to forget all internal ingroup conflicts in situations of threats to the ingroup, and (3) the readiness to unite against an outgroup. Ingroup primacy can decrease or increase the influence of identity salience on the conflict behavior of ingroup members.

The salience of social identity cannot be used as a single explanatory factor for the impact of social identity on personal perception and behavior. It is also important to study the meanings of identity that are contained in group beliefs, norms, values, goals, and worldviews. I analyze the development of the meaning of social identity through eight defining components. On the basis of the prevalence and composition of different components, I further describe different *modes* of the meaning of identity and introduce the concept of *dominant* identity—a single identity with prevailing narratives of threat.

The chapter stresses the possibility to choose social identity as one of the most important characteristics of social identity in the real world and discusses group and individual ability differences in adopting new identities. It also stresses that an acquired social identity has a greater impact on a person's behavior that an ascribed one.

In this chapter, I discuss three methodological approaches to the classification of social identity: ideographic, component, and taxonomical. On the basis of two dimensions, (1) the form of a person's relationship and (2) the level of involvement in a group, the chapter suggests that social identity has four *types:* positioning, dyad, descriptive, and collective. It also suggests that the content of social identities can vary and reflects different *forms* of social identity (cultural, reflected, and mobilized). It then describes the specificity and dynamic of these forms. Finally, it presents the concept of the *locus of self-esteem,* which depends on the sources of satisfaction with ingroup and pride (internal, based on high confidence, or external, based on favorable comparison between groups), and explains its impact on conflict intentions.

The first three studies explore the impact of identity salience. Study I examines the effect of identity salience on the perceptions of and interactions with outgroup members. It compares people with and without salient social (ethnic) identities. Study II analyzes the structure of consciousness of people with salient and nonsalient ethnic identities by examining the constructs of consciousness reflected in the perception and estimation of other ethnic groups. Study III tests the proposition that people with salient ethnic identities are more similar in values to their ethnic groups than people with nonsalient ethnic identities. It shows that people with salient ethnic identities attribute values to other ethnic groups that are in opposition to the main values of their own ethnic groups.

The next three studies explore the meaning of identity. Study IV analyzes the components of the meaning of ethnic identity: language, history, culture, and religion/ideology. The results show that a shared history is the most important component of the meaning of ethnic identity for representatives of two ethnic groups. Study V examines the meaning of ethnic, national, regional, and Soviet identities for two ethnic groups through an analysis of stereotypes and attitudes connected with each identity. Study VI analyzes the different meanings of social identity by examining the constructs of consciousness associated with each of the social identities.

Chapter 5 shows that the development and disappearance of any social identity results in a reorganization of different levels of the social identity system. The development of a new identity has several forms. I explain that differentiation, integration, and mechanisms of competition are all important characteristics of this development. I explore several factors that influence the formation of a salient identity: the existence of a majority or even the prevalence of people relating to specific social categories, threat or negative attitudes toward the ingroup, a change in the social situation or balance of power, and changes in a person's goals and values.

Cultural changes also have a significant impact on transformations in social identity systems. In the chapter, I analyze the processes of cultural adaptation and its influence on the social identity of a person and explore the dynamics of social identity during several processes: (1) the adaptation of immigrant minority groups within a new society, (b) the adaptation of minority groups in new independent states, and (c) the adaptation of new minority groups after a regime change or revolution.

Study I analyzes the structure of the system of social identities of Crimean Tatars and Russians, showing the main components, interconnections, contradictions, dynamics, and development of identity systems.

The third part of this book explores interrelations between social identity and conflict. Chapter 6 describes two frameworks within which intergroup prejudice has been analyzed: social identity theory and realistic conflict theory. The relationship between the salience of identity and attitudes toward outgroups, as well as the attribution of goals, is discussed. The chapter also examines three components of prejudice and stresses that research findings provide sufficient empirical information about stereotypes and emotions but shed considerably less light on the behavioral component of prejudice. I define *the readiness for conflict with an outgroup* as the willingness and eagerness to defend one's own group in situations of real or perceived threat from other groups, control actions of the members of other groups that can be potentially dangerous or unpleasant for one's own group (or can increase the status of other groups), or take revenge on members of the other groups.

Social identity and feelings of relative deprivation are interconnected and can strengthen each other. Members of an ingroup with a more salient social identity will evaluate an outgroup through standards of ingroup identity and feel more deprived, whereas relative deprivation influences the salience of social identity by increasing ingroup solidarity. This chapter shows that minority groups have more salient social identities and stronger ingroup biases. They are also more socially mobile and ready for transformations. In many situations, ethnic conflicts are connected with the opportunity for minorities to assimilate or with the level of permeability of social borders.

In situations of perceived competition between groups, all actions of outgroups are interpreted in terms of their aggressive motivation and goals and the possible threat to an ingroup. The chapter explores the different contexts of intergroup relations that lead to the perception of the outgroup as a threat. In situations involving a lack of information, ingroup members tend to use their beliefs and stereotypes as a basis for forecasting outgroup behavior and for taking actions against the outgroup.

Chapter 7 presents the "Four C model," which illustrates the four stages of identity-based conflict: comparison, competition, confrontation, and counteraction. It is acknowledged that counterpoised interactive communities can peacefully coexist for centuries, holding multiple and cross-cutting identities. Nevertheless, even in peaceful and cooperative communities, the process of reproducing ingroup identity (e.g., the socialization of children, or accommodation to the changes in intergroup relations) is the basis for the perception of "positive We–negative They." This is influenced by factors such as unfavorable perceptions of an outgroup, the tendency to evaluate the outgroup negatively, relative deprivation or disadvantage, asymmetrical status, and the history of conflict with the outgroup. In situations of competition, perceived or real conflict, a threat strengthens this negative evaluation and influences the attribution of such stereotypes as aggressiveness, anger, and antagonism. The perception of an outgroup as a threat is mostly based on the attribution of negative goals to outgroups through the interpretation of current intergroup relations. Such factors as information failure, credible commitments, and the security dilemma can reshape social identities, provoke identity conflict, and generate situations where individuals tend to choose one identity among others. These dominant identities take the form of a mobilized collective identity and contain ideologies and attributed intentions. In a politicized field of intergroup relations, ingroups position themselves positively as they define the outgroups as opponents or enemies and attribute aggressive intentions to them. Fighting with the outgroup is viewed as necessary for ingroup survival.

Study I explores the impact of ingroup primacy on the readiness for conflict behavior for ingroup members with different levels of social identity salience. Study II shows that both the salience of identity and the attachment to the ingroup's interests contribute to the readiness of ingroup members to fight for their goals; however, the readiness to fight against outgroup goals is only an effect of interest. The salience of identity contributes only to the readiness to fight for ingroup goals and does not influence the readiness to fight against outgroup goals. Study III shows that ingroup identity, ingroup support, and outgroup threat and interests have a significant impact on the readiness to fight for ingroup goals. Nevertheless, the readiness to oppose outgroup goals is connected only with ingroup interests.

The specially designed experimental study IV shows that situational identity, rather than ethnic identity, determines more conflicts. It also discusses several possible interpretations for this effect. Study V concludes that a salient ingroup identity influences the development of attitudes and stereotypes toward foreign conflicts. This also impacts the perceptions of interconnections between situations in one's own region and those in the region of conflict.

Chapter 8 stresses that the movement from colonialism and totalitarianism to political pluralism is connected with the construction of a state and the reshaping of national identities. In addition to contributing to the escalation and the self-perpetuation of identity-based conflicts, national identity building in postcolonial and postcommunist societies may also create superordinate peaceful identities and opportunities for conflict resolution. The chapter describes two approaches to the study of differences between patriotism and nationalism and suggests that a new national identity can embody a different level of development for positive stereotypes of one's own nation (patriotism) and negative stereotypes and attitudes toward the other nations (nationalism). I suggest the following structure of national identity: (1) salience of national identity, (2) satisfaction by fulfillment of its functions, and (3) adoption of a national culture. The chapter describes three different concepts or ideas of national identity: ethnic, multicultural, and civic.

Study I shows that, in some cases, the adoption of a national identity does not create a common meaning or a sense of unity. Rather, some ethnic minorities use loyalty to a nation to accomplish their own goals and receive more benefits. The readiness for conflict behavior can be reinforced if the state provides social and personal security and helps to increase the social status of a given ethnic minority. National identity can reduce this readiness to fight only if ethnic minorities do not hold ethnocentric views and are ready to adopt national identity. Likewise, these ethnic minorities should perceive the state willing and able to provide more opportunities and defend the rights of their ethnic groups.

Study II suggests that the position of a minority within the nation can regulate the impact of ethnic and multicultural concepts on the readiness to fight with other groups. The civic concept of national identity significantly reduces the readiness for conflict among ethnic minorities.

The fourth part represents implications for identity conflict management. Chapter 9 explores various conflict reduction approaches by using the theoretical framework of intergroup contact, realistic conflict, and common identity theories. I introduce a model for resolving identity-based conflicts that includes early warning, conflict analysis, identity management, and conflict resolution. In conclusion, the methods and techniques for the management of identities, including identity-based training, management of multicultural communities, identity reconstruction workshops, and negotiation of national identity, are introduced and discussed.

I joked about my work, calling it "A Cookbook for Identity Studies," because throughout the book, the insights from the theoretical analysis are supported by examples of qualitative and quantitative research. I hope that the book will help students and researchers design their studies of social identity, formulate their research questions and hypotheses, develop innovative models and variables, identify new methods of study, and interpret their results in innovative ways.

THE REGIONAL CONTEXT

The research presented in this book was conducted in Crimea, Ukraine, from 1998 to 2003. Crimea has a tradition of a multiethnic society. For several centuries, this area was one of the most multiethnic regions in Europe. Crimea was a nominally independent khanate of the Ottoman Empire until 1783, when it was annexed by Russia. After the Russian Revolution, Crimea was independent from 1917 to 1918 and then incorporated in the Soviet Union as an autonomous republic of the Russian Federation in 1921 (for additional reading on Crimea, see Bilinsky 1999; Motyl 1992; Sasse 2002; Shevel 2000).

Before World War II, the total population of Crimean Autonomic Soviet Socialist Republic was 1,126,529 people. According to the process of division into districts (zoning) in 1935, the territories with a predominance of certain ethnic groups were isolated into independent administrative units. For instance, in the Alushta, Balaklavsky, Bakhchisaray, Karasubazarsky, Kuibyshev, Sudak, and Yalta regions, the majority of populations included Crimean Tatars, while in the Biyuk-Onlarsk and Telmansky areas Germans were the majority and in the Larindorff and Fraidorff districts Jews were the majority. Finally, 177 Tatar, 130 Russian, 40 German, 32 Jewish, 72 Greek, Armenian, Bulgarian, and other regional self-regulatory bodies were created. Moreover, hundreds of ethnic schools were established, and newspapers and magazines were published in the languages of several ethnic groups.

The Stalinist repressions, which originated in the growing nationalism and chauvinism, caused massive arrests among population. First of all, hundreds of religious buildings of various ethnic groups were destroyed (mosques, temples, synagogues, etc.). As a potential enemy, the German population was subject to repressions, and in 1938 the German national schools, districts, and self-regulatory bodies were liquidated. At the very beginning of the World War II, 50,200 Germans and their families were expelled from their places. In April 1944, after the liberation of Crimea, 2,230 Germans were deported.

On May 18–20, 1944, the deportation of the Crimean Tatars began. According to different data, between 187,859 and 188,626 people were expelled to Uzbek SSR, Mariisk ASSR, and the Gorky, Sverdlovsk, and Kostroma regions. The majority were old people, children, and women. During the deportation, about 80,000 houses, 500,000 cattle, 360,000 square hectares of land, 360 bee gardens, and 40,000 tons of agricultural provisions were confiscated. Simultaneously, all Crimean Tatars were dismissed from the Red Army and sent to special settlements. The total number of the deported Crimean Tatars exceeded 200,000. Along with the Crimean Tatars, 9,620 Armenians, 12,420 Bulgarians, and 15,040 Greeks were deported.

In total, 228,392 people were exiled from Crimea. The living and working conditions in new resettlements were very hard; in the period between 1944 and 1948, 44,878 people (approx. 20% of the total number of deportees) died of starvation, diseases, and acclimatization. The deportation resulted not only in the destruction of the ethnic education system and national culture, but also in the creation of misconceptions about treachery. Deported ethnic groups were considered "second-class" people.

In 1989, the restriction measures regarding the return of all deported ethnic groups from Crimea were nullified. The declaration of the Supreme Council, issued on November 14, 1989, declared the illegal actions taken against deported ethnic groups as criminal activities. Starting in the end of 1980s, the massive return of the Crimean Tatars, Armenians, Germans, Bulgarians, and Greeks changed the ethnic composition of Crimea.

Regional administrations were not ready to solve the problem of the living conditions of people who had returned. There were no legal grounds, specific programs for financial assistance, construction materials, working places, resident registration, and so forth. As a consequence, numerous meetings, pickets, and "self-seizures" of lands took place in different areas.

By the initiative of the Crimean administration between 1987 and 1989, a campaign against Tatars was conducted in the mass media and at working places. The aim of such activities was to "condemn radical activists of Tatar nationality." All these actions resulted in the formation of hostile attitudes towards repatriated civilians. One of the most serious events, which took place in October 1992, was the destruction of a Tatar building and the arrest of 40 Crimean Tatars in the village of Krasny Yar (Alushta district). This incident caused massive Tatar movements—for example, an attempt to capture the building of Crimean Supreme Council.

However, the national Ukrainian government took actions to avoid future interethnic conflicts. One of the most important areas in the national policy of Ukraine was the structure of the assistance for the returning persons. "The Declaration of Nations Rights of Ukraine" (November 1, 1991) established the policies and guaranteed equal rights for all ethnic groups living on the territory of the republic. In order to coordinate all efforts of various regulatory bodies, several institutions were established in Crimea: the Crimean Republican Committee on ethnic groups' affairs, Intergovernmental (Ukrainian-German) Commission of the deported Germans' issues, the Foundation of deported Crimean peoples, and the Board of deported Armenians, Bulgarians, Greeks, and Germans. So, by the middle of 1992, the system of government institutions dealing with the issues of return and accommodation of deported ethnic groups was formed in Crimea. The Ukrainian State Committee on Ethnic Affairs (SConEA) was established in November 1993.

However, the general concept of the state ethnic policy and required legislation were in the developmental stages, so the government's activities in this sphere were inconsistent and compromised. The deported ethnic groups' problems were often considered as regional issues at the local level. The majority of positive resolutions were not implemented, because of the lack of financial resources. For instance, according to the Resolution of the Cabinet of Ministers of Ukraine (N 636, August 11, 1995), 20 million *grivnas* were assigned for necessity of capital constructions for deported civilians; however, the amount of money was not received in full. The budget appropriations on the accommodation of deported people are constantly reduced. For example, in 1995, the financial support for the accommodation of deported peoples decreased 17 times in comparison with 1992, and at the end of the 1990s, the budget for accommodation was further reduced by 30 percent. In 2000, when the project began, more than 11,000 families were waiting for living spaces. Under such conditions, the local government had to build no less than 700,000–800,000 square meters of living spaces. According to SConEA estimations, the development of housing can take 30–35 years, which would prevent the returning of 250,000 people to the Crimean peninsula.

In the 1990s, the population of Crimea was nearly 2.5 million. Ethnic Russians comprised 64 percent of the population, 23 percent were Ukrainians, 10 percent were Crimean Tatars, and 3 percent were Belorussians, Armenians, Greeks, Germans, Jews, and others. Thus, Crimea was the only large-scale administrative-territorial unit of Ukraine where the ethnic majority consisted of the ethnic Russian population. Besides, according to the census of 1989, more than a half of Crimean Ukrainians recognized the Russian language as their native tongue. At the same time, the Crimean Tatars considered Crimea as their only motherland, where they formed as an ethnic group. The Crimean Tatars considered the Russian politics tough and dangerous for the Islamic nations. They view Russians as a threat to their security despite the fact that the Russians inhabiting the peninsula at the end of 1990s were not responsible for the tragedy of the Crimean Tatar people. The denial of ethnic problems at the legislative level, unstable state policy and economy, weak political movements, low mass media impact on the formation of positive image of multicultural Crimea, and absence of special educational programs debilitated the formation of tolerance and ethnic coexistence. Among the subjective factors are the mutual mistrust, biases, and negative images of "other" ethnic groups.

Thus, the Crimea of the 1990s had substantial potential for ethnopolitical violence. The resettlement changed the ethnic balance of the population through the insertion of an ethnically divergent group and resulted in land and property disputes and citizenship claims by the new arrivals. Crimean Tatars received state donations and funds for resettlement. This fact increased negative attitudes among Russians, who also experienced economic deprivation. The Russians increased their irredentist autonomy claims after the collapse of the Soviet Union, even though they had better access to jobs and education than Crimean Tatars. The unraveling of the communist system of the government also posed the challenges of a new political institution building, social reorientation toward the market economy, and the definition of new concepts of post–Cold War national security for Ukraine as a newly independent state.

The process of reintegration of ethnic minorities showed that Russians and Crimean Tatars differed in their conceptions of the legitimacy of their positions in Ukraine (Korostelina 2000a, 2003). The Crimean Tatars consider it legitimate to reclaim their possessions and reestablish a national-territorial autonomy. The Russians aspire toward establishing closer relations with Russia and perceive the Crimean Tatar autonomy as a step toward Crimean incorporation in the Muslim world. Conversely, Crimean Tatars fear that local autonomy will never be granted if Crimea is part of Russia. In addition, Crimean Tatars repeatedly protest the denial of their citizenship rights, access to education, employment, and housing. In May 1999, 20,000 Crimean Tatars joined in protest against these discriminatory practices, which in turn provoked a negative reaction from the ethnic Russian population, which felt threatened.

In the situation of social and economic crisis, the conflict of rights, interests, intentions, and expectations made this region tremendously explosive and required effort for a peaceful solution. Hence, the goals of Russians and Crimean Tatars were incompatible with the formation of a common national identity. The meaning of national identity varied among politicians and peoples, and representatives of ethnic groups had different concepts of national identity. Thus, in the beginning of the twenty-first century, the program of integration and acceptance of a common Ukrainian national identity was still unresolved.

PART I

UNDERSTANDING SOCIAL IDENTITY

CHAPTER 1

SOCIAL IDENTITY AS SOCIAL PHENOMENON AND SCIENTIFIC CONCEPT

1.1. THE CONCEPT OF SOCIAL IDENTITY

Social identity is now considered one of the most popular and controversial concepts in social science. Probably no other social phenomenon has received such intensive and rapt scrutiny from philosophers, psychologists, sociologists, political scientists, and anthropologists. Social identity has become a prism through which the most important aspects of social life are explored and assessed. At the same time, it is one of the most diffuse and loose concepts in social research. As Brubaker and Cooper (2000) recently argued, the term "tends to mean too much (then understood in a strong sense), too little (then understood in a weak sense), or nothing at all (because of its sheer ambiguity)" (1). In this book, I will analyze social identity as a feeling of belonging to a social group, as a strong connection with social category, and as an important part of our mind that affects our social perceptions and behavior.

Research shows that social identity, rather than being primordially intrinsic and inherent, is socially constructed and influenced by the processes of existing social structures. Postmodern theories have radically challenged the traditional conceptions of identity by arguing that the idea of the immutable and invariable person in the liberal humanistic approach is anachronistic and incomplete. Conceptions of the person should be expanded to acknowledge that identity is socially determined and in an evolving state of flux (Butler 1990; Novotny 1998; Young 1997).

Many modern philosophers contend that the new century can be called the "era of identities." Social identity provides individuals with a sense of protection from the risk of interpersonal opposition and saves them from solitude by establishing boundaries and a sense of a common space within a group. As J. Friedman (1999) stresses, in the world of globalization, people have gone from destroying established borders to erecting boundaries in every possible area of social reality.

These boundaries are not created to enclose or protect existing communities, but to develop the possibilities for establishing groups with new social identities. F. Barth (1981) defines social identity as a product of the process of border formation: it is articulated at the boundary and is defined and moderated by the contrast between "them" and "us." It is only *after* the establishment of borders that the myths of a historical past and common ancestry appear, with the new social and political roots of identity thoroughly concealed under the cover of invented stories.

Bauman (1999, 2002) shows that the main problem of an individual at the beginning of the new millennium is not how to develop a chosen identity and have it accepted by others (an important aspect during the era of modernism), but which identity to choose and, subsequently, how to be ready to change this identity if it is ineffective in certain socioeconomic conditions. In his work, he describes identity as an aspect of human experience: "Instead of something obvious and *given* it began to look like something problematic and a *task*" (1999: 29).

A person is not concerned about finding his or her place in a social class, securing that place, or avoiding expulsion from it, but is instead worried that this class or group will change or disappear. Giddens (1991) stressed the active nature of identity in his conception of self-identity. He described the individual self as a "reflected project" (2) characterized by processes of reflection and revision and stressed that identity "has to be routinely created and sustained in the reflective activities of the individual" (52–53).

Despite their changing nature, social identities can be characterized as relatively stable and fixed. As Kellner (1992) stressed, in a postmodern world "there is still a structure of interaction with socially defined and available norms, customs, and expectations, among which one must choose, appropriate and reduce in order to gain identity" (142). In spite of the increasing number of possible social identities that an individual can choose from, he or she still depends on others to develop and perform these identities: identities "available" for individuals are "embedded in coherent and integrative social practices" (Kempny and Jawłowska 2002: 4). Barth (1969) stressed that identity is generated, confirmed, and transformed in the process of interactions between groups and individuals; it is a dialectic between similarity and difference. Social identity is always formed through complex interrelations with other people and reflects their perceptions and behaviors.

In a globalized world, "local" identities, such as regional or ethnic ones, do not arise or exist on the bases of particular groups, spaces, or territories. Globalization transforms these identities in such a way that they become more interconnected, inclusive, and open to the world. At the same time, by eliminating the distinctions between different cultures and regions, globalization provokes strong resistance from small groups and leads to a higher salience. As Kempny and Jawłowska (2002) stress, "Despite globalizational tendencies and boundary blurring, people still persist in maintaining or even highlighting their cultural differences" (10). Even under the pressure to modify the meanings and structures of identities and the boundaries between them, groups tend to develop and strengthen symbolic differences (Cohen 1986). As Melosik and Szkudlarek (1988) point out, the contemporary world is characterized by two tendencies: to diminish differences and their importance for individuals and to reshape strict distinctions.

In the middle of the last century, Erikson (1974) described the problems he found among adults as an "identity crisis." This was the first time this term was used to describe the state of patients who had lost their sense of "I" and time continuity. Identity crises, as Erikson explained, are pathological, and those suffering from them require medical help, particularly during adolescence. From his research, Erikson concluded that the identity of a healthy person provides a sense of self-permanence and continuity.

Today, the concept of an identity crisis is much more significant than a simple pathology or stage of development. The feeling of lack of self-resemblance and permanence is now experienced by a wider array of people in the world. Melosik and Szkudlarek (1998) describe the formation of social identity as a dilemma: by achieving a goal, I lose freedom; by becoming someone, I cease to be myself. The world consists of numerous opportunities for a person, and the acceptance of social identity provides a sense of confidence and stability, leading to a loss of alternate opportunities as identity decisions are made. As Lasch (1979) notes, social identity can be accepted or rejected as if it were a dress or suit, since it is a result of free choice and entails no commitments. Bauman (2002) emphasizes the tendency in the postmodern stage of modernity "to trade off a lot of security in exchange for removing more and more of the constraints cramping the exercise of free choice, which in turn generates the widespread sentiments of fear and anxiety" (28). People strive to overcome fear and uncertainty and therefore adopt a strong social identity. Thus, in reality, the freedom of choice becomes a limitation of options.

E. Hobsbawm (1994) addressed the main paradox of the development of social identity, stressing that in an unstable, indefinite, and mobile world, men and women seek out a group with which they can form strong, everlasting bonds. Social identity becomes a surrogate for society: it serves as a "home" that no longer exists in an individualized world of globalization and is perceived as a comfortable shelter that provides protection and certainty. By affording security and assurance, social identity deprives individuals not only of their freedom of choice but of their individuality as well, determining their behavior on the basis of group norms, goals, and beliefs.

For the study of social sciences, social identity creates a conceptual bridge between individual and social levels of the analysis of social reality. Thus, social identity serves as a link between an individual's psychology and the structures and processes of large social groups. As a result, the term "social identity" is now included in all fields of social science and has become an important part of numerous theoretical conceptions, from psychoanalytical theories to the models of nation building. The field of psychoanalytic studies focuses on the role of social identity in ethnic conflicts and cycles of violence

(Volkan 1997, 2004). Anthropological research has shown the manifestation of social identity in culture, displaying its meaning and its impact on group boundaries (Barth 1969; Cohen 1986). Social psychologists analyze social identity in the process of intergroup relations, prejudice, and group conflicts (Tajfel and Turner 1986; Turner et al. 1987). Sociologists evaluate it to analyze the interrelations between personality and society (Giddens 1991; Jenkins 1996). Political scientists explore its role in domestic and international conflicts (Brubaker 1996; Fisher 1997; Gellner 1994; Gurr 1970).

All these approaches analyze social identity as a dynamic construct that determines interrelations between individual behavior and social reality. Nevertheless, their understandings of the roots and mechanisms of social identity as a phenomenon vary, as do their methodological approaches and interpretations of results. In particular, they highlight the discrepancies in focusing on either cognitive or motivational aspects of social identity, on either intergroup relations or ingroup similarities, and on contradictions in the understanding of the role of identity in social processes.

1.2. IDENTIFICATION AND IDENTITY

The terms "identification" and "identity" are often used interchangeably, as though they characterize the same social phenomenon. In this study, I consider identity and identification accordingly as a state and a process that leads to this state.

The term "identification" first appeared in 1914 in Sigmund Freud's *Group Psychology and Analysis of Ego* (1959). Freud defined it as an unconscious connection between child and parent and as a mechanism of interaction between individuals and social groups. He considered identification with a group leader as the basis for group formation and as one of the latent forms of the Oedipus complex. Now, most scholars analyze identification as a mechanism of individual socialization that influences the formation of an individual's consciousness.

Identification is a permanent, incomplete, and open process of socialization that prompts one to search actively and independently for one's own personality and strengthens the subjective component in the formation of self-conception. This identification process is determined by culture and social reality. Thus, identification has both emotional and cognitive components. The emotional component usually develops during the first stage of a positive relationship or as a result of positive feelings. The cognitive component is based on emotional connections that lead to an acceptance of values, beliefs, attitudes, and worldviews. As soon as a person recognizes similarities in perception and evaluation of the world with other group members, he or she feels a stronger positive emotional connection with the group.

Thus, identification fulfills two main functions: (1) realization of the individual need to belong to a group that provides protection and confidence and (2) inclusion of a person into a system of social relationships. Several types of groups serve as objects of identification:

1. primary groups (family, friends);
2. "primordial" groups (ethnic, religious);
3. socially constructed groups (nation, political party);
4. contact groups (colleagues, mates, associates);
5. symbolic groups (generation).

An individual's ability to control the processes of identification can vary. In some situations a person can have an impact on the mechanisms and outcomes of identification, but in most of the cases he or she does not have control over the processes. The early processes of identification are more difficult to control. For example, identification with the family is mostly an uncontrolled development period in which a person accepts the rules, principles, traditions, and values of the family as a social group. Even by opposing or conflicting with the family, a person follows already adopted behavioral models. As Ackerman (1970) stresses, identification with the family includes involvement in the family's expectations, aspirations, anxiety, gladness, and joys.

The feeling and understanding of "we-ness" is a result of social identification processes. This feeling of identity cements a group as a social aggregate and leads to common forms of thinking and behavior. An individual's emerging social identity can be maintained, changed, or reconceptualized in the process of social interaction. The history and culture of a society determine social identity; however, people with specific identities are active builders and developers of history and culture. This reciprocity serves as a mechanism in the reproduction and reconstruction of social identities. Social identity is also a positively internalized self-image that shows how individuals perceive themselves through social relations. It provides a feeling of adequacy and stability regarding changes in the social world and grants the individual the ability to make sufficient decisions in complex social situations.

Several parameters characterize identity, such as actuality, salience, and valence. The actuality of identity has two meanings. Some scholars analyze it as the most obvious specific category for an individual. Usually, actuality is measured by first asking an individual, "Who are you?" and then listing different categories (usually five) that best characterize him or her. The criterion of actuality in this context is determined by the presence or absence of a social category. If a person mentions this category among the five answers, this identity is considered actual for him or her. Other researchers stress the importance of intergroup relations. In their opinion, the actuality of social identity must be analyzed through a comparative study of these categories within different groups. In this context, the emphasis is put on the relative actuality of social identity. These two approaches can be applied simultaneously and complement each other.

Several factors influence the actuality of social identity, including inter-group or categorical context. Identity becomes actual only in the process of comparing an ingroup with an outgroup or a specific category. In this case, the main feature of the group or category determines the actuality of the complemented identity. Thus, when one interacts with people from another ethnic group, ethnic identity becomes actual. If one is going to another country, the actuality of one's national identity increases. Women in groups where men prevail have actual gender identities, and men in groups where women prevail also develop actual gender identities. The stronger the difference between complemented categories, the higher the actuality of a particular identity becomes. Another factor that strengthens the actuality is threat (real or perceived) or conflict between groups. If members of an out-group pose a threat to the ingroup or offend and insult its members or the ingroup itself (including its values and beliefs), the actuality of the ingroup identity rises immediately. Existing, open, or latent conflicts between groups also strengthen the actuality of social identity.

The second characteristic of identity is salience. Disputes exist over the different approaches to understanding salience; however, most scholars agree that salient identity is the most important identity for an individual. One's salient identity characterizes one's core position within other identities and does not depend on the situations of intergroup relations. It influences one's thinking and behavior even in situations lacking an opposing category or identity.

I will later analyze the salience of identity in detail, but it is important to stress the problem of the interrelation between actuality and salience. Most authors use them as interchangeable terms or do not make distinc-tions between them. But some scholars point out important differences. Thus, Hutnik (1986) analyzes actuality as a level of awareness and salience as a measure of centrality. In my opinion the actuality of identity represents the reflection and understanding of social context and is determined by the specificity of intergroup relations. The salience of social identity is character-ized by both the level of awareness and the centrality among other identities. Therefore, the social identity can be actual but not salient (e.g., regional identity, which is not important for an individual, may become manifested during travel to another region), but salient identity is always actual for an individual. As I will later discuss, if social identity remains actual for a long time, it can become central and salient.

The third characteristic is valence, which shows the positive or negative connotations of a particular identity. Since social identity provides a person with security, self-esteem, and a degree of certainty, it has a positive valence in most cases. But some research shows that it can also be negative (Clark and Clark 1939). People with negative valence of their ethnic or racial identity tend to make friends with members of other ethnic groups. The relationship between the salience and the valence of identity was analyzed in several research programs, with the results showing that in most cases, salient social identities are connected with positive valence.

1.3. Theoretical Approaches to Social Identity

The last several decades have seen a rise in the study of social identity as a concept in the understanding of social processes. Social identity has been and is still used for the analysis of sociopsychological phenomena on a number of different levels, including individual, group, cultural, and societal. To make a short overview of the theories of social identity, it is useful to combine them into groups of disciplines and thought (see, e.g., Huddy 2001; Deaux 1996).

Social Identity as Interrelations between Individual, Group, and Society

Social Identity as a Membership
This group of theories (Reid and Deaux 1996; Rosenberg and Gara 1985) analyzes social identity as part of individual self-conception and of the self that has been influenced by membership in a specific social group or category, and as a set of shared behaviors and socialization. A person will internalize his or her membership in this group and will perceive it as a part of his or her own personality. The meaning of this identity can be found in the answer to the question "Who am I as X?" where X is the group or social category. This meaning is often used in the study of socialization and internalization processes. Research in the framework of this paradigm applies this theory to the development of gender-based identity (Skevington and Baker 1989), ethnic and racial identity (Cross 1991; Phinney 1990), and cultural identity (Ferdman 1995).

Social Identity as a Role
Sociological theories of role interaction stress the importance of the structure of one's social system, which includes functional roles, status positions, and the interrelations between the two. According to this approach, a social group is a set of individuals who interact by accepting different interconnected roles. Individuals have different social identities depending on their roles and positions within a group. In this context, social identities can be considered internalized rules, expectations, and norms connected to specific social roles. By accepting a social role, a person puts himself or herself in a specific position in relation to others and in relation to the social system as a whole. Thus, role identity is also a type of self-identity, because it reflects different types of personalities.

In contrast with personal social identity, role identity is defined in the process of interaction with others within a broad intergroup context (Stryker, Owens, and White 2000). This understanding of social identity is close to the concept of the "interconnected self" developed by Markus and Kitayama (1991) in their analysis of cultural differences during the processes of personal development. Role identities include, but are not limited to, professional (doctor-patient, teacher-scholar), familial (parent-child, husband-wife), and attraction-based (friendship and love) relationships. This identity can also reflect the interpersonal relations between individuals such as colleagues and club or community members.

Role identities are interconnected because one person's behavior influences, and depends on, other people's behavior. Every role, even stable and fixed, has to take into account the features, needs, and skills of the other people who are involved in complementary roles. Therefore, role identities reflect the influence of social norms and expectations on a person, along with the influence of social roles and intergroup relations on the person's self-conception. Jenkins (1996) posits that categorization and the attribution of a specific category to a person form the basis of identity. It is important who attributes this category, how important or prestigious he or she is to the person, how other people react to this attribution, and how long this category has been in use. Jenkins describes two types of social identity: nominal, which indicates a name or title; and virtual, which characterizes the real embodiment of identity. Nominal identity reflects the external part of identity, while virtual identity exhibits its content. People can have similar nominal identities, with very different meanings reflected in their virtual identities. As a result, their behaviors will be diverse. Changes in nominal identity can produce changes in virtual identity, and there is the possibility of a reverse process. The dialectic relations of nominal and virtual identity, Jenkins stresses, reflect the interactions between internal and external in the process of psychic functioning.

On the basis of Barth's work (1981), Jenkins emphasizes that an ethnic group can remain even if its group members change their social identity. The preservation of group boundaries in interethnic relations provides this stability. The intergroup differences strengthen the perception of ingroup similarity. Jenkins describes ingroup similarity as a social construct that symbolically exists in the lives of group members and can influence their behaviors. It develops on the basis of symbols and exists in languages, rituals, and dresses, creating the content of nominal identity. Real features of behavior in groups are individualized and reflect the content of virtual identity.

Collective Social Identity

While social identity influences the perception and assessment of a situation, this theory of social identity emphasizes the processes related to the formation of social identity, but pays less attention to the content of a specific social identity. Thus, it is important to distinguish social identity as a result of identification with a group from collective identity, the sets of norms, values, and ideology that this identity contains. The term "collective identity" is connected with the study of social movements in sociological literature (Klandermans 1997; Taylor and Whittier 1992). The concept of collective identity not only includes shared experiences, attitudes, beliefs, and interests of ingroup members, but is also connected with the processes of actively creating group images, goals, and ideas of self-representation.

Thus, collective identity can be described through the achievement of a collective aim for which this group has been created. In this context, the term "collective identity" determines the interconnection between social identity (on individual and group levels) and collective actions in the political arena (Gamson 1992).

Social Identity and Intergroup Relations

Social Identity Theory and Categorization Theory
Sociopsychological theories of social identity analyze the structure of social systems by putting emphasis on intergroup relations and categorical distinctions (Tajfel and Turner 1986; Turner et al. 1987). This approach considers social groups to be communities of people who share common characteristics, social experiences, and behaviors. Social identity, in this context, is a result of the processes of identification with other group members. All group members have similar social identities, beliefs, and attitudes. While personal social identities reflect the level of presentation of group or categorical membership in personal self-conception, group social identity is connected with the perception of a person as an integral part of a social group.

The theory of social identity was developed on the basis of experiments with simple social categorizations. The experiments showed that different bases for categorization—the color of one's eyes, appreciation of the art of Kandinsky and Klee, nominations for observers and students—provided sufficient conditions for the development of intergroup favoritism and intergroup prejudice and discrimination (Allen and Wilder 1975; Billig and Tajfel 1973; Brewer and Silver 1978; Doise and Sinclair 1973; Tajfel et al. 1971). Experimental situations have demonstrated that under certain conditions, minimal intergroups (in which groups are defined only by name) can be formed even without any other criteria for affiliation. During this research, participants considered that they were divided into groups only for the convenience of experimental procedures; they did not have contact with one another, nor did they have any reasons to believe in the similarity of interests and attitudes among members of their group. The results of these experiments showed the effect of ingroup favoritism. It appeared that the simple categorization connected with the introduction of a new social category was sufficient for the development of the positive estimation and support of group members. These results became the basis for the development of a new framework for social categorization: social identity.

The theory of social identity (Tajfel 1978, Tajfel and Turner 1986) stresses that together with personal identity, an individual has a social identity that is reflected in his or her membership in different groups. This identity is an important part of self-conception and influences the individual's perception of himself or herself and of society as a whole. Social identity is developed through the affiliation of individuals to different groups, along with a determination of their position in society. Individuals perceive themselves as members of a group and identify themselves with it in order to distinguish between their groups (ingroups) and outgroups.

People with similar social positions and common histories have comparable social identities. Therefore, social identity is connected not only with the perception of similarities within an ingroup (common history, attitudes, values, etc) but also with the perception of differences between this group and the members of other groups or categories. The more salient social identities are, the more people differentiate their groups from those of others.

The theory of social identity stresses the importance of two aspects: cognitive and emotional. According to Tajfel and Turner (1986), social identity is "that part of an individual's self-concept which derives from his knowledge of his membership in a social group (or groups) together with the value and emotional significance attached to that membership" (255). The cognitive basis of social identity is the process of social categorization and intergroup comparison. Therefore, the cognitive component is connected with the emotional one, which reflects such feelings of belonging to a group as love, hate, amity, and enmity. This cognitive-emotional involvement strengthens a person's social identity. One of the most important ideas of the theory is the need for positive social identity, which can be achieved in the comparison among groups with positive overestimation of their ingroups, otherwise known as the phenomenon of ingroup favoritism.

Turner et al. (1987) further developed the conception of group identity in the theory of social categorization, in which they posited that "depersonalized" meaning has led to a change in perception: a person is now viewed not as a unique unit but as part of a system of interchangeable social identities. This identity, characterized as collective or "we" identity, is a result of a person's identification with the group as a whole. Group identity develops not as a result of interpersonal relations between members of a group, but as a product of a common, shared membership in this group. Individuals categorize themselves as members of social categories, perceiving and estimating themselves in terms of these categories. Since people belong to a number of groups, they have multiple presentations of their selves.

The theory of categorization describes group processes in terms of the functions of self-conceptions and stresses group process influence on self-categorization, perception, and learning. Personal and social identities are explained as different levels of self-categorization. Personal identity is connected with categories of self that describe an individual as uniquely different from other people (within ingroups). Social identity is connected with social categorizations of "us" and "others," categories of self that define the individual in terms of a shared similarity with the members of a specific social category in contrast to other social categories (we against them, ingroup against outgroup, men and women, ethnic and racial groups, etc.). This theory suggests that when we think and perceive ourselves as "we" and "us," we define ourselves in terms of "others" who exist outside our personality. Social identity cannot be reduced to personal identity and analyzed in the theory of categorization as "social collectivity." We can identify ourselves with various categories that have different levels of comparison and diverse subjective meanings of self.

Group social identity has complex interrelations with self-conception. First, when social identity develops, a person acquires new social features. The boundaries between the self and other members of a group weaken in comparison with new boundaries between ingroup and outgroup. The victories and defeats of a group become part of a person and influence his or her perception and estimation of the world. Second, the person's attitudes, beliefs, and behavior become part of a group and influence the differentiation from other groups, thus strengthening unity and solidarity within the ingroup.

According to social categorization theory, the processes of identification have three stages. During the first stage, individuals define themselves as members of a social group; in the second, they learn the stereotypes and norms of the group; and in the third, group categories influence the perception and understanding of all situations in a particular context. Salient social identity leads to an individual's depersonalization. This process strengthens the perception of similarities with the other members of the ingroup and of differences from the members of outgroups and decreases personal differentiation from other people. This theory demonstrates that the "collective self" explains most group phenomena and why individual interests do not play an important role in group dynamics.

This theory interprets differentiation as a process of interaction between the "readiness" of a person to use particular categories, the "conformity" between these categories, and the real stimulus that represents these categories (Oakes 1987). Categorization is described as a dynamic process that depends on the context of situations and is influenced by the multitude of interrelations within this context (Oakes, Haslam, and Turner 1998). The principle of *metacontrast* stresses that differences within an ingroup are smaller than those between ingroup and outgroup. This principle describes the formation of categories on the basis of intergroup similarities and intergroup differences and shows that they are not independent, but are parts of the process of categorization. Metacontrast helps to analyze intergroup differences by comparing them with ingroup ones. It creates a sense of cognitive clarity that leads to perceptions of the world in different categories.

The group prototype serves an emotional function (Hogg 1992). According to the categorization theory, people identify themselves with a group on the basis of similarity with the ingroup prototype. When autostereotyping occurs, the ingroup becomes important for the individual because the individual turns out to be strongly interconnected with other ingroup members. As Hogg (1992) stresses, the main conclusion is that identity results from unity among ingroup members and ingroup relations, but also is a product of positive attitudes toward the prototype.

The theory of categorization stresses two main sources for instability of identity: ingroup cohesion and changes in the group prototype. As research shows, in relevant contexts the perception of differences within the group is less significant than the estimation of differences between the groups. The effect of an outgroup's homogeneity contributes to the perception and evaluation of the outgroup as more homogenous in comparison with the ingroup. This assessment of categorization (as variant and dependent on context) leads to the understanding of similarities and differences as contingent on situations of comparison. People who can be perceived as different in one context (e.g., a cardiologist and pediatrician in a hospital) will seem more similar in another situation (e.g., in comparison with a physicist), without any changes in their position. In the process of categorization, differences turn into similarities, and vice versa.

Thus, three basic elements are central for the theories of social identity and social categorization: the existence of category, identification with it, and the processes of social comparisons. The first can be described as a "label"; the second is intimately connected with the acceptance of the category on emotional, cognitive, and behavioral levels; while the third is reflected in the positive estimation of an ingroup.

Activity Approach for Social Identity

This approach was developed in the framework of activity psychology (Leont'ev 1978, 1982; Vygotsky 1978, 1989). It emphasizes objective conditions that connect social groups with the structure of intergroup activity. The theory of social categorization analyzed some aspects of intergroup activity, such as status differences between groups, minority-majority relations, and forms of organization among intergroup interaction (competition and cooperation). However, in comparison with cognitive-oriented theories, the activity approach stresses that social categorization of group members can act as a mediator for the impact of objective situation on social behavior. In their research, Ageev (1990), Ageev and Tolmasova (2000), and Yadov (1993, 1995) show several determinants of intergroup interaction that have an impact on social identity: goals and criteria of the estimation of intergroup relations, levels of the dependency of an individual on a group, and the successes and failures of ingroup activity.

One of the most important problems of studying social identity in the activity approach is related to the interrelations between consciousness and unconsciousness. Social identity is analyzed as interrelations among different self-images in the structure of internalized roles in society and as an ideal representation of a person's position in the social world in the quest for self-meaning. Depending on the perception and assessment of social situations and conditions of activity, a person can have different levels of awareness about his or her social identity. Situational identity is characterized by the absence of integration with personal meanings and values and by the lack of understanding of social position. On the other hand, transsituational identity reflects the significance of social relations and is integrated in a person's disposition. Situational identity can become transsituational through an increasing awareness and acceptance by the person. Unconscious social identity is not integrated with the meanings and values of a person and does not fulfill connotation function. One's awareness of social identity depends on one's relationship with society and on one's attitudes and disposition. Only deliberate social identity provides personal meaning for practice and activity. In this context, social identity is composed of the accepted social meanings and the understanding of a person's role in society. It is evident that the development of one's social identity influences the formation of individual worldviews and one's role in this world.

Therefore, one may not have a social identity

Psychodynamic Approach to Social Identity

The most important representative of the psychodynamic approach to social identity, Vamik Volkan (1988, 1997, 2004, 2006), described large group identity as "tens of thousands, or millions, of people—most of whom will never meet one another in their life times—sharing a permanent sense of sameness" (2006: 15). This theory tries to explain how group identity is adopted by individuals and can prevail over individual identity, describes the dynamics and structure of group identity, and shows how it contributes to the development of intergroup conflict.

As Volkan stresses, individual identity can be perceived as a garment that belongs only to the individual who wears it and that, among other things, protects him or her from the harmful effects of the environment. But every individual who belongs to an ethnic group (or any basic identity group for that matter) also has a group identity, or "we-ness." Group identity is like a "large canvas tent" that protects individuals as if they were family members (Volkan 1997: 27). As long as the tent remains strong and stable, held erect by the leader, the members of the group do not pay much attention to it—that is, they do not have the need to constantly prove or express their ethnic identity. If the tent is shaken or disturbed, however, those who are under it will become collectively preoccupied with trying "to shore it up" again. The group identity supersedes individual identities and becomes a matter of major concern (Volkan 1996).

The main components of Volkan's theory of group identity are (1) chosen traumas and glories, (2) shared reservoirs, (3) minor differences, (4) differentiation and integration, and (5) projection.

The development and preservation of group identity require strong internal components that show the main content of group identity and the specificity of intergroup relations. Volkan describes these as *chosen glories* (important, usually mythologized and idealized achievements that took place in the past) and *chosen traumas* (losses, defeats, humiliations—also mythologized—that are usually difficult to mourn). They are "a shared mental representation of the event, which includes realistic information, fantasized expectations, intense feelings, and defense against unacceptable thoughts" (Volkan 1997: 48). They help individuals to unite around powerful ideas of group gains and losses. Volkan describes them as events evident to ingroup, but I consider that they are usually real events from the history of the group but do not always have actual historical significance. They are chosen because of the current state of relations with other groups and provide "explanations" for poor economic conditions or minority status.

These ideas of glories and traumas are linked to real or symbolic objects: *suitable targets of externalization* (STEs) (or shared reservoirs), determined either by culture (familiar objects of a child's environment) or by parents and other adults. STEs are such symbols as flags, songs, special dishes, places of worship, religious icons, memorials, certain animals, people, and groups of people (Volkan 1997). Positive STEs, or reservoirs of good representations, are associated with decent and trusted people such as parents, friends, leaders, and allies. Negative STEs, or reservoirs of bad representations, are associated with terrible memories, threats, and enemies. STEs tie people together, unite groups, and transfer meaning to new generations.

Members of a group do not always integrate positive and negative STEs in their group image. Most of the time they use negative STEs to describe other groups and positive STEs to portray their own group. In this case, the integration of positive and negative and pleasant and unpleasant in the group image is not complete. As a child wants to "rid himself of unintegrated 'bad' aspects of his world" (Volkan 1997: 90), groups try to project negative images onto other groups. Minorities can easily become suitable targets for the externalization (or projection) of the negative feelings and images of majorities (Volkan 1988). Volkan stresses the human tendency to split away and externalize the negative aspects of oneself—the dimensions one wishes not to acknowledge, or for which one will not or cannot take responsibility.

If the real or psychological borders between groups are not clear and groups share similar characteristics, behaviors, and beliefs, the group identity can be at risk. To be able to protect the uniqueness of the group and project negative images onto other groups, people have to stress minor differences between groups. Such differences are reinforced by enemy images and dehumanization of the members of other groups. These perceptions and intentions can lead to the policies of "ethnic cleansing," massacres, and genocides.

Social Identity and Culture

The concepts of identity and culture in anthropology intersected until the 1960s, when identity was understood as based not on real but on socially sanctioned notions of cultural differences. "While ethnic identity should be taken to refer to a notion of shared ancestry (a kind of fictive kinship), culture refers to shared representations, norms, and practices" (Eriksen 2001: 43). The theory of self-formation (Holland and Lave 2001; Holland et al. 1998) helps resolve the recent debate in anthropology by stating that *identity* replaces culture as the major concept of the field. Authors examine the processes by which people are constituted as agents as well as subjects of culturally constructed, socially imposed worlds. The theory stresses that identities are formed in history and practice through the collective work of evoking, confirming, or declining participation in collective practices.

Through these practices, people position themselves and others, revolving from experiencing their scripted social positions to becoming involved, on the basis of their knowledge and commitment, in cultural worlds. Identities form and exist in the process of identification, and enduring struggles and historical struggles are "crucibles for forging identities" (Holland and Lave 2001: 3).

The current research in anthropology shows that both identity and culture are part of the same complex processes; the understanding of social and individual actions requires focusing on both social identity and culture. Eriksen (2001) points out that people deeply involved in their cultures are taught to identify with abstract, mythically rooted communities of people of "the same kind" through schools and mass media: "It is based on a sometimes ambiguous mix of kinship and locality; it has well developed myths of origin and myths of past suffering; and it distinguishes clearly between 'us' and 'them'" (61). Peacock (2007) stresses the moral dimension of identity; he understands it as civic virtue, functioning as a Weberian "ideal type." He emphasizes that identity is a root for orientation to a good, moral framework that is acquired like language in childhood, that requires a dialogue with others to persist, and that defines communities much as language and other markers of culture do.

Social identity as a Function of Borders between Groups

As I stressed earlier, Barth (1981) perceives social identity as a product of the process of border formation: it forms at the boundary and is defined in the relationship between "them" and "us." Horowitz (1975) points out that intergroup boundaries are constructed in social life just as they are constructed in the laboratory. Cultural and political elites play an important role in the process of boundary enlargement or contraction, stressing the resemblances and disparities that define the group and its boundaries. Horowitz describes how "artificial ethnicity" develops through the creation of larger ethnic agglomerations connected to political competition in the whole territory. Cultural sociologists also study the context factors that shape boundaries, including the cultural repertoires, traditions, and narratives that individuals have access to (Lamont 2000; Somers 1994; Swidler 2001). They analyze the meaning of boundaries within and across societies as a result of cultural membership and stress their incorporation in the environment. On the basis of a large number of historical case studies, McAdam, Tarrow, and Tilly (2001) show the constitution of social actors through boundaries. They show that the invention and borrowing of boundaries, as well as encounters between previously distinct and competing networks, lead to the formation of categories of social actors.

Cohen (1985, 1986) shows that communities recognize clear boundaries that represent distinctive ways of life and may often mobilize themselves by perceiving these boundaries as endangered—as under threat from the outside. Kriesberg (2003) also stresses the importance of the clarity of group boundaries in mobilization of conflict parties. The clear recognition of inter-group differences and socially defined categories reinforces the willingness of group members to fight for power and resources.

Tilly (2005) stresses that social identities "center on boundaries sepa-rating us from them" (7). On each side of the boundary, people sustain interrelations within the ingroup; they also develop interrelations between their groups across the boundary. According to Tilly, the elements of social boundary include distinctive social relations on either side of an intermedi-ate zone, distinctive relations across this zone, and shared representations of this zone itself. This intergroup boundary, as well as relationships within ingroups and across the boundary, is reflected in the narratives of both groups and creates the basis of collective identities. Narratives of groups can contradict or complement one another, but they always have mutual impact. Tilly (2005) emphasizes the importance of group boundaries in people's lives: "People everywhere organize a significant part of their social interac-tion around the formation, transformation, activation, and suppression of social boundaries" (132).

The boundaries between groups can be defined as "any contiguous zone of contrasting density, rapid transition, or separation between internally con-nected clusters of population and/or activity for which human participants create shared representations" (Tilly 2005: 132; see also Abbott 1995; Lamont and Molnar 2002). This description of boundaries includes ingroup relations, intergroup relations across the boundary, and shared representa-tions of the boundary.

Analyzing the process of boundary change, Tilly (2005) describes two clusters of mechanisms: (1) those that precipitate boundary change and (2) those that constitute boundary change and produce its direct effect. These mechanisms can occur more or less simultaneously, but a precipitant always plays a causation role. The precipitating mechanisms include encounter (interaction between previously separate or indirectly linked groups; e.g., new immigrants), imposition (creation of new boundaries where they did not previously exist), borrowing (using already existing models of categories to install similar boundaries), conversation (communication between parties that modify relationship and representations), and incentive shift (changes in boundary-maintaining incentives). The mechanisms that constitute bound-ary change include inscription/erasure (increasing or decreasing the impor-tance of the border and intergroup differences), activation/deactivation (increasing or decreasing the salience of the boundary), site transfer (moving members of groups from one side of the boundary to the other), and reloca-tion (combining constitutive mechanisms).

Boundary change is connected with the development of conflicts and strongly impacts the intensity and forms of collective violence. Tilly (2005) discusses the mechanisms leading to ethnic cleansing: boundary imposition and boundary activation. Through the analysis of major European episodes such as the genocide of Armenians and Greeks of Anatolia around World War I, the Holocaust during World War II, the deportation of Crimean Tatars,

Chechens, and other peoples in the Soviet Union, and the Yugoslavia War in 1990, Tilly shows that imposition—or the drawing of a new, previously nonexistent border—led to expulsion and extermination. Thus, the Nazis successfully developed a boundary between Jews and non-Jews: The Nazis' Nuremberg Laws issued in July 1935 identified a Jew as a person with at least 25 percent of Jewish ancestry and strictly prohibited marriage of Jews with non-Jews. During 1930s, Jews were forced to emigrate, leaving their goods behind. In 1941, the systematic killing of Jews, Poles, and Bolsheviks strengthened the border between them and other peoples. Tilly also stresses that political boundaries usually aim to defend insiders from the threatening outsiders. Political leaders and governments support these boundaries or their transformation, which leads to stronger political exclusion.

1.4. SYSTEMIC APPROACH TO THE STUDY OF SOCIAL IDENTITY

The research is generally devoted to social and psychological processes of the influence of group membership on social identity and the impact of social identity on the group members' behavior and perceptions. However, social identity has historically not been analyzed as a systemic phenomenon with complex structures and specific interrelations within identities and relative development.

The systemic approach to social identity can help analyze this phenomenon because social identity is a structure with complex interrelations among different identities, all of which are involved in the processes of development and functioning. There are several types of systemic approaches: complex, structural, and integral. Using multiple methods of research, complex approaches analyze social identity as a set of components, but do not examine the interconnections among these components, the specificity of the structure, and the relationship between the components and the structure. Structural approaches include the research of compositions (subsystems) and the structure of objects but do not pay attention to the interrelations between subsystems and the phenomenon holistically. Integral approaches analyze the relations among parts of a system, as well as the relations between the parts and the whole.

Systemic approaches are useful tools for researching complex, multilevel phenomena such as social identity, because they help find knowledge gaps about the concept and help define areas of ambiguity for further research. Most importantly, on the basis of interpolations, one can forecast the features of the absent parts. The main task of the structural approach is to analyze and synthesize systems. In the process, the system is singled out from the environment, thus allowing the structure and its components, functions, integral characteristics (features), and interrelations with the environment to be defined. Systemic approaches reflect the structure and dynamics of phenomena. This orderliness can be described in terms of levels, stages, periods, layers, and so forth.

The study of social identity as a system requires analysis on several levels. First, social identity has to be examined as a part of its class or type, which defines the regularities of its development and functioning. Social identity is a component of the complex system of identity (together with individual identity). The problem of interrelations and interconnections between social and individual identity is complicated and needs further research. In an analysis, one should assess the interactions among the components of the identity system, as well as the main determinants that influence the dominance of one of the identities.

Second, social identity has to be considered as a system with specific characteristics. This conception helps stress its unity, including the interconnections among components in the processes of development and functioning. A larger analysis of the structure, functions, and dynamics of social identity will be taken up later.

Third, social identity has to be analyzed systematically in relation to the set of subsystems that influence its operation. This analysis includes different types of social identities, problems of salience and actuality, the specificity of the development of acquired and assigned identities, and the interrelations with stereotypes and attitudes, all of which will be explored later.

Fourth, social identity has to be characterized by its external interactions. Its impact on the development and resolution of social conflicts will be analyzed. Social identity is a powerful determinant of intergroup differentiation, prejudice, and discrimination. At the same time, it can be used to achieve tolerance, commonality, and peaceful coexistence.

Part II

Social Identity as a System

CHAPTER 2

SOCIAL IDENTITY IN THE
SYSTEM OF IDENTITY

2.1. INTERRELATIONS BETWEEN SOCIAL AND INDIVIDUAL IDENTITY

The interrelation between social and individual identity is one of the most complex and contradictory conundrums in social science. Most identity theories clearly state that identity has two main components: individual or "self" identity (which includes role identity) and collective or "we" identity (which includes group identities and social categories). Thoits and Virshup (1997) defined individual identity as a result of identification with a particular type of "person" and social identity as a result of identification with a group or category. Social identity is usually described in terms of group similarities and reflects shared interests, values, and beliefs, while individual identity is defined as a set of individual features and provides a basis for differentiating an individual from other people. These features have a certain constancy, or at least continuity in time and space.

The notion of individual identity reflects the idea that each individual is unique. The term still does not have a common definition, but all theories concur that individuals are aware of their being distinct. This understanding can be developed only through interaction, through which individuals assess themselves as identical to or different from others. In other words, individual identity includes self-sameness, continuity in time and space, as well as differentiation from other people. Its stability depends on the social context and can change over time.

Those studying identity conclude that there is the continuous problem of conflict between social and individual identity. The absence and presence of differentiation are analyzed as two poles, between which human behavior develops. It is hard to imagine how a person can feel himself or herself as identical to and different from the same people simultaneously. The majority of scholars emphasize that these two types of identity are incompatible (Deschamps and Devos 1998; Tajfel and Turner 1986; Tajfel and Turner 1979). Nevertheless, the current research shows that they are compatible. Jaromowic (1998) found that personal conformity demonstrates positive interaction between group identification and personal differentiation by following ingroup norms. However, researchers have not proved that this phenomenon exists in different cultural contexts. Below, I will discuss some theories that describe the interrelationship between social and individual identity.

The differentiation between individual and social identity explicitly began with the development of psychological thinking. At the end of the nineteenth century, William James (1890) stressed the differences between "I" and "Me" and pointed out the idea of duality in self-representation. This idea had a significant influence on Mead's theory of social identity (1934), which analyzed the result of unconscious processes on the adoption of group norms, customs, expectations, and beliefs. In contrast to social identity, individual identity was developing in the process of self-reflection or the understanding of the "self." Therefore, social identity, or "Me" in Mead's terminology, evolves from a group's behaviors and attitudes, whereas individual identity, or "I," characterizes a unique person with individual perception and evaluation of social situations. "I" and "Me" are deeply interconnected: a person makes his or her contribution to the development of society, and society influences the formation of the person. This understanding of the interrelations between individual and social identity is reductive and cannot adequately describe the complexity of these interconnections, which, as I will show below, are unique for everyone and characterize him or her with an inimitable personality.

Breakwell (2004) stressed these interrelations, describing them as the parts or aspects of individual identity. This identity has the following structure:

1. Biological organism as the core aspect of identity (however, in time, it loses its significance);
2. Content of identity, which includes all characteristics that a person uses to describe himself or herself;
3. Evaluation of the content on the basis of social norms and values;
4. Subjective time connected with the development of identity.

As Breakwell points out, social identity plays the initial role in the process of personal development, during which its categories are assimilated, forming the basis for the content of individual identity. Once formed, individual identity begins to influence social identity in this dialectic relationship. Thus, the interconnection of three processes—biological, social, and personal—influences the development of individual identity.

This development has crisis periods in which a person will find or adopt new values, ideas, and kinds of activities. The idea of premature identity reflects the interrelations between individual and social identities. This identity is a result not of independent search and choice, but of identification with other people and groups. On the basis of experimental results, Marcia (1980) revealed the different "statuses" of identity as results of individual identity development crises:

Diffuse identity, which characterizes people with no clear goals, values, and intentions;
Premature identity, which characterizes people who do not live through the crisis but have goals and values;
Moratorium identity, which characterizes people in the state of crisis;
Achieved identity, which characterizes people who successfully went through the crisis and have personal goals, values, and beliefs.

Habermas (1990) stresses that I-identity is a combination of individual and social identity and analyzes both identities as two dimensions of the balancing I-identity. Individual identity, the vertical dimension, provides connections through a person's history. Social identity, the horizontal dimension, helps meet the requirements of all role systems, which include a person. To maintain this balance, a person uses different techniques of interaction, demonstrating his or her identity and trying to meet the role expectations of a partner.

Unlike Breakwell and Habermas, Tajfel and Turner (1979) analyze the interrelations between social and individual identity as conflictual in nature. In 1974, Tajfel emphasized the existence of two opposite poles in a person's behavior. On the one end of the continuum (which is ideal and probably cannot be found in society) is the interaction between two or more individuals, whose behavior is completely determined by their interpersonal relations and individual characteristics; it has no impact from groups and other social categories. On the other end of the continuum are the interrelations between two individuals that are totally determined by their membership in different social groups and social categories and are not influenced by their interpersonal relations.

These two poles connect interpersonal attitudes and intergroup behavior. Individual identity reflects interpersonal behavior that is characterized by a differentiation between the individual and others, while social identity reflects intergroup relations that are characterized by a differentiation between groups (or between "we" and "they'). Tajfel stresses that, depending on the situation, an individual will act as a person actualizing individual identity or as a member of a social group actualizing social identity. This choice is connected with the need for positive self-evaluation and self-esteem and improving self-representation. If an individual cannot have high self-esteem in the context of interpersonal comparison, he or she will tend to increase self-evaluation by connecting with social groups, estimating them more positively in comparison with other groups.

Turner et al. (1987) developed this idea further by stressing that an individual emphasizes differences between groups only if she or he could not develop high self-esteem in interpersonal relations and perceives intergroup differences as the only way to achieve positive self-evaluation. If an individual can accomplish his or her search for high self-esteem in interpersonal relations, he or she will not have intergroup prejudice. In other words, if an individual achieves positive identity by identifying with a group, the intergroup differences for him or her will be more significant than interpersonal. In the interpersonal context, the intergroup differences will not be important. Thus, individual and social identities are antagonistic: The stronger the individual identity, the less the similarities a person will find between himself or herself and other ingroup members, and the less salient the ingroup identity is. The stronger the social identity, the fewer the differences between a person and other ingroup members, which creates a basis for depersonalization. Depersonalization is connected with the processes of autostereotypization, which leads an individual to perceive himself or herself as strongly connected with an ingroup, but not as a unique personality with distinctive characteristics.

Turner et al. (1984, 1987) explain the opposition between individual and social identity by describing three levels of self-categorization:

1. The *high level*—categorization as a human being—is connected with human identity, which is based on comparison among biological species (commonality of human race, differentiation with other forms of life);
2. The *middle level*—belonging to a specific group—is connected with social identity, which is based on ingroup-outgroup (i.e., intergroup) comparisons;
3. The *low level*—perception regarding the uniqueness and exclusivity of personality—is connected with individual identity, which is based on interpersonal comparisons within an ingroup.

If a person perceives himself or herself at one of these levels, the other two levels become irrelevant. As Turner et al. (1987) stress, the salience of one categorization is fundamentally antagonistic to that of the other levels: it leads to a sense of similarity within a class and differences between classes and produces a decline in the perception of in-class diversity and interclass likeness.

Evidently, the introduction of these three levels does not resolve the basic contradiction between individual and social identity. According to the theory of social categorization, they continue to be in a relationship of negative interdependence. But research over the last twenty years has helped discover ways of resolving this dilemma. One such study shows ingroups perceived as more heterogeneous in comparison with outgroups, which means that, together with intergroup differentiation, a person can perceive differences between ingroup members.

The attempt to use this idea for resolving the contradiction between social and individual identity is connected with the development of the covariation hypothesis between interpersonal and intergroup differentiation in the works of Deschamps and Doise (1978) and of Deschamps and Devos (1998). As their research shows, the accent on ingroup similarity does not necessarily lead to the perception of intergroup differences. The covariation hypothesis suggests that when a person is placed in a dichotomous social context between two groups reflecting mutually exclusive categories, sociocentrism and egocentrism occur simultaneously. Sociocentrism reflects intergroup differentiation and intergroup prejudice, and egocentrism is connected with differentiation between a person and other people.

For the verification of the hypothesis, a special study was conducted at a women's college: 88 girls within the 16- to 20-year-old bracket were separated into two groups. The first group was also divided into two subgroups on the basis of their preferences regarding modern artists. The second group was not divided into subgroups and was not connected with the preference for an artist. The experiment confirmed not only the existence of intergroup discrimination in the first group and the absence of discrimination in the second, but also the presence of a more salient interpersonal differentiation in the first group than the second. In other words, the rise of intergroup differentiation led to more salient interpersonal differentiation. Further research confirmed these results; however, it also showed that in some situations, the opposition of individual and social identities could be so strong that the two have to be analyzed as orthogonal (Deschamps and Devos 1998).

Serino (1998) described the interrelation between individual and social dimensions through several strategies, where interrelations between similarities and differences cannot be described only by the processes of assimilation and differentiation. On the basis of this interaction, a notional prototype simultaneously reflected a conformal standard of category and the differences between the category's prototype and peripheral members. Individual identity includes not only personal traits but also common group features, which can have different forms and levels of development among group members.

2.2. Cultural Dimensions as Determinants of the Interconnection between Social and Individual Identity

I suggest that the analysis of cultural dimensions can provide a key to the problem of interrelations between social and individual identity. Cultural differences go beyond the sphere of communication processes and include such areas as traditional values and beliefs, standards and ritual of behavior, norms of interpersonal relations, and social structure and hierarchy. These cultural differences also have a significant impact on the formation of social and individual identity.

People exist in a complex system of interrelations with their social environment: culture influences the values, beliefs, attitudes, and behavior of persons just as they influence their cultural environment. The differences among cultures can be described on the basis of ten features: national character or basic individuality, perception, conception of time, conception of space, thinking, language, nonverbal communication, values, behavior, and social groups and relations.

Changes in one feature can lead to changes in all the features. These features can be characterized as the parts, processes, and results of three main categories of culture. This classification reflects a model of culture developed by Trompenaars and Hampden-Turner (1997, 2000), who suggest that culture is a set of three circles: (1) main attitudes and views, (2) norms and values, and (3) products.

Sociologists describe two main types of relations to the public goods: one based on group priority (collectivistic orientation) and the other on individual priority. In their research, Hofstede (1980, 2001), Markus and Kitayama (1991), and Triandis and Gelfand (1998) further developed the early ideas of Durkheim (1969). Collectivistic orientation characterizes societies where the group is perceived as primary and the person secondary. Individualistic orientation puts the person at the center of the society.

The "collectivism-individualism" duality applies to the dichotomy between the cultures of the East and those of the West. For example, Hofstede (1980) shows that most individualistic cultures flourish in English-speaking countries, beginning with the United States and Great Britain, whereas most collectivistic cultures can be found in Asia and South America (Taiwan, Hong Kong, Singapore, Japan, Peru, and Colombia). Of course, collectivism can be realized in different forms. For example, "contextual collectivism" thrives in Japan, and "simple collectivism" in Korea (Triandis and Gelfand 1998).

Sociocultural dimensions have been studied in sociology as the culturally determined dichotomies that serve as bounds for the development of personal choice; in social psychology, they have been studied as the systems of value orientations; in cross-cultural psychology, they have been studied as a universal psychological phenomenon. In all these conceptual schemas, the sociocultural dimensions create a continuum of cultural variation and lead to the study of culturally and socially determined communications and interrelations among groups.

In his groundbreaking research, Triandis (1988, 1995) shows that cultural characteristics change with environmental transformations, forming what he calls specific cultural syndromes. A cultural syndrome is an explicit set of values, attitudes, beliefs, norms, and models of behavior that distinguish one group or culture from another. Triandis describes individualistic and collectivistic cultures as idiocentric and allocentric. The normative structure of groups in allocentric cultures significantly differs from that in idiocentric ones. Markus and Kitayama (1991) also assess the connections between these two orientations and psychological functioning.

The principle of group profit is a collectivistic norm; the principle of individual benefit is typical to individualistic norms, though it also includes recognizing the interests of others and the norms of exchange. The norms of exchange have two different interpretations: one is based on the principle of justice, while the other takes the survival of the most adopted individuals as its reference point. These two interpretations create different foundations for attitudes toward public welfare: the first one exhorts to "play honestly," while the second advocates rational behavior. The differences between allocentric and idiocentric cultures are also reflected in other normative rules, including justice, law, and distribution of power, rights, responsibilities, and resources.

In collectivistic cultures, power is perceived as an attribute of a group; the will of this group can be expressed in different ways such as by a majority of votes, via the opinion of elders (or the elite), or by charismatic leadership. The belief that power is used for the interest of the group attaches legality to the authority—a belief that is more important than prescribed procedures of decision making and voting. When the connection among individuals is interpreted as following the principle of survival, the notion of legitimacy has another meaning. Power is considered legitimate if it is based on the will and agreement of the parties and will always depend on procedural criteria of the establishment and use of power.

A collectivistic paradigm implies a common responsibility for the well-being and morality of each group member, as well as a sense of cooperation, share holding, support, help, and intimate contact among group members. An individualistic paradigm assumes that each person is responsible for his or her own destiny and that all social responsibilities rest on an implicit social contract. The differences between individualism and collectivism are shown in Table 2.1 (based on the ideas of Triandis 1988, 1995, Trumbull, Rothstein-Fisch, and Greenfield 2000).

Table 2.1 The Differences between Individualism and Collectivism

Differences	Individualism	Collectivism
Content of self	Individual differences	Social categories
Way for self-actualization	"Do what I want"	"I am not a burden for my group"
Values	Independence and individual achievement	Interdependence and group success
Norms	Self-expression, individual thinking, personal choice	Adherence to norms, respect for authority, group consensus
Regulation of behavior	Personal attitudes and estimation of cost-profit	Ingroup norms
Roles	Egalitarian relationships and flexibility in roles	Stable, hierarchical roles (dependent on gender, age)
Goals	Personal goals more important than group goals	Group goals more important than personal goals
Differences between groups	Not salient	Salient
Understanding the physical world	Knowable apart from its meaning for human life	Understanding in the context of its meaning for human life
Property	Private property, individual ownership	Shared property, group ownership
Type of relations	Horizontal	Vertical

Demographic characteristics and social class have a strong impact on these cultural dimensions. As research shows, people with high levels of education are more individualistic in their values and behavior than their compatriots with lower levels of education, the inhabitants of towns and cities are more individualistic than people who live in the countryside, men show more individualistic behavior than women, and younger people are more individualistic than their elders. Noricks et al. (1987) showed that Americans after the age of 56 considered their social context and other people in their decision making more than during their earlier years of life. People who lived in other countries and studied in foreign institutions can also change their attitudes.

The dimension "individualism-collectivism" is not apolitical and can be characterized by several parameters. Triandis and **Gelfand** (1998) described two types of cultural dimensions: horizontal and vertical. Horizontal collectivism is characterized by perceptions of a person as a part of a group in which members are equal. Vertical collectivism also suggests the attachment of a person to a group, but disclaims the equality of its members. Horizontal individualism connects the conceptions of autonomy and equality. Vertical individualism implies the autonomy of individuals, but denies equal rights and opportunities for all.

The dimension "individualism-collectivism" also includes other parameters. For example, Parsons (1951) suggested the existence of a parameter that characterizes "self-oriented behavior based on personal interests" and "group-oriented behavior based on common interests of a group." Another parameter, uncertainty avoidance, was proposed by Hofstede (2001). Cultures with a low tolerance for uncertainty and ambiguity tend to create a rule-oriented society that institutes laws, rules, regulations, and controls in order to reduce the amount of uncertainty. A high tolerance for uncertainty is reflected in a society that is less rule-oriented, more readily open to change, comfortable with more and greater risks, and more tolerant; consequently, such societies are more individualistic. As research shows, cultures with a low tolerance for uncertainty are characterized by a strong tendency for group agreement and a low tolerance toward new or different people. These tendencies lead to a high level of anxiety, which is connected with a fear of disapproval from a group, and to the search for an absolute truth, a need for a formal rules and norms, and low motivation of achievement (Oberg 1960; Taft 1977).

Psychological analyses of group dynamics and group mentality show that individualism and collectivism are ingrained in the psyches of individuals and are connected with the identification of the collectivity. The processes of individuation and social identification lead to identity formation. The development of self-conception also includes cognitive differences between "Me" and "Not Me" (as differentiation from other people) and identification with the subjects of the social world (acknowledgment of similarity with other people and connections with groups). Individuation leads to the perception of the social world as composed of a set of varied objects (individuals), and thus this process creates the differential system "Me- Others." Identification, on the contrary, eliminates the distinction between objects and forms a conception of the "self" as identical or similar with others. If the notion of group becomes the leading cognitive category, the social world is divided into ingroups and outgroups, and this process forms the differential system "We-They."

Reykowski (1997) suggests that the process of forming group identity (and collectivistic orientation) depends on the type of socialization a child receives, such as an education that accents obedience, conformity toward groups norms, and respect for group values, as well as traditions and symbols that lead to the development of collectivistic orientation.

I consider that two processes—individuation and social identification—"compete" with each other during the formation of an identity: the less developed the process of individuation, the more salient the process of social identification, and vice versa. Collectivistic culture, to a significantly greater extent than individualistic culture, contributes to the development of group identity and creates more possibilities for the manifestation of this identity among members of the society. Among representatives of individualistic cultures, individual identity is developed as initial and basic and usually dominates in the dyad of social and individual identity. In this context, a person perceives and estimates the world from an individual point of view and takes an individual approach to situations. In collectivistic cultures, group identity is formed before personal identity and becomes a leading one throughout a person's whole life. Social identity influences the system of stereotypes and attitudes shared with other members of a group. In these cases, individual identity can only become independent if a person changes his or her social environment, switching to the one with a dominant individualistic culture.

Much of the research on cultural dimensions confirms that members of collectivistic cultures are more likely to discriminate against representatives of other groups. Thus, the Polynesians show more discriminatory behavior than the Europeans, and the Greeks discriminate against others more than the French (Triandis 1995). Hinkle and Brown (1990) stressed that the interrelations between social identity and intergroup comparison are stronger in collectivistic cultures than in individualistic cultures. Results show that the outcome of comparison among groups is important only for members of groups in collectivistic cultures. Other studies demonstrate that representatives of both individualistic and collectivistic cultures discriminate against outgroups in the minimal intergroup situation, but that representatives of individualistic cultures are less discriminatory (Morales, López-Sáez, and Vega 1998). Crocker and Luhtanen (1990) found that intergroup discrimination is connected with group esteem, but not with self-esteem: people with high group esteem demonstrated stronger discrimination against members of an outgroup.

I believe that this phenomenon can be explained through identity theory. In collectivistic cultures, group identity is dominant and determines positive attitudes toward ingroup members as well as aloof, negative attitudes toward outgroup members. Thus, a high level of differentiation between "us" and "others" leads to the differentiation of behaviors: positive toward the ingroup and negative toward other groups. The more salient a social identity, the more impenetrable the intergroup boundaries, and the more difficult the contact with representatives of outgroups. In individualistic cultures, where individual identity prevails, members do not distinguish people using categories of "us" and "others"; rather, they communicate with everyone following the single formula of "Me" and "They." Therefore, negative attitudes toward outgroup members are not salient in individualistic cultures. Consequently, a salient group identity suppresses the positive relationships with representatives of other groups.

Clearly, therefore, types of culture have an impact on the process of identity formation. Such dimensions as individualism-collectivism influence the degree of a person's dependence on a group, orientation toward personal or group values and goals, and the readiness for interaction with representatives of other cultures. The cultural dimension has significant effect on interrelations between social and individual identity in the system of identities and on the leading role of one of these identities in a person's life and his or her social interactions.

To gain a deeper understanding of the impact of cultural dimensions on the structure of an identity system, it is important to distinguish between belonging to a category and the internalization of its meaning. Barth (1981) considers the differences between (a) nominal identity, which is based on name, and (b) virtual membership, which is based on experience. In another research, this dyad was analyzed as a difference between (a) category, which unites people on the basis of common characteristics that are evident for others, and (b) group, members of which know about their sameness and describe themselves on the basis this similarity (Jenkins 1996). Young (1997) understands this dyad as representing differences between association, in which a person is associated with a group but maintains a sense and understanding of individual identity, and membership, in which the group constitutes a part of members' personalities. Scholars consider that an association is equivalent to an addition of an adjective to a person's self-description and does not constitute a common experience or worldview, whereas membership in a group influences the very identity of a person. Turner (1987, 1994) describes these two different experiences using the terms "membership" group, which does not have a significant impact on identity, and "reference" group, which does significantly influence and alter individual identity.

I see this difference as a differentiation between a categorical group and a group of membership. Groups can be described as categorical if a person describes himself or herself using this category only: I am a father, I am a doctor, or I am a woman. This group satisfies all main criteria of the group: the person realizes the features of prototypes or typical members of this group, shares common characteristics of the members of this category, and can understand the differences with the members of other categories. For example, a woman who characterizes herself as a mother knows what it means to be a good mother, which features she has as a mother, and how women who do not have children are different from her. But despite these categorical similarities, she does not necessarily share the values and goals of all people in this category (mothers), does not have close contact with a "group of mothers," and is not interrelated with them. She can stay at home or go to work, but in either case she may not necessarily have close contact with other mothers. In the categorical group, a person characterizes himself or herself as an individual and interacts with other people from this individual position.

In a membership group, a person has continual, intimate contact with other members of the group; shares their values, beliefs, and feelings; and participates in efforts to reach the common goals of the group. He or she interacts with other people not as an individual but as a member of the ingroup dealing with members of either ingroups or outgroups and orienting primarily around the stereotypical features of those members. In a membership group, a person characterizes himself or herself as a member of the group, stressing his or her similarity and closeness with other ingroup members. Thus, to extend our previous example, a woman can become a member of the local mothers club, meet with them every week, and work together with others to improve (for example) the ecological situation or state of education in their community. A woman aligning herself in membership terms will share values, goals, and beliefs and experience group commonality.

The prevalence of categorical groups or membership groups is one of the main characteristics of individualistic or collectivistic cultures and is one of the most important influences on the process of identity formation. The categorical groups prevail in individualistic cultures and influence personal orientation and the supremacy of individual identity. Collectivistic cultures are characterized by the prevalence of membership groups, which influences the formation of group orientation and social identity as a basic one. The same group can operate both as a categorical group and a group of membership, depending on the orientation of its members. For example, a member of an ethnic group can draw his or her goals and values from the group, share his or her destiny with the group, and actively fight for the rights of the ingroup or discriminate against members of other groups. In this case, the ethnic group is operating as a group of membership. But if a person only ascribes to an ethnic group, characterizing himself or herself by ethnicity, and does not share group goals and beliefs, does not participate as an active member of the group, and does not perceive the world in terms of ingroups and outgroups, the ethnic group is operating as a categorical group. Categorical and membership groups are identified in the field of social categorization theory, but authors do not analyze the differences between them as well as the outcomes of affiliation with each of these group types. I suggest that categorical groups be described in terms of a role theory of identity and membership groups in terms of a group theory of identity.

In individualistic cultures, a person's development is based on a reflection of his or her own behavioral and personal characteristics; the process of self-representation reflects an understanding of the differences between the person and others and is mostly realized on the level of conscious.

In collectivistic cultures, groups and intergroup relations have a significant impact on personal development. A person perceives the group and intergroup processes as primal and seldom analyzes them; the process of self-representation, which is based on group characteristics, therefore contains many unconscious components. The prevalence of conscious and unconscious elements in self-representation and worldview is one of the most important characteristics of individualistic and collectivistic cultures. Therefore, the identities of representatives of individualistic cultures are realized after individual reflection. The identities of representatives of collectivistic cultures contain group beliefs and values that are adopted unscrutinized and are therefore not well realized and partly unconscious.

Study I. The Structure of Narratives in Collectivistic and Individualistic Cultures

The above findings concerning collectivist and individualistic cultures suggest the following proposal: in collectivistic cultures with a predominant social identity, such concepts as close relationships with family and the ethnic group, social recognition, and group support determine the character of individual perceptions, understandings, and interpretations of the social reality; in individualistic cultures with a predominant individual identity, the most important concepts reflect personal growth, individual achievements, and close relationships with one's partner.

This study was conducted together with my Ph.D. student Olga Dzhuzha. To verify this proposition, we created the following unfinished "fairy tale."

> *A father of two brothers died and left land and a house to the older brother. The younger brother, smart and brave, went on a journey to find his destiny. After encountering different troubles and adventures, he found a sacred cave. In the middle of the cave, he saw a patterned trunk. He opened the trunk and . . .*

Our respondents, the representatives of collectivistic culture (Crimean Tatars) and individualistic culture (Russians), were asked to complete this fairy tale. Their stories were analyzed using a special system of codes that identified 6 main and 14 auxiliary themes. The main themes included the following: (1) own people, motherland; (2) returning to family, family reunion, union with relatives; (3) loss of the sense of life, loss of life; (4) self-realization, understanding of own personality, personal growth; (5) love, new partner, new family; and (6) professional realization, work, job. The list of auxiliary themes included (1) social recognition, (2) help, (3) involvement, (4) achievements, (5) self-affirmation, (6) close relationships, (7) returning, (8) separation, (9) endless search, (10) deception, (11) ordeal, (12) struggle, (13) gain, and (14) defeat.

Each main and auxiliary theme was measured by its intensity on a five-point scale outlined as follows: (1) leading; (2) one of the leading; (3) salient, repeating; (4) mentioned several times; and (5) mentioned one time.

The findings showed that the main themes for Crimean Tatars involved returning to family, family reunion, motherland, and ethnic group. Their auxiliary themes stressed help, involvement, social recognition, and close relationships. Such main themes as self-realization, understanding of own personality, personal growth; love, new partner, new family; and professional realization, work, job prevailed in the narratives of Russians. The most important auxiliary themes for them included self-affirmation, achievements, close relationship, and social recognition. The results were examined using factor analyses of main themes and auxiliary themes for each ethnic group—Russians and Crimean Tatars.

Analysis revealed three factors among the main themes of the Crimean Tatars' narratives.

Factor one includes two main themes: (a) returning to family, family reunion, union with relatives (with weight 0.65), and (b) professional realization, job (with weight –0.82). Interpretation: The most important theme in the narratives of the Crimean Tatars is that of returning to the family and uniting with it once again. This theme far outweighed the values of a professional career, an interesting job, and so forth.

Factor two takes in two main themes: (a) people, motherland (with weight 0.56) and (b) loss of self (loss of the sense of life, loss of life) (with weight −0.87). Interpretation: In the Crimean Tatars' narratives, the connection with one's ethnic group, land, and motherland is the most important condition of life, of understanding the self. One can feel fulfilled only in living within one's ethnic group, and in one's homeland.

Factor three contains two main themes: (a) love, new partner, new family (with weight 0.72) and (b) self-realization, understanding of own personality, personal growth (with weight −0.83). Interpretation: Love and relationship with one's partner are more important than self-realization. Family values prevail over the values of personal growth and development.

Analysis revealed five factors among the auxiliary themes of Crimean Tatars' narratives.

Factor four contains three auxiliary themes: (a) social recognition (with weight 0.83), (b) achievements (with weight 0.77), and (c) help (with weight 0.66). Interpretation: Social recognition can be attained only by providing help to the ingroup. This represents a person's most important achievement.

Factor five contains four auxiliary themes: (a) involvement (with weight 0.40), (b) endless search (with weight −0.80), (c) separation (with weight −0.75), and (d) self-affirmation (with weight −0.33). Interpretation: Involvement in the ingroup is perceived as the happy end of the quest for a meaningful life. Self-affirmation leads to separation from the group and an endless quest for fulfillment. People can be happy only through their connections with others and their identification with a group.

Factor six includes three auxiliary themes: (a) involvement (with weight 0.47), (b) returning (with weight 0.40), and (c) deception (with weight –0.86). Interpretation: If a person is connected with an ingroup, the social environment becomes trustworthy, stable, and safe from any threats. Deception is the result of solitude and absence of fellowship.

Factor seven includes three auxiliary themes: (a) ordeal (with weight 0.85), (b) self-affirmation (with weight 0.64), and (c) returning (with weight −0.33). Interpretation: Individuals experience a sense of inner peace on returning home. People who seek self-affirmation must endure suffering and struggles in life. The only way to overcome such ordeals is to return home.

Factor eight contains three auxiliary themes: (a) returning (with weight 0.48), (b) defeat (with weight −0.90), and (c) separation (with weight −0.47). Interpretation: Returning home (to the ethnic group, the motherland) is perceived as a gain through unity with the family and ingroup. Separation from the group and the attainment of personal autonomy seemed to be a major hardship.

Additional factor analysis included such variables as the salience of ethnic identity in addition to both main and auxiliary themes. This analysis revealed one main factor that includes five components: (a) salient ethnic identity (with weight 0.81), (b) ethnic group, motherland, people (with weight 0.79), (c) social recognition (with weight 0.33), (d) deception (with weight −0.40), and (e) separation (with weight –0.34). Interpretation: Ethnic identity is associated with unity with an ethnic group, the motherland, and land as well as with social recognition by the ethnic group. Separation from the ethnic group is considered an act of deception.

Consequently, analysis shows the following features in the narratives of Crimean Tatars:

1. Separation, self-affirmation as an independent person, personal development, and growth are perceived as negative, connected with defeats, deceptions, and ordeals. The search for personal autonomy is seen as endless and fruitless, the results of which extend beyond the boundaries of the narrative. Thus, the concept of personal development does not retain adequate models in collectivistic cultures.
2. Enhancing one's professional career and achievements in work are viewed as an act of separation from the ingroup, as interests subdominant to family and ethnic group values. Social recognition can be achieved only through uniting with the ingroup, providing it help, and participating in it.
3. The most acceptable, wise, and successful choice a person can make is the choice to return to the ingroup—to achieve reunion with the family, ethnic group, and motherland. This choice is perceived as the safest for the person's psychological health, defending him or her from external threats and providing confidence and trust. Returning to the ethnic group terminates all ordeals and defeats, as well as all attempts for self-realization, which is not viewed as important or desirable. The most significant goal for a person in collectivistic culture, therefore, is social recognition.
4. The most esteemed way of life in collectivistic culture is immersion within a unified group. Ethnic identity serves as a guarantor of personal security

and stability in the social environment. Group values and perceptions dominate personal opinions and attitudes.

Analysis revealed three factors among the main themes of Russians' narratives.

Factor one includes three main themes: (a) love, new partner, new family (with weight 0.82); (b) professional realization, job (with weight 0.68); and (c) loss of the sense of life, loss of life (with weight –0.52). Interpretation: The presence of a loving partner (or nuclear family) and a successful professional career enables one to achieve a fulfilling life.

Factor two contains two main themes: (a) self-realization, understanding of own personality, personal growth (with weight 0.89) and (b) loss of the sense of life, loss of life (with weight –0.58). Interpretation: Another important factor of personal integrity is self-realization, which promotes an understanding of one's personality.

Factor three includes three main themes: (a) loss of the sense of life, loss of life (with weight 0.36), (b) returning to family, family reunion, union with relatives (with weight –0.78), and (c) own people, motherland (with weight –0.68). Interpretation: A good life is also rooted in family, one's ethnic group, and the motherland. They are important sources for stability and a general sense of life. All three factors are connected with self-realization, a sense of personal life, and personal development.

Analysis revealed three factors among the auxiliary themes of Russians' narratives.

Factor four comprises five auxiliary themes: (a) struggle (with weight 0.78), (b) ordeal (with weight 0.75), (c) gain (with weight 0.63), (d) achievements (with weight 0.62), and (e) self-affirmation (with weight 0.60). Interpretation: Self-affirmation is a result of gains and achievements attained through life's struggles.

Factor five contains four auxiliary themes: (a) returning (with weight 0.85), (b) close relationship (with weight 0.65), (c) gain (with weight 0.43), and (d) ordeal (with weight 0.35). Interpretation: Returning from travel to family and home and developing close relationships with loved ones represents a gain in the struggle with life's ordeals.

Factor six includes three auxiliary themes: (a) social recognition (with weight 0.78), (b) self-affirmation (with weight 0.50), and (c) achievements (with weight 0.38). Interpretation: Social recognition is perceived as a result of successful self-affirmation and achievements. Thus, it is connected with personal development and the acknowledgement of personal achievements.

Additional factor analysis of the Russians' narratives included such variables as the salience of ethnic identity in addition to both main and auxiliary themes. This analysis revealed one main factor that includes five components: (a) social recognition (with weight 0.80), (b) salient ethnic identity (with weight 0.66), (c) achievements (with weight 0.35), (d) self-affirmation (with weight 0.35), and (e) professional career, work, job (with weight 0.34).

Interpretation: For the Russians, ethnic identity was one component in a complexity of social recognition and personal achievement.

Consequently, our analysis showed the following tendencies in the narratives of the Russians:

1. The integrity of self is the most important concept. The avoidance of the loss of self is possible only through professional self-realization and happiness in one's nuclear family (defined as one's spouse and children and not connected with previous generations). Having achieved these two goals, a person can stop his or her search for self-affirmation. The ethnic group and the motherland also contribute to one's personal integrity, but their role is less significant than that of professional career and nuclear family.
2. The most appropriate and successful means for attaining personal integrity is individualistic self-affirmation, which is connected with personal development. Additionally, a person must endure struggles to attain self-awareness.
3. The narratives are characterized by marginality: the search for personal integrity is described through both (a) separation, personal development, and autonomy and (b) returning to the ingroup and reconnecting with the ethnic group and the motherland.
4. Social recognition considered results from personal growth and professional achievements. The respect from the society and ingroup is based on independency and personal accomplishments than on help and participation in the ingroup.
5. Ethnic identity is part of a complexity of achievements and centers on pride in one's Russian identity and self-realization as a professional, spouse, and parent. Personal attitudes and worldview are more important than group norms and perceptions.

Study II. The Study of Social Identity, Attitudes, and Readiness for Conflict Behavior in Individualistic and Collectivistic Cultures

The transition from polymodal individual and social identities to a single, dominant group identity, including a fixed We-They duality, reflects interrelations between attitudes and identity. Two main theories of intergroup relations, social identity theory and realistic conflict theory, give contradictory explanations for the interconnection between identity and attitudes. Realistic conflict theory considers conflicts of interest between groups as well as negative attitudes toward members of the outgroup as initial factors in the formation of ingroup identity. Social identity theory suggests that strong identification with the ingroup leads to the development of intergroup prejudice, negative attitudes and conflict behavior.

To examine the causal relationship between social identity and attitudes, I conducted a study of the interconnections between social identity, attitudes and readiness for conflict behavior. I hypothesize that this relationship can be described by a basic model (see Figure 2.1).

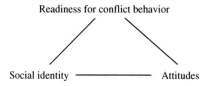

Figure 2.1   A basic model of interconnections between social identity, attitudes, and readiness for conflict behavior.

Residents of select towns and villages in Crimea were interviewed during September 2001, just after the events of September 11. The research was conducted in cities of Simferopol, Sevastopol, Yalta, and Dzhankoy and rural areas around these cities. The sample was stratified by location, number of resettlements, and rural-urban status. The participants were Russians (257) and Crimean Tatars (257) and equally distributed across these locations. Of the participants, 41 percent were male and 59 percent were female; 38 percent were between 20 and 30 years old, 32 percent between 30 and 45, 18 percent between 45 and 60, and 12 percent above 60; 58 percent were residents of towns and 43 percent residents of villages. Participation was voluntary. The respondents were provided with a questionnaire and selected answers from the list.

They were also tested using Triandis's INDCOL scale (1995) for collectivistic-individualistic cultures. The scale includes 32 items like the following: the decision of where to work should be made jointly with one's spouse, if one is married, and it is reasonable for a son to continue his father's business. Results show that Russians perceive their ethnic group as collectivistic on the basis of the parameter of orientation to group and individualistic on the basis of the parameters of openness to change, orientation to interaction with other groups, and weak social control. Crimean Tatars estimate their group as highly collectivistic on the basis of all parameters (see Table 2.2).

The study of readiness to defend ethnic and religious group shows that Crimean Tatars are readier to defend the norms and values of their ethnic group than Russians, who show a higher readiness to defend the safety of their ethnic group (see Table 2.3).

The differences between the two ethnic groups are significant with respect to a willingness to defend the ethnic group. Interestingly, Crimean Tatars show a higher readiness to defend the safety, norms, and values of the religious group than the Russians.

I conducted regression analyses of the interrelations among national, ethnic, religious, and regional identities, attitudes, and readiness to defend ethnic and religious groups. The analysis showed that the national identity of the Crimean Tatars is connected with individual and group readiness to defend the values and norms of their religious group. These findings confirm the results of previous research (Korostelina 2001, 2002), which showed that national identity motivates Crimean Tatars to preserve the cultural independence of their group. The ethnic identity of Crimean Tatars is connected

Table 2.2 Parameters of Individualism versus Collectivism (in Percentage)

Ethnic Group	1A	1B	2A	2B	3A	3B	4A	4B
Russians	62	38	58	42	79	21	43	57
Crimean Tatars	100	0	8	92	41	59	55	45

Note: Group orientation (1A) – Self-orientation (1B)
Openness for changes (2A) – Resistance for changes (2B)
Openness for interaction (3A) – Denial for interaction (3B)
Strong social control (4A) – Weak social control(4B)

Table 2.3 The Readiness to Defend Ethnic and Religious Groups among Russians and Crimean Tatars

Readiness to Defend	Ethnic Group		Religious Group	
	Safety	Norms and Values	Safety	Norms and Values
Crimean Tatars				
Individual	2.2163	2.2974	2.2305	2.2555
Group	2.3541	2.3840	2.3008	2.3758
Russians				
Individual	2.3268	2.1868	2.0039	2.0118
Group	2.3125	2.2568	2.1137	2.1490

with individual and group readiness to defend the safety, values, and norms of an ethnic group.

The religious identity of the Russians is connected with individual and group readiness to protect the religious group and individual readiness to defend the values and ideas of the ethnic group. The religious identity of Crimean Tatars is connected with all factors except individual readiness to defend the safety of the ethnic group. The most significant interconnection was found in the individual and group readiness to defend the safety of the religious group and individual readiness to defend the norms and values of the religious group.

The ethnic and regional identity of Russians and regional identity of Crimean Tatars were not closely connected with the readiness to defend the ethnic and religious group through violent means. Interestingly, religious identity is connected with the readiness to defend the ethnic group, especially its norms and values, by any methods and actions. Religious identity is connected with the readiness for conflict behavior of representatives of both ethnic groups.

Consequently, the readiness to defend ethnic and religious groups using violent methods is connected with religious identity. For Crimean Tatars—Muslims with a very salient ethnic and religious identity—religious identity is significantly connected with seven of eight possible indexes that confirm the importance of this identity for representatives of collectivistic cultures.

The results of analyses of interrelations between types of social identity and attitudes show that the national identity of Crimean Tatars is connected with ideas about opposition between religions, the split within the Muslim world, and the support for jihad. The belonging to the Ukrainian nation weakens opinions about unity and the tolerance of Muslims. The national identity of Russians is connected with attitudes about opposition between religions.

The ethnic identity of Russians is connected with attitudes that Talibs are terrorists and the perceived relation between terrorism and the Muslim religion.

The religious identity of Crimean Tatars is connected with the belief that Muslims support jihad (which carries negative connections), that Talibs are terrorists, and that it is important to unite against terrorists. The religious identity of Russians is connected with the concept of opposition between religions and the perceived relation between terrorism and the Muslim religion.

The regional identity of Crimean Tatars is connected with the belief that war in Afghanistan is just. The regional identity of Russians also is connected with the support of the war in Afghanistan, as well as with attitudes about the split between the Muslim and Western worlds.

Thus, the social identity of Crimean Tatars is more strongly connected with particular attitudes toward terrorism than is the social identity of Russians. Each of the ethnic, national, and religious identities of Crimean Tatars exhibits 3 of 8 possible interconnections with attitudes; regional identity is connected with only one attitude. For Russians, more significant interconnections were found for regional identity (3 connections out of 8); each of the religious and ethnic identities had two interconnections; only one interconnection was found for national identity. The strongest connection with social identity was found for the following attitudes of Crimean Tatars: the opposition of the Muslim and Western worlds, the belief that Talibs are terrorists, and the idea that a split within the Muslim world is exacerbating the war on terrorism. For Russians, attitudes about the opposition of the Muslim and Western worlds have the most significant interconnections with social identity.

The analysis of interconnections between attitudes and individual readiness to defend an ingroup shows that for Russians, the readiness to defend the safety of their ethnic group is connected with attitudes regarding the link between terrorism and the Muslim religion, the concept of opposition between religions, the support for jihad by Muslims, the perception that Talibs are terrorists, and the importance of the unity of the world in the war on terrorism. Individual readiness to defend the norms and values of an ethnic group or a religious is also connected with attitudes about the association between terrorism and the Muslim religion, the concept of opposition among religions, the split within the Western world, the support for jihad by Muslims, the belief that Talibs are terrorists, support for war in Afghanistan, and the importance of the unity of the world in the war on terrorism.

Individual readiness to defend the safety of the religious group among Russians is connected with attitudes about support for jihad by Muslims and support for the war in Afghanistan. Individual readiness to defend the norms and values of the religious group is connected with attitudes about the association between terrorism and the Muslim religion, support for jihad by Muslims, the belief that Talibs are terrorists, and the importance of the unity of the world in war on terrorism.

For Crimean Tatars, the readiness to defend an ethnic group is connected with attitudes about the split within the Western world, support for jihad by Muslims, and vigilance in the war on terrorism. Individual readiness to defend the norms and values of the ethnic group is connected with attitudes about opposition between religions, the split within the Muslim world, and support for jihad by Muslims. Individual readiness to defend the safety of the religious group among Crimean Tatars is connected with attitudes about support for jihad by Muslims. Individual readiness to defend the norms and values of the religious group is connected with negative attitudes toward the war in Afghanistan.

Thus, the attitudes of Russians were more significantly connected with individual readiness to defend the ingroup than the attitudes of Crimean Tatars. For Russians, our study showed 19 significant interconnections (12 on the level $p < .001$), while for Crimean Tatars, only 8 interconnections were found (3 on the level $p < .001$). For Russians, individual readiness to defend the norms and values of the ethnic group revealed the highest number of significant interconnections with attitudes (7 out of a possible 8 connections). Significant interconnections with attitudes were also found for the individual readiness to defend the safety of the ethnic group (5 interconnections). For Crimean Tatars, more significant interconnections with attitudes were found for the readiness to defend the safety, as well as the values and norms of the ethnic group (3 connections for each).

The analysis of interconnections between perceived group readiness to defend the ingroup and attitudes shows that group readiness to defend the safety, as well as the values and norms of the ethnic group among Crimean Tatars is not connected with any attitudes. Perceived group readiness to defend the safety of the religious group among Crimean Tatars is connected with the attitude that Muslims support jihad, and a perceived group readiness to defend the values and norms of the religious group is connected with attitudes about the split within the Western world.

For Russians, the group readiness to defend the safety of the ethnic group was connected with attitudes about support for jihad by Muslims, the belief that Talibs are terrorists, and the importance of the unity of the world in the war on terrorism. Group readiness to defend the norms and values of the ethnic group was connected with attitudes about the association between terrorism and the Muslim religion, the concept of opposition between religions, the split within the Western world, support for jihad by Muslims, the belief that Talibs are terrorists, and the importance of the unity of the world in the war on terrorism.

Group readiness to defend the safety of the religious group among Russians was connected with attitudes about support for jihad by Muslims. Group readiness to defend the norms and values of the religious group was also connected with attitudes about support for jihad by Muslims.

Thus, perceived group readiness to defend the ingroup is less strongly connected to attitudes than to individual readiness. The tendency for the prevalence of interconnections between readiness and attitudes among Russians was confirmed for group readiness to defend the ingroup. Group readiness to defend the norms and values of the ethnic group among Russians had more significant interconnection with attitudes (6 connections out of a possible 8); 3 significant interconnections were found for group readiness to defend the safety of the ethnic group. For Crimean Tatars, group readiness to defend the safety, norms, and values of the ethnic group did not have any significant interconnection with attitudes.

Consequently, the social identity of Crimean Tatars was more strongly connected with the readiness to defend the ingroup than was the social identity of Russians. The religious identity of Crimean Tatars displayed a higher number of interconnections with attitudes (7 significant connections out of 8). The study reveals four significant connections with attitudes for ethnic identity and two connections with attitudes for the national identity of Crimean Tatars. No interconnections were found for regional identity. For Russians, connections with attitudes were found only for religious identity (3 significant interconnections). The national identity of Crimean Tatars was connected with individual and group readiness to defend the norms and values of the religious group. The ethnic identity of Crimean Tatars was connected with individual and group readiness to defend the safety of the ethnic group and with individual readiness to defend the norms and values of the ethnic group. The religious identity of Russians was connected with individual and group readiness to defend the safety of the religious group, and with individual readiness to defend the norms and values of the ethnic group. Therefore, the readiness to defend the ingroup was connected with religious identity for both groups and with ethnic identity for Crimean Tatars. No connection with readiness to defend the ingroup was found for regional identity.

The social identity of Crimean Tatars was more strongly interconnected with attitudes toward terrorism than was the social identity of Russians. Each of the social identities of Crimean Tatars (ethnic, national, and religious) displayed three significant interconnections with attitudes; for regional identity, only one significant interconnection was found. For Russians, regional identity exhibited three significant interconnections with attitudes; religious and ethnic identities exhibited two significant interconnections with attitudes; and only one interconnection was found for national identity.

The social identity of Crimean Tatars was more connected with the readiness to defend ingroups than with attitudes. Indeed, 13 interconnections were found between social identity and the readiness to defend the ingroup

(6 on the level $p < .001$), while 10 interconnections were revealed between social identity and attitudes (only 1 on the level $p < .001$). The social identity of Russians was more strongly connected with attitudes than with the readiness to defend ingroups. Accordingly, 8 interconnections were revealed between social identity and attitudes (4 on the level $p < .001$), while 3 were found between social identity and the readiness to defend the ingroup (2 on the level $p < .001$).

The attitudes of Russians were more strongly interconnected with individual readiness to defend the ingroup than the attitudes of Crimean Tatars. Thus for Russians, the study revealed 19 significant interconnections (12 on the level $p < .001$), while for Crimean Tatars only 8 significant interconnections were found (3 on the level $p < .001$). Among Russians, individual readiness to defend the norms and values of the ethnic group had the highest number of interconnections with attitudes (7 out of a possible 8 interconnections). Significant interconnections with attitudes were also found for individual readiness to defend the safety of the ethnic group (5 interconnections), as well as for individual readiness to defend the norms and values of the religious group. For Crimean Tatars, individual readiness to defend the safety, norms, and values of the ethnic group had 3 interconnections with attitudes. Only one significant interconnection with attitudes was found for individual readiness to defend the religious group.

This study reveals fewer interconnections between attitudes for perceived group readiness to defend the ingroup than attitudes for individual readiness, while it confirms the tendency for a prevalence of interconnections between readiness and attitudes among Russians. Group readiness to defend the norms and values of the ethnic group among Russians had more significant interconnections with attitudes (6 connections out of a possible 8); 3 significant interconnections were found for group readiness to defend safety of ethnic group. For Crimean Tatars, the group readiness to defend the safety, norms, and values of the ethnic group does not have any significant interconnection with attitudes.

The results of my research provide the opportunity to revise the basic model of interrelations among attitudes, readiness to defend the ingroup, and social identity (Figure 2.2). For the Crimean Tatars, data gathered during our study show the following number of significant correlations:

Between social identity and readiness to defend ingroup: 13 significant correlations (8 at $p < .001$ level).

Between social identity and attitudes: 10 significant correlations (1 at $p < .001$ level).

Between readiness to defend ingroup and attitudes: 8 significant correlations (3 at $p < .001$ level).

Consequently, for Crimean Tatars, social identity is the initial factor in the formation of conflict behavior. The readiness for this behavior strongly

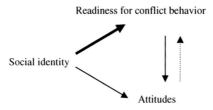

Figure 2.2   The model of interrelations between attitudes, readiness to defend ingroup, and social identity for Crimean Tatars.

Figure 2.3   The model of interrelations between attitudes, readiness to defend ingroup, and social identity for Russians.

influences attitudes; social identity also has an impact on attitudes. The basic model therefore takes the form shown in figure 2.2.

For Russians data gathered during our study shows the following number of significant correlations:

Between social identity and readiness to defend ingroup: 3 significant correlations (2 at $p < .001$ level).
Between social identity and attitudes: 8 significant correlations (4 at $p < .001$ level).
Between readiness to defend ingroup and attitudes: 19 significant correlations (12 at $p < .001$ level).

Consequently, for Russians, attitude is the initial factor in the formation of conflict behavior and the development of social identity, and it has a strong influence on the readiness for conflict behavior. The basic model therefore takes the form shown in figure 2.3.

Consequently, for representatives of collectivistic cultures salient social identity plays a determinant role in the formation of conflict behavior. The ideas of connection with an ingroup, subordination to it, and unity with its members are more important than individual autonomy. Social recognition and respect are the results of help for and involvement in the ingroup. A salient social identity influences attitudes and the perception of the situation: group values and perceptions dominate individual opinions and attitudes. People are ready to fight for and defend ethnic identity to ensure personal security and social stability. A salient social identity influences the readiness to defend the safety as well as the ideals and values of the ingroup by using any methods including violence. The attitudes and readiness for conflict behavior are interconnected; however, the readiness for conflict behavior occupies the primary position.

For representatives of individualistic cultures, personal development and achievements are more important than involvement and connections with an ingroup. Social recognition and respect are the results of personal success, professional accomplishments, and self-realization. The personal perception and estimation of a situation (attitudes) precedes and determines the readiness for conflict behavior. Attitudes have a strong impact on social identity. A salient social identity also has an influence on the readiness for conflict behavior; nevertheless, attitudes can increase or decrease this influence. For representatives of collectivistic cultures, strong belonging to an ingroup determines the readiness for conflict behavior, whereas for representatives of individualistic cultures, individual estimation of a situation carries the strongest impact on the readiness for conflict behavior.

CHAPTER 3

SOCIAL IDENTITY AS A SYSTEM

3.1. MODELS OF SOCIAL IDENTITY

For the last several decades, the prevailing model of identity was identified as the "onion model," also known as the "circle" or "*matreshka* model." This model describes identity as a set of circles, where the internal circles symbolize the most important layer of identity and the exterior circles symbolize salient identities, which are considered less important than situational identities. Although this model stresses the multiplicity of identity and demonstrates different levels of identity salience, it does not reflect the interrelations and dynamics within identity systems.

The model proposed by Worchel et al. (2000), which is extremely different from the "onion model," suggests that several identities can influence a person's behavior. For example, both individual and social identity can have comparable importance for a person or one of them can dominate. The authors posit that individual identity consists of several components. The first, personal characteristics, contains features that do not result from group membership and that stress a person's originality or uniqueness: personality traits, physical characteristics, skills and abilities, personal experience, and personal aspirations. These characteristics also influence intergroup relations and social identity (several studies have confirmed the impact of self-esteem, need for affiliation, and cognitive complexity on intergroup relationships). Consequently, personal characteristics affect intergroup relations directly or through ingroup identity.

The second component of individual identity is the presence of an intragroup identity that includes individuals' roles within their ingroup and their relationship with it. Worchel et al. posit that this dimension can be described as a personal characteristic and can also serve as a measurement for ingroup behavior. Thus, a person can be a leader or a follower, have low or high social status, and have positive or negative relations with the ingroup. Intragroup identity is unique and will change if a person becomes a member of another group. Like personal characteristics, intragroup identity affects intergroup behavior directly or through intergroup identity.

The third component concerns group membership, which reflects the categorization of the world into groups and membership in groups. This dimension is connected not only with ingroups but also with outgroups, because the development of the meaning of group membership requires a clear definition of intergroup boundaries. The fourth component is a sense of group identity that is connected with the context of social interaction and reflects ingroup identity by characterizing it through the stressed differences with outgroups. Several studies analyzed group identity as "group beliefs" (Bar-Tal 1990, 1998) or "collective self-esteem" (Luhtanen and Crocker 1992).

The model proposed by Worchel et al. (2000) disputes the idea of an oppositional relationship between individual and social identity and shows the possibility of a positive relationship between them. It also overcomes the "individual–social identity" dichotomy by developing a multidimensional approach for the study of identity that influences behavior. In addition, it stresses the importance of interconnections among all four dimensions of identity.

Interrelations between social identities are illustrated in the conception of comparative identity (Ros, Huici, and Cano 1994; Ros, Huici, and Gomez 2000). This conception describes the connections between different social identities that affect intergroup relations and intergroup differentiation. Ros et al. (2000) define comparative identity as "the comparison of degree of identification with two categories at different levels of inclusion (identification with the category at the lower level minus identification with the category at the higher level)" (82). They show that the level of identification with other categories has an effect on the salience of identity. In their research, they found significant differences between groups based on comparative identification with a specific region in Spain and stressed the importance of assessing the salience of both national and regional identities for a complete understanding of intergroup relations. Moreover, comparative identity appeared to be a more significant indicator of regional identity salience than of just the level of identification. Thus, the group with a low level of regional identity salience and a high level of national identity salience shows strong national (ingroup) favoritism. The intensity of this favoritism was significantly lower for the group with a high level of regional identity salience and a low level of national identity salience.

Another example of research reflecting the interrelations between identities is the conception of crossed categorization proposed by Crisp and Hewstone (2000). This conception is based on the idea that, despite laboratory research conducted on identity, in the real world a person can have multiple social identities and can be described by different categories (Arcuri 1982; Deschamps and Doise 1978). Crossed categorization reflects the intersection of two categories (e.g., religious and ethnic, national and regional). By crossing ethnic and gender categories, the authors received four groups: Welsh Female, Welsh Male, English Female, and English Male.

As their research showed, group differentiation in the case of cross categorization (one ingroup and one outgroup category) is significantly lower than that in the case of single categorization (both outgroup categories). Research has also confirmed the existence of strong interrelations between gender and minority/majority identity: for minorities, men are more likely to think of themselves in gender-stereotypic terms and to identify with their gender than are women, as they are the members of a lower-status group (Swann and Wyer, 1997).

Adler (1994), Crenshaw (1998), and King (1988) stress that an individual's system of identities is not simply a combination of that person's ethnic, multicultural, and civic identities, but rather a system in which identities have multiple effects. Some approaches to conceptualizing multiple social identities exist. According to Brewer's classification of identity theories (2001), theories of person-based social identity (Cross 1991; Phinney 1990; Skevington and Baker 1989) suggest that one's self-concept consists of different stereotypes, attitudes, and values that one receives from membership in groups. Some of these particulars may be more salient than others, but they all serve as parts of a single representation of the individual self. Theories of relational social identity assume that the self is a set of discrete identities, each of which can be differentiated from a person's other role identities. This system is organized and structured, and it determines which identity will be salient in a particular social context (Stryker and Serpe 1994; Stryker 2000). Theories of group-based social identities suggest that one's identity system depends on the social context (Turner et al. 1994), but that some social categories can be relatively stable across time and situations (Abrams 1999). The idea of the fluidity of identity in social categorization theory (Turner et al. 1987) grew out of research on situational identities in laboratory settings. However, research into ethnic identity shows a remarkable stability over time (Alwin, Cohen, and Newcomb 1990; Ethier and Deaux 1994; Sears and Henry 1999).

3.2. The System of Social Identities

Applying the insights of this scholarship to identity formation, I define identity as a system that involves core identities, short-term identities, and situational identities. Core identities are fairly stable and dominant: they exist for a relatively long time and change only in situations of considerable social shifting; some core identities remain through an individual's entire lifetime. Short-term identities are inconstant and reflect temporary ingroup and intergroup relations. Situational identities are connected with, and depend on, concrete situations. They are a "building material" for short-term and core identities.

All identities are interrelated, and correlations among subsystems of core identities are stronger and firmer. If social identities are stable, a person can have several salient identities simultaneously. Since social identities exceed the bounds of the individual "self" and determine the relationship with other people, the system of social identity becomes compound and multi-faceted. As social identities are shared with members of other ingroups and connect persons with them, the redefinition of and the separation of one's identity from the system become a complex task for a person.

The theory of social identity stresses that each identity is formed as a result of an individual's membership in an ingroup and of an opposition to or comparison with members of an outgroup (Tajfel and Turner 1979, 1986). The existence of an outgroup and an ingroup's negative and conflict-ridden relations with it strengthen group identity (consider, e.g., the effect of simple social categorization: Allen and Wilder 1975; Billig and Tajfel 1973; Brewer and Silver 1978; Brewer and Miller 1984; Doise and Sinclair 1973). The position, achievements, and losses of the group as a whole are incorporated into the self and respond to personal outcomes (see, e.g., Hirt et al. 1992).

The results of this research and numerous other studies encourage us to understand social identity as an open, unstable system. The factor of asymmetry, the element of chance, and feedback play important roles in the development of such systems. Asymmetry reflects the relative or significant decrease in the importance of other groups and categories if a person becomes strongly involved in a new group. Salient group identity changes a person's relations with the social world from symmetrical (equal with all groups) to asymmetrical (ingroup-centric or superior). The other factor, feedback, stresses the importance of comparison (opposition) with an outgroup for identity development. Thus, the social identity system does not develop in adaptation to a situation or social content, but becomes a permanent reproduction of stable imbalance with environment. Thus, changes occur in outgroups, and negative or conflict relations with them strengthen ingroup identity.

One identity can influence another identity's development, increase or decrease its salience, and strengthen or weaken its impact on attitudes and behavior. In particular contexts of intergroup relations—when an individual is in a minority position, suffers from discrimination, or engages in conflict—different identities become strongly interconnected and reshape one another.

Identity system is also open to personality and serves certain psychological functions for group members (see below). The needs for individual security and social status can change the structure of identity system. If a new identity begins to perform the necessary functions, it can lead to the disappearance of old identities. If one of the identities stops fulfilling its functions, it gradually loses its significance and vanishes.

Even a small disturbance or minor impact can move an identity system away from its equilibrium position—force the system to become unstable and make a person's behavior unpredictable. Changes in social environments, relationships between groups, status, power, and the supremacy of ingroups and outgroups will or can lead to the reorganization of identity systems, contradictions, and even identity crises. Thus, short-term identities will change but core identities can remain.

However, even in the situation of the destruction and disappearance of their respective social groups, identity-related processes continue to be organized in the same way as they were within the whole system in the past. This can be interpreted as the *memory of an identity system* and can lead to a sense of contradiction in one's system of identities. Consider, for example, the Soviet identity of the populations of the former Soviet Union. Despite the disappearance of the common "Soviet people," this identity still occupies a leading place as a core identity among middle-aged and elderly people.

Thus, social identity reflects not only the current situation but also the history and structure of society in the past. Possible changes in the future can influence it. For example, a person planning to join college can begin to feel close to an upcoming student community by sharing the members' values and attitudes and by participating in some events even before entering college, thus becoming a real member of the group. Rogers (1961) postulated that a sense of identity involves seeing ourselves as we really are—who we have been, who we are, and who we will become. Thus, a sense of identity can only be attained when we discover and chart our own destinies in life. As Tajfel (1969) observed, situations of rapid social change in outgroup and ingroup relations play an important role in structuring people's visions of the future. When an identity system functions according to its "memory" without reference to the present or future, it leads to contradiction in the system of identities.

The problem of identity stability invokes numerous discussions among scholars. On the one hand, social identities, like ethnic identity, demonstrate high stability over time: they are more stable than other social and political attitudes. At the same time, research confirms their mobility and fickleness. Turner et al. (1987) illustrated the strongest advocates of the changeability of identity. The idea of fluidity and instability of identity was built on the research on situational lab identities, while the research on ethnic identity showed remarkable stability over time (Alwin, Cohen, and Newcomb 1992; Ethier and Deaux 1994; Sears and Henry 1999). As research demonstrates, manipulation with the number of men and women and changes in the prevalence of one gender's representatives in the experiment had a strong impact on gender identity. A temporary group prototype or a typical group member that embodies a group's main characteristics influences spontaneous rise and change in identity. In their study, McGarty et al. (1992) created small groups of three and five persons to assess their opinion on different topics, looking for the main person whose opinion coincided to a high degree with the group's opinion and a person whose opinion was very different from the group's opinion. This experimental manipulation helped to show the effect of prototype and high fluidity of identity.

However, other research stresses the stability of identity in shifting social contexts. It is hard to assume that in real life the prototype will change the same way as in laboratory research. As studies of stereotypes have shown, there are numerous ways to rationalize the differences between a group member and the group's majority, without excluding this member from the group. People do not notice or dissemble such information (i.e., a member's characteristics being different from the typical characteristics of other members). One exception from the stereotypic "rule" does not change regularity. Thus, for example, the attempts to change the basic prototype of a feminist woman into a typical clerk and housewife were not successful (Huddy 2001).

On the basis of the postmodern view on identity, social identity can be considered sufficiently fluid and changeable depending on the social context. It does not mean that such identities as ethnic, national, or religious can disappear or rise in a moment. But the salience, meaning, and content of these identities are exposed to changes. In some countries, such as Afghanistan, Iran, Turkey, Pakistan, and the Republics of Central Asia (during the Soviet period), national identity began to develop after borders of the countries had been established. In Central Asia, nineteenth-century populations and dialects blended into one another, making the most salient identification in the region tribal and clan based (for a more in-depth analysis, see Manz 1994 and Roy 2000). No relationship between ethnicity and statehood existed at that time, because the Muslim dynastic state ruled over a very multiethnic population. In 1924/25, after the October Revolution, the Soviet government developed a "National Delimitation" plan *(natsional'no-gosudarstvennoe razmezhevanie)* in order to create territorial and linguistic nations on the basis of the Western model. The main idea of this plan was that the administrative boundaries of the five new Central Asian republics were to be connected with ethnic boundaries. In 1936, the Soviet constitution further solidified the new national frameworks by granting the republics of Turkmenistan, Uzbekistan, Kazakhstan, Kyrgyzstan, and Tajikistan the status of union republics. During the Soviet period, each ethnic group became more rooted in and committed to its Soviet-demarcated territory and indigenous Central Asians gradually came to dominate their republics demographically, linguistically, and politically.

Iran, Turkey, and Pakistan also achieved statehood before acquiring a coherent sense of national identity (see Zürcher and Schendel 2001; Wassem 2007). Thus, nation building became a political project implemented by authoritarian elites. Pakistani nationalism, unlike Indian nationalism, was not based on a historically established and geographically well-defined political entity. The partition of India involved not only independence from the colonial rule but also separation from mainstream Indian nationalism. Since the distinction between Muslims and Hindus played a key role in mobilizing the large Muslim population of British India in favor of Pakistan, the Two-Nation Theory had a strong impact on the formation of national identity in Pakistan. The Muslim League, in pursuit of its project of carving out a state for Muslims in India, had to first "separate" Muslims from Hindus as a self-conscious political community and then create a Pakistani identity in the context of a Hindu-Muslim dichotomy. This led to an exclusive focus on Islamic identity, almost by default. The existence

of conflicting social and political interests poses a challenge to the definition of national identity in Pakistan. National identity contained different,
even controversial, values, beliefs, and worldviews that led to an inconsistency in attitudes and opinions among the young generation, an overall
instability in society, negative attitudes and prejudice toward other peoples,
and conflict intentions.

Consider Indonesia, where from the 1920s to the 1940s, political elites
debated and struggled to define the meaning of the Indonesian national
identity: the nationalists stressed the principles of self-determination, democracy, and modern political institutions; the Islamists called for a nation based
on Islam; the socialists supported communist programs; and the integralists
developed the idea of a nation as a common family (for a more in-depth
analysis, see Anderson 1991 and Tan 2006). In 1945, the political elite
stressed the necessity of a territorial and national unity that would unite religion, class, and regional and cultural groups. As a basis for the new national
identity, five principles were developed: (1) nationalism or Indonesian unity,
(2) humanitarianism, (3) Indonesian democracy through consultation and
consensus, (4) social justice, and (5) belief in God.

These principles served as a unifying ground for different groups, which
were united into a single Indonesian nation-state. The inauguration of Pan-
casila (*pancha* means "five," and *sila* "principle") as the official ideological
and philosophical basis of the Indonesian nation initiated a long process of
negotiation and construction of national identity. The principles of tolerance, social justice, and unity were mixed with integralism, which is rooted in
the traditions of the Javanese aristocracy and anti-Enlightenment European
thought. The differences between the political elite remained unresolved
throughout the 1950s and the first part of the 1960s and led to an open
conflict between groups.

These illustrations prove that several factors influence the development
of and changes in both the salience and meaning of social identities. First,
the state itself can categorize people into ethnic, regional, political, or other
groups. By stressing the position of minorities and affirmative action, by
developing regional administrative units, and by monitoring elections and
political debates, the state can post boundaries and reshape social identities.
Second, the elite and leaders can and will manipulate social identity and add
an ideological context according to their political aims. I will discuss this
dynamic in Chapter 7. Third, international communities, by intervening in
ethnic conflicts, can reshape the meaning of the terms "ethnicity," "indigenous rights," "right of self-determination," and so forth. In postwar Bosnia,
the new program "Separate but Equal" strengthened intergroup boundaries
and intensified perceptions of difference, thus sufficiently reshaping the
social categorization of identity and increasing identity salience. Fourth,
the media is a powerful source in forming and sustaining social identities by
stressing a real or imaginary outgroup threat, developing strong prototypes,
and reshaping values and beliefs.

3.3. FUNCTIONS OF SOCIAL IDENTITY

The research on the functions of social identity can be divided into two groups. The first emphasizes general functions, such as the motives for accepting social identity. As mentioned earlier, the theory of social identity considers the need for positive social identity and high self-esteem as the main motive in the process of ingroup identification. Studies show that in situations of low status, strong group identification protects individuals from the feeling of personal discomfort.

Brewer's theory of "optimal distinctiveness" (1996, 2000, 2001) suggests that people have the dual need for distinction from a group (intercategory contrast) and for inclusion in it (intracategory assimilation). These two needs are components of a homeostatic model that describes a person's permanent search for the balance between differentiation and inclusiveness. Thus, a person who feels excluded from ingroup interaction will search for a group or social category that can provide strong feelings of inclusiveness. A person deeply involved in interactions with a large group will search for a more differentiated group that has some level of individualization among its members. According to this model, groups that are exclusive rather than highly inclusive engage more attachment and identification, because they satisfy both of these needs simultaneously (Brewer 2000).

Another basic function of social identity is the reduction of uncertainty (Hogg 1996; Hogg and Abrams 1993). According to this approach, a person will experience uncertainty while engaged in the processes of interpreting and understanding the world. Social identity can provide access to social consensus and can give one the opportunity to use this consensus as a basis for self-verification. The need for self-verification is described as a drive to establish and maintain a coherent self-image. As Hogg and Abrams (1993) note, perceived agreement creates the categories that we use for identification and the prototypes that we internalize. Further studies confirm the interrelation between the level of uncertainty and the disposition toward identification with specific categories.

Rabbie, Schot, and Visser (1989) described the perceived interdependence among individual members of a group as a basis for identity. This approach suggests that the main motivation for identity is the self-interest that derives from the awareness of a common fate: the perceived common treatment and outcomes that result from ingroup membership. Thus, people believe that their individual achievements and failures are connected with those of other group members. This positive interdependence leads to cooperation and a very salient identity. In a study of gender consciousness and political activism, Gurin and Townsend (1986) confirm the functional role that a sense of common fate has in the formation of identity.

The second approach to studying the functions of social identity defines a set of functions that certain social identities fulfill. In their research, Clary et al. (1998) discovered six functions of social identity: self-defense, altruistic and humanitarian values, benefits related to career, social interactions, the understanding of self, and personal growth. Aharpour (1997) in his study described five functions: help and rewards, distance and detachment, intergroup comparison, social learning, and self-categorization. Deaux et al. (1999) described seven: the understanding of self, positive interpersonal comparison, collective self-esteem, cooperation within a group, intergroup comparison and competition, social interaction, and romantic attachment. All of these functions provide opportunities for the realization of different individual and group needs. The first three functions are connected with personal needs and the development of self-conception. The relationship between any two members of an ingroup is associated with the functions of social interaction and romantic attachment. Ingroup cooperation, intergroup comparison, and competition reflect the relationship among all group members. As further research shows, only five of these functions are connected with the salience of social identity: the understanding of self, positive interpersonal comparison, collective self-esteem, cooperation within a group, and social interaction.

An analysis of social identity functions also requires the examination of a person's involvement in a group. This entails a study of not only the level but also the character of this involvement. Kelman (1997a) describes six patterns of personal involvement in a social group that are based on two motivational bases for extending loyalty to the group: sentimental (a feeling of shared identity with ingroup members) and instrumental (the perception that the ingroup meets a member's individual needs and interests) attachments. He stresses that these two sources of attachment are analytically separate, but influence and reinforce each other. He also addresses three types of orientation to the group: the acceptance of group rules, obligation to follow them, and expectations of fair share of resources (rule orientation); identification with and emotional involvement in group roles (role orientation); and sharing of the group's values and commitment to the group (value orientation). A rule-oriented loyalty is superficial and brief, but arises easily in the context of stressing a group's symbols and rules. A role-oriented loyalty reflects an enthusiasm and desire to participate in group life. A value-oriented loyalty is more stable and deep and serves as a basis for the formation of salient social identities.

Although the list of functions served by social identity is long and diverse, the definition of these functions requires further research. I propose the following list of social identity functions: (1) increasing self-esteem, (2) increasing social status, (3) personal safety, (4) group support and protection, and (5) recognition by ingroup. Below, I describe the results of my research on the importance of these five functions for different types of social identity and interactions among them.

Study I. The Functions of Social Identity

By using specially designed surveys in different towns and villages of Crimea, the study was conducted several times during 1998–2001. The sample was stratified by location, number of resettlements, and rural-urban status.

The participants were Russians (235) and Crimean Tatars (216), distributed across these locations in equal proportions. Of them, 43 percent were male and 57 percent were female; 37 percent were between 20 and 30 years old, 31 percent between 30 and 45, 16 percent between 45 and 60, and 14 percent above 60; 55 percent were residents of towns and 45 percent residents of villages. Participation was voluntary. The respondents were provided with a questionnaire and asked to select answers from a list.

This study aimed to examine the impact of the functions of social identity on its salience. I analyzed the importance of the functions for three social identities: ethnic, regional, and national. The results are presented in Table 3.1.

Therefore, for Russians, ethnic identity provides social status and recognition; regional identity provides self-esteem, personal safety, group support and protection, and recognition by group; and national identity provides social status and support. As a study of the dynamic of social identity (see Chapter 5) proves, the most salient identity for Russians is regional identity, which fulfills four functions for ingroup members.

For Crimean Tatars, ethnic identity provides self-esteem and recognition by group and national identity provides personal safety, group support and protection, and social status. As research on the dynamic of social identity shows (see Chapter 5), the most salient identity for Crimean Tatars is ethnic identity. Thus, for them, self-esteem and recognition by group are the most important functions. In fact, the study of structures of consciousness reveals that only Crimean Tatars used the category "Deserving Respect." Despite the fact that national identity ranks only third among the social identities for Crimean Tatars, it serves three functions, which are connected with security and status. One can explain this fact by stating that national identity is developing and Crimean Tatars connect all their hopes of increasing status and security with a new national identity.

To explore the interconnections between different functions of social identity, a factor analysis for the two ethnic groups was conducted. It

Table 3.1   The Importance of the Functions of Social Identity

Identity	Ethnic Group	Functions				
		Self-Esteem	Social Status	Personal Safety	Group Support and Protection	Recognition by Group
Ethnic	Russians	0.64	0.69	0.67	0.66	0.71
	CT	0.57	0.22	0.34	0.28	0.31
Regional	Russians	0.88	0.66	0.81	0.79	0.76
	CT	0.20	0.17	0.14	0.17	0.20
National	Russians	0.62	0.69	0.59	0.71	0.67
	CT	0.11	0.45	0.37	0.42	0.28

revealed four factors for each group. For Russians, these factors include the following:

1. Social status (0.76) and recognition by group (0.72) provided by ethnic identity;
2. Personal safety provided by national identity (0.70);
3. Self-esteem provided by regional (0.80) and ethnic (0.70) identities;
4. Social status provided by regional identity (0.71).

For Crimean Tatars, these factors include the following:

1. recognition by group provided by regional (0.82) and national (0.79) identities;
2. self-esteem provided by regional (0.88) and ethnic (0.88) identities;
3. personal safety (0.70), group support (0.72), and social status (0.82) provided by ethnic identity;
4. personal safety provided by national (0.81) and regional (0.72) identities.

Thus, for Russians, the function of social status is most important and is provided by ethnic and regional identity. These two identities also provide another important function: self-esteem. For Crimean Tatars, the basic function is personal safety, which is provided by ethnic, regional, and national identity. Possibly, it is connected with the history of deportation. Analysis confirms the importance of two other functions: self-esteem and recognition by the group, which are provided by ethnic identity.

Consequently, the importance of the functions of social identities differs among ethnic groups. These functions influence the salience of identities: if an identity provides most of the functions, it becomes salient. The salience of identity is also connected with the fulfillment of the most important functions. If ingroup members attach important functions to a new identity, it develops into a salient identity and can replace other identities that previously provided the corresponding functions. The study of functions of social identities can help understand the basic needs of a particular group and develop an early warning for triggering events and situations. Thus, if social status is the most important function for ethnic identity, any threat to the status of an ethnic group or its members can provoke negative reactions and conflict activities. If self-esteem is the most significant function for national identity, any threat to the self-respect of a national group can inflame the readiness for conflict behavior. The 12 cartoons of Islam's Prophet Muhammad published by the Danish newspaper *Jyllands-Posten* in September 2005 provoked mass protests and outrage among Muslims throughout the world. The depictions that included incendiary images, such as Muhammad wearing a turban shaped as a bomb with a burning fuse, were perceived as offensive and threatening to the self-esteem of Muslims.

CHAPTER 4

COMPONENTS OF THE SYSTEM
OF SOCIAL IDENTITY

4.1. SALIENCE OF SOCIAL IDENTITY

Salience can be said to be the most important component of identity, and it can be influenced by such factors as permeable or impermeable group boundaries, positive or negative intergroup comparisons, identity distinctiveness, and socialization (Berry et al. 1989; Brewer 1991, 2001; Tajfel and Turner 1979). Salience can vary on a continuum from strong to weak: each identity can be very salient, salient, or nonsalient. As Phinney (1991) shows, persons with a high salience of ethnic identity have strong feelings for their group memberships, evaluate their groups positively, and are interested in their groups' culture and history.

Stryker (1969) has argued that various identities exist in a hierarchy of salience, and one identity can be invoked over others not only because of its salience but also because of the level of commitment to that identity. One highly salient identity can prevail over another. Because of the hierarchy of salience, these identities may exhibit stable or situational characteristics. Stryker noted that if an identity is salient for a long period, it becomes a central identity and has a strong influence on behavior. At the same time, Ting-Toomey et al. (2000) noted that for some individuals, being forced to confront interpersonal issues arising from difference, such as stereotypes, prejudice, and discrimination, increases the salience of ethnic identity.

Several findings confirm that the importance or dominance of social categories reinforces identification choices. For example, McGuire et al. (1978) found that children representing ethnic minorities in their classes tended to describe themselves in terms of ethnic groups, while children in the families with a prevalence of one gender (such as the only girl in a family of five brothers) stressed their gender identity in self-description. Ellemers, Spears, and Doosje (1997) showed that people with salient identities find that they have much in common with the other members of their ingroups and do not want to leave the ingroups even in situations of threat. A salient social identity influences the level of satisfaction in ingroup activities (Wann and Branscombe 1990). Identity theory also indicates that numerous, authoritarian, and powerful outgroups influence the development of a salient identity. When it is institutionalized in a social system, the asymmetrical mix of different influences on a salient identity leads to development and change within an individual's structure of identities. Research has shown that even disproportion between groups can increase the salience of identity. As Kinket and Verkuyten (1997) demonstrated in their research, situational salience (e.g., percentage of Dutch and Turkish students in the classroom) affects a weak rather than a strong identity.

According to Oakes's functional approach to salience (1987), the use of a category in a given context depends on the accessibility of the category and the fit between the category and reality. As Huddy (2001) argued, four factors influence the acquisition of identity: the valence of group membership, the defining social characteristics of typical group members, the core values associated with membership, and the characteristics of common outgroups that help to define what an ingroup is not. Gerson (2001) maintains that social practices influence the development and salience of identity: "what people do and how they conceptualize or represent what they do as constituting membership in various groups" (183).

To understand the nature of a salient identity in the system of social identities and its impact on conflict behavior, I have analyzed identity formation in the processes of socialization and acculturation. From the first days of life, each person shares culture, language, religion, geographic region, and so forth with others. Through everyday interactions with parents, grandparents, neighbors, and peers and through education at different social institutions (kindergarten, school, church), a person absorbs values, beliefs, and ideas about the world from others. Group characteristics influence socialization processes, and each society affects the dynamism and specificity of this influence (see Chapter 2 for a comparative analysis of individualistic and collectivistic cultures). As studies show, different features can compose the content of social identity: color of skin, physical characteristics, history, religion, customs, and so on. I propose the following three factors as determinants of the salience of different social identities:

1. *Level of differences.* From early childhood, a person aspires to understand the world by analyzing the similarities and differences between things, events, people, and groups. As the theory of social categorization stresses, these differences play an important role in processes such as cognitive development.

2. *Prevalence of intergroup or interpersonal contact.* By analyzing the impact of collectivistic and individualistic cultures on the dominance of social and individual identity (see Chapter 2), I have shown that social identity is the leading identity in collectivistic cultures and affects a person's perceptions and behavior, while individual identity dominates in individualistic

cultures. As research shows, within any culture, social identity becomes more salient in the context of groups. Thus, men and women identify more strongly with gendered groups and describe themselves in terms of typical gender characteristics in intergroup contexts (man and woman) than in intragroup contexts (man-man and woman-woman) (Gaertner et al. 1999). In such situations, the contradiction "We-They" becomes more significant than the contradiction "Me-You."

In the context of intergroup relations, a person perceives others in terms of ingroups and outgroups. The judgments and opinions about members of outgroups are created on the basis of intergroup comparisons, while those about members of an ingroup are developed through intragroup comparisons. Outgroup homogeneity, as proposed by the social categorization theory, results in the perception of outgroups as more homogenous when compared with ingroups. Relations with other people as typical members of outgroups strengthen identification with ingroups and lead to the formation of a salient social identity.

3. *Competition among groups.* I will discuss this factor in detail in Chapters 6 and 7. Here I just want to stress that the competition for scarce resources, power, information, and independent positions significantly strengthens the salience of a corresponding social identity. As the theories of social identity constantly stress, the negative comparison with outgroups is related to strong identification with one's ingroup. During the process of comparison, people project their negative feelings, desires, and ingroup stereotypes on members of other groups; these "congeal" in the forms of shared reservoirs and chosen traumas that reshape negative attitudes toward members of outgroups (Volkan 1997, 2004).

The proposed model demonstrates the constructivist approach to social identity salience. The first two factors—the level of differences and the prevalence of intergroup or interpersonal relations—are connected with culture and the psychology of group dynamics. The third factor, competition, stresses the role of the political and economic aspects in the formation of a salient social identity.

The salience of social identity is connected with the *primacy of ingroup,* which is defined as the feeling of supremacy of ingroup goals and values over individual ones. This primacy contains several components, such as (1) predominance of ingroup aims over individual ones, (2) the readiness to forget all internal conflicts in a situation of treat to the ingroup and (3) the readiness to unite against outgroups. The higher the level of ingroup primacy for ingroup members, the stronger their willingness to disregard their own goals and values and to follow the ways of behavior required by the ingroup.

The ingroup primacy can increase or decrease the influence of identity salience on the conflict behavior of ingroup members. Some groups require a high level of ingroup primacy as a condition for group membership; other groups provide opportunities for maintaining a balance between individual and ingroup values and goals. If high ingroup primacy is required, the salience of ingroup identity will lead directly to intergroup prejudice and conflict behavior. If it is not required, ingroup members with salient identities can still rethink and revise their attitudes toward an outgroup and, subsequently, their readiness for conflict behavior is defined on the basis of individual experience. It will reduce the impact of identity salience on intergroup prejudice.

4.2. MEANING OF SOCIAL IDENTITY

The salience of social identity cannot be used as a single explanatory factor for the impact of social identity on individual perceptions and behavior. The meaning of identity is contingent on group beliefs, norms, values, goals, and worldviews. Bar-Tal (1990, 1998) describes beliefs as views that all group members share because these views are crucial for a group. He describes three types of beliefs that become group beliefs:

1. Those that are practical and purposeful in the process of group formation and meet the need for group belonging,
2. Those that reflect a sense of commonness for group membership, and
3. Those supported by leaders as the most significant for a group.

Group norms define which actions are important for group members, which are prohibited, and which are necessary in specific situations (Homans 1950); they regulate the behavior of group members and serve as criteria for estimating this behavior. Norms can be included in the meaning of identity if they provide unique characteristics to the group and are shared by all people. Values characterize a sense of life and world and serve as measurements for the estimation of objects, actions, and events. To influence identity meaning, values have to be shared by all group members who believe in the immutability and importance of their group. Shared values increase the salience of social identity and define group boundaries. Several features, including confidence and centrality, characterized group beliefs and values. Usually, group beliefs, norms, and values are perceived as real facts and have a high level of confidence. A decrease in trust frequently leads to the weakening of social identity and to group disintegration. Centrality defines the importance of beliefs and values for group members and the structure of values; some values can be more significant and vital than others. Groups vary on the basis of the level of confidence and centrality of values. High levels of trust and centrality of the majority of values, norms, and beliefs characterize religious groups. Other groups can have less central values and beliefs, thus providing fewer reasons for confidence.

The meaning of social identity develops on the border between groups and constitutes both the content of group membership and the specificity of interrelations with outgroups. It contains the following components:

1. *Ingroup traditions and values (culture).* This component reflects the specificity of interrelations within ingroups, cultural characteristics, values

and beliefs, holidays and customs, ways of life, and worldviews. It is a basic characteristic of all groups that portrays an ingroup's everyday experiences.

2. *Ingroup language.* It concerns the native language(s) of an ingroup, other common spoken languages, and the influence of worldview and perception on individuals and groups through specific grammatical orders and linguistic structures.

3. *Characteristics of ingroup members.* This component includes ingroup prototypes as well as stereotypes, valued individual features, and characteristics of the most prominent ingroup members.

4. *Ingroup history.* This element contains historical events, names, and situations that are important for ingroups and that assist in defining their development. Chosen traumas and glories, fairy tales and legends, and heroes are essential parts of ingroup history.

5. *Ingroup Ideology.* This component reflects the main ideas, goals, aspirations, and aims of an ingroup.

6. *Interrelations with outgroups.* This element contains the norms and traditions of interconnections between ingroups and outgroups; the history of relationships, benefits, gains, and loses that resulted from the interrelations; the record of discriminations; and differences in status and power.

7. *Reverberated identity.* This element refers to an ingroup's identity that results from comparisons with outgroups. It includes all ingroup characteristics that develop in apposition to outgroup characteristics. To understand "who we are," it is important to define "who we are not" on the basis of "who the others are."

8. *Outgroup image.* This component reflects stereotypes, attitudes toward outgroups, and the perceived characteristics, culture, and history of outgroups that help define intergroup borders and stress differences between ingroup and outgroup.

Usually, the meaning of social identity is multimodal and contains all of these components. The prevalence of one or some of them leads to a different *mode* of the meaning of identity. The dominance of such components as ingroup traditions and values, characteristics of ingroup members, and reverberated identity leads to a *depictive mode* of the meaning of identity (e.g., Amish people). *Ideological modes* of the meaning of identity are characterized by the prevalence of an ingroup ideology and of interrelations with outgroups (political parties). If ingroup history and interrelations with outgroups become the most important components, the meaning of identity is in a *historical mode*. The national identity of people in the Dominican Republic contains a prevailing historic mode: during survey interviews, all Dominicans described history as a main source of ingroup pride and identity (ICAR student report, 2005). Lastly, the dominance of a reverberated identity, outgroup image, and interrelations with outgroups defines a *relative mode* of the meaning of identity.

Conflict and violence between groups can lead to the transformation from multiple identities with multimodal meaning to a single identity with prevailing threat narratives—a *dominant* identity. A dominant identity replaces all other core social identities and becomes the most salient and actual identity prevailing in the system of social identities. Moreover, it overcomes individual identity and influences the perception of situations pertaining to ingroups and outgroups. Even among representatives of individualistic cultures, dominant identities can influence the weakening of individual values and attitudes and of individual responsibilities and positions, thereby forcing people to perceive themselves in a dichotomous context: "ingroup-outgroup." They always have the form of a mobilized identity, and the most important components of their meaning are interrelations with outgroups and negative outgroup images. They lead to the perception of the world in terms of a positive "We" and a negative "They." Fighting with the outgroup becomes the main goal and condition for individual and ingroup survival.

Consider Japan's invasion of China in 1931. The Chinese soldiers in Nanking immediately ran or surrendered when the Japanese army invaded, which led to the further dehumanization of Chinese soldiers. Surrender was considered an impossible act of weakness and the ultimate violation of the strict code of military honor that the Japanese soldiers had been ingrained with since childhood. Consequently, the Japanese did not perceive the Chinese prisoners of war to be human. This attitude transferred from the soldiers to the Japanese civilian population. Over 20,000 Chinese women aged 7 to 77 years were raped and then murdered or turned into sex slaves or "comfort women" for the Japanese soldiers. Chinese men were forced to rape their own children or mothers at gunpoint for the amusement of the Japanese soldiers. Chinese soldiers were doused with gasoline and burned, others were buried alive or were forced to bury alive their friends and family, and many were decapitated. After six weeks of violence, the Japanese Imperial Army had murdered 300,000 people in Nanking alone.

The example of East Timor and Indonesia shows how changes in the meaning of ingroup identity can lead to the changes in attitudes and policies toward outgroups (for a more in-depth analysis, see Tan 2006). After the Indonesian independence in 1945, the sovereignty, national unity, and territorial integrity of the Indonesian state were considered sacred and nonnegotiable. The idea of a united Indonesian nation-state unifying different groups was the core concept of the meaning of national identity. In 1974, East Timor began to establish new institutions, develop education and infrastructure, and shape nationalist ideologies. The Indonesian government perceived this development as a sign of aspirations for independence and began to recognize East Timor as a threat and a potential enemy. In order to preserve unity and hegemony as the main principles of the meaning of national identity, the Indonesian government began invasion and brutal occupation of East Timor.

In 1984, the new Indonesian president B. J. Habibie declared the consolidation of democracy as the most important national interest. On the basis of this new meaning of national identity, the government saw the policies toward East Timor as inconsistent with the vision of Indonesia, a country that was stressing human rights, independence, and self-determination. "For these policymakers, resolving the East Timor issue was intertwined with achieving their political project of building a new and just Indonesia where democracy and human rights would have a central place. They had turned the Suharto regime's understanding of Indonesia's national interests vis-à-vis East Timor on its head" (Tan 2006: 201). Thus, changes in the meaning of national identity led to changes in Indonesia's policies toward East Timor.

The processes of group formation and the development of the meaning of identity are simultaneous; however, there are times when one of these processes can outstrip the other. The meaning of identity can be created before the formation of a group (e.g., religious sects, political parties, groups of volunteers, clubs). If this occurs, the set of beliefs, values, and norms is defined at the beginning, and from this foundation, group formation begins. More often, the meaning of identity develops after the definition of group boundaries and the creation of groups.

Ingroup identity can have different meanings if an ingroup exists in different regions or countries (like diasporas) or among different subcultures and subgroups. Thus, for the Karen people who live in Thailand and Burma, national identity has a very different meaning (for a more in-depth analysis, see Buadaeng 2007). In Burma, the Karen have a sense of pride because they believe themselves to be superior to all other groups. This belief stems from the fact that missionaries and colonizers provided higher education to the Karen and granted them with high-rank positions in the government. The British enabled them to have permanent settlements in the more fertile lowland areas and supported their governing power. As an expression of their gratefulness for the higher status they have been given, the Karen showed their "loyalty" to the British Empire by supporting the British army attacks on the Burmese army, as well as by participating in the suppression of Burmese revolts. After the independence of Burma in 1948, a fight between the Karen and the Burmese government started and continues to this day. On the other hand, the Karen in Thailand live mainly in mountainous areas of the north and west as forest conservation-oriented people with rituals in relation to each type of forest. Their missionary activities in Thailand had only started in the 1950s, but the Thai government controlled this situation in order to integrate these hill tribes into the Thai society. Thus, the Karen never asked for a separation from the Thai society and felt that they were a part of it. These two positions in different societies—dominant in Burma and inferior in Thailand—influence the variation in the meaning of the Karen's identity: superior and independence-oriented in the first case, and peaceful and nature-oriented in the second.

We also have to separate internal meanings (of ingroup identities) and external meanings (of outgroup identities). Often, members of ingroups and outgroups have different understandings and ideas about the core values, beliefs, and norms of a specific ingroup. This misconception results in incorrect interpretations of ingroup activities and actions. Thus, Russians in Ukraine desire close relations with Russia, including cultural and economical exchange between the two countries, the legal status for Russian as a second national language, and opportunities for the cultural development of their group. They do not want Ukraine to join Russia or become a part of Russia themselves, because they have significant disagreements with the Russian policy, including the war in Chechnya, and want to develop a new sense of identity that is neither Russian nor Ukrainian, but a "salubrious" mix of the two: Ukrainian Russians. Nevertheless, many Ukrainians perceive this group as a "fifth column" that seeks a dependent relationship with Russia, or even to join Russia as a republic. Many Ukrainians equate Russians with Soviets and blame them for all communists' crimes in spite of the fact that many Ukrainians were among the leaders of Soviet Union's Communist Party, including the general secretaries Khrushchev and Brezhnev. These different—ingroup and outgroup—meanings of the Ukrainian Russian identity have led to internal conflicts and opposition.

The meaning of ingroup identity can have a significant impact on the perception and behavior of group members. Research stresses the importance of meaning in both shaping identities and determining conflict or tolerant behavior (Deaux 1996; Huddy 2001; Gurin, Hurtado, and Peng 1994; Simon and Hamilton 1994). Breakwell (2004) showed that different meanings of the European identity have shaped the reactions of Europeans to policies designed to create the European Union. The meaning of the African American identity influences the readiness to support programs designed to improve the situation of other minority groups (Sellers et al. 1998). Research also shows that the meaning of national identity can influence attitudes toward other groups and political situations; thus individuals with a nativist sense of the American identity (such as being Christian) regard immigrants negatively and see the adoption of American customs as an obligation for them (Citrin, Wong, and Duff 2000).

4.3. ASCRIBED AND ACQUIRED IDENTITY

Many postulates of the theory of social identity are derived from a minimal intergroup situation. In a famous experiment, people were ascribed to two groups on the basis of their preference for the artworks of Kandinsky and Klee. They did not have a choice of group and an opportunity to analyze interpersonal and intergroup differences so as to adopt ascribed identities. On the basis of these results, the theory of social identity suggests that the salience of group membership is the most important determinant of identity. For example, men who work surrounded by women's majority must have a salient gender identity, and Hispanic Americans who live in a predominantly African American community must have a strong racial identity. This approach to identity is very deterministic and excludes individual perception and preference.

The choice of identity is one of the most important characteristics of social identity in the real world. However, it can impact the development of ingroup cohesion and intergroup discrimination, even in laboratory experiments. In their study of identity, Turner et al. (1984) divided participants into two groups and asked them to solve cognitive problems in small teams. In the first group, participants could choose their team; in the second, they were assigned to one of the teams. The results showed that the opportunity to choose one's group increases the loyalty to this group and one's identification with it. Thus, the members of the wining teams demonstrated a higher level of self-esteem and cohesion when they were assigned to teams. However, participants who chose their team showed more self-esteem and group cohesion in situations of team loss. Further research confirms the impact of identity acquisition on intergroup discrimination. Laboratory studies showed that the salience of group identity increases in a situation that provides the possibility of group choice, while it decreases and results in the formation of negative attitudes toward other groups in situations of competition for resources.

The acquisition of social identity depends on individual differences in the ability to adopt a new identity. Duckitt (1989) suggests that authoritarian behavior can be explained in particular by a strong individual tendency for identification with a dominant social group, such as that of whites in the United States or Christians in Europe. It is possible that people who are less open to new experience or intolerant prefer ascribed identities to acquired ones and feel uncomfortable in situations of multiple choices. In their study of individual differences in identity acquisition, Perreault and Bourhis (1999) analyzed the impact of ethnocentrism, authoritarian behavior, and the individual need for certainty regarding the salience of social identity. In laboratory experiments, they found that all three personal characteristics are correlated with the strength of ingroup identification, but that ethnocentrism has the most significant effect. People who show antipathy toward outgroup members are more inclined to adopt new identities in the laboratory context. Other research showed that motivational factors, such as high self-esteem, the need for belonging to a group, the need to be unique, and the need for certainty, also can be determinants of salience for an acquired identity.

Groups differ on the prospects for a person to choose membership in these groups. Group permeability and the level of uncertainty in social environments are factors that affect the acquisition of social identity. Studies on the impact of group permeability show that members of groups with a low social status are more disposed to deny their membership and identity. Nevertheless, Wright (1997) demonstrated that group permeability has to be extremely strong in order to influence an individual's decision to leave an ingroup. In his study, he confirmed the correlation between identity salience and permeability of boundary: members of groups with permeable boundaries have low levels of social identity salience.

Groups also differ on the level of uncertainty about group membership. Theories of social identity are based on the idea of known and fixed membership and use empirical research to analyze groups with distinct relationship and boundaries. However, membership in some groups, especially political or ideological ones, cannot be described as clear and fixed. For many people, the boundaries of political groups (except political clubs and organizations) are indefinite, uncertain, and, sometimes, incomprehensible. Huddy (2001) analyzed this question by introducing the notion of the dyadic "group boundaries–meaning of identity." Other scholars stress that group boundaries would be a sufficient condition for understanding group membership if all group identities are simply assigned to group members. Nevertheless, when social identity is acquired, the meaning of group identity has a significant impact on the process and results (as outcomes) of identity adoption. Thus, even though many Germans feel a deep anxiety about being connected with German nationalism and do not want to show their patriotic feelings, the German identity is salient. In laboratory experiments on sharing resources, German students decided that other German students would not discriminate against Jewish students, but Jewish students were predicted to discriminate against Germans. This perception arose from the historical relationship between Germans and members of the Jewish faith, but it is not a product of social identity salience.

Huddy (2001) posits four factors that influence the process of social identity acquisition: the valence of group membership, identification with a prototype, the basic values, and differences with outgroups.

1. *Valence of group membership.* As research shows, a group identity never becomes salient when others estimate a group negatively, and its boundaries are permeable. Individual differences in perceptions regarding the ingroup valence also affect the formation of an ingroup identity. Some Americans, for example, are proud of their international image and are glad to meet fellow compatriots outside the United States; others expect anti-American feelings and actions and stay away from other Americans. Some commercial firms even use this perception and propose that Americans wear T-shirts, bags, and caps with Canadian symbols while traveling in foreign countries. Moreover, the valence of identity also depends on the meanings associated with the symbols adopted by various groups. For example, during World War II, the Ukrainians who collaborated with Nazi divisions, such as "SS Galichina," used a symbol with three teeth. After independence, this symbol became a part of the Ukrainian flag and provoked different feelings and senses of identity among eastern and western Ukrainians.

2. *Identification with a prototype.* The social categorization theory stresses the importance of group prototypes in defining group membership and understanding the behavior of group members; similarity with an ingroup prototype strengthens social identity. This approach suggests that the analysis of group prototypes can explain how and when similarities are

developed—which forms the basis of identity—and describes the people who are prepared to adopt this identity. For example, if conservative men from southern American states typically serve as representatives of the American Republican Party, working women from northern states will feel distant from this same party.

3. *Basic values.* In addition to the characteristics of typical members, such as clothes, language, and lifestyle, social identity is developed on the basis of main values. In the study of the values of German and Jewish students, Schwartz and Bilsky (1990) asked participants to rank 19 terminal and 18 instrumental values on the basis of individual preferences and as a perception of their ethnic groups. Individual and group lists were interconnected; however, the correlation was more significant for the Jewish than for the German students. The authors explained this fact by concluding that the group identity of German students is less salient. In my research of the values of Russian and Crimean Tatars, I also found stronger interconnections between individual and ingroup values among Crimean Tatars, whose ethnic identity is more salient than that of Russians (see study below).

4. *Differences with outgroups.* Outgroups not only stress intergroup boundaries but also define identity by emphasizing the information about typical outgroup characteristics that is different from ingroup features. For example, feminists were defined as women who were not housewives and did not look at their career indifferently. After independence, the national identity of Pakistan was developed in contrast with the Indian identity.

Thus, early research on social identity suggested the stability and predetermination of social identity by culture, social environment, and other people, whereas current research stresses the ability of a person to choose, acquire, or reject social identity. The latter completely changed the understanding of identity as ascribed or given from birth to view it as something that develops as a result of free individual choice. As I discuss in Chapter 1, religion, education, social position, and sexual orientation can be subjects for preferential selection. Migration, high diverse rates, affirmative action, and secondary education can lead to the reevaluation of and changes in social identity systems.

Individual choice is possible even for social identities that have been considered stable for a long time: ethnic and racial. Nagel (1995) studied the increasing number of people who identified themselves as "American Indian" in national censuses. From 1960 to 1990, the number of people who used the American Indian identity as a self-descriptive category increased threefold. As Nagel suggested, this fact could not solely be explained by birth rate increases, and thus he concluded that these data provided evidence of changes in social identities. He found an increase in this identification among people who lived in towns or states without reservations, were married to people of other ethnic or racial groups, and spoke English. In other words, the percentage of such people increased in social contexts where individuals could exercise the freedom to choose identities. The possibility to acquire or reject this identity is lesser for American Indians who live with reservations or use this identity for administrative goals.

Another great example is the identity of blacks in Argentina. In 1810 black residents accounted for about 30 percent of the population of Buenos Aires, but in 1887 their numbers decreased to 1.8 percent. Reel (2005) discussed two popular myths: a yellow fever epidemic in 1871 that devastated the black population and the war with Paraguay in the 1860s. Recent research using distinct methods such as door-to-door surveys and analysis of DNA samples shows that black Argentines did not disappear, but mixed with other population. The DNA analysis showed that 10 percent of those that identified themselves as white had African genes, but because of strong racial prejudice, they denied their racial identity and wanted to believe that they were white by counting even "one drop of white blood" (Reel 2005). The development of the Argentinean national identity in the nineteenth century was based on the idea of a "white country with European roots," and the government conveniently pretended that the black population had disappeared, and did not reflect those of African ancestry in its censuses.

Ethnic identity is also a matter of choice in mixed families. Children of American immigrant families where grandmothers are Italian and English and grandfathers are Polish and Swedish have a great possibility to chose one of these ethnic identities or even acquire a new one: American. In multicultural regions, such as the Balkans, where families have a mix of ethnic and religious groups, children choose their ethnicity, and even siblings can acquire different ethnic identities.

Acquired social identities have a greater impact on a person's behavior than ascribed ones. In many cases, people who adopt new religious, ethnic, or national identities show stronger devotion to ingroup beliefs, values, and norms than people with ascribed identities. An acquired identity can completely change the structure of the social identity system: it can become the most salient identity, replacing other core identities and modifying their meanings. Any changes in social environments or ingroup relations will have a lesser impact on acquired identities than on ascribed ones.

4.4. TYPES OF SOCIAL IDENTITY

There are three methodological approaches to the classification of the types of social identity: ideographical, component, and taxonomical approaches. The ideographical approach defines the types of social identity on the basis of membership in different social groups:

- Family: father, daughter, wife;
- Professional: teacher, driver;
- Regional: inhabitant of the city, state, north;
- Religious: Muslim, Orthodox, Protestant;
- National: citizen of the country, American, Russian;

- Ethnic: French, Russian;
- Political: Democrat, communist, socialist;
- Class: working, middle.

The component approach is connected with the analysis of elements within social identity. By conducting factor analysis together with the study of interrelations among factors, Klink et al. (1997) described two components of social identity: cognitive and evaluative emotional. Ellemers, Kortekaas, and Ouwerkerk (1999) expand this research and describe three aspects of social identity: self-categorization, group self-esteem, and group loyalty. These aspects depend on a group's status and relative size.

The taxonomical approach stresses the existence of several classes of social identity. Deaux et al. (1995) proposed the combination of 64 forms of social identity taken from previous research into specific classes. The cluster analyses of the data showed five different classes of social identity: interrelations, vocations, political relations, ethnicity/religion, and social position. These classes are characterized by central or peripheral positions, collective or individual nature, social desirability and status, and the extent to which an identity is acquired. These criteria can serve as a basis for further differentiation within each class.

Collectivism and individualism were analyzed as determinants of differences between the types of social identity in several studies. Thus, Brown et al. (1992) described two dimensions that influence group differences: an accent on relations and the absence this accent. Luhtanen and Crocker (1992) proposed a new notion of collective self-esteem that is based on belonging to a group and is developed in intergroup relations. Prentice, Miller, and Lightdale (1994) showed two types of social identity: one based on group interconnection and the other on identification with a group. Brewer and Gardner (1996) used three levels of analysis (individual, interpersonal, and group) to define the three forms of self-concept: individual, relations based, and collective. For our analysis of social identity, two levels are important: relations based and collective. Social identities that reflect relationships develop in dyadic interrelations; collective social identities are a result of membership in groups.

The following two types of social identities reflect the forms of personal relationships: interpersonal or intergroup. As mentioned earlier, the two types of groups based on the level of involvement are the categorical group and the group of membership. I suggest that the forms of personal relationships and the level of involvement in groups constitute four types of social identity. Table 4.1 summarizes the distinction between these four types.

A *positioning identity* reflects situations when a person identifies oneself or herself with a specific category of interpersonal relations, but is not deeply involved in it and does not acquire the norms, values, and beliefs associated with this position in society. For example, when a person is asked to be a mentor, he or she associates with this position or thinks about himself or herself in these terms, but does not feel a sense of responsibility, does not like

Table 4.1   Types of Social Identity

Level of Involvement in Group	Types of Personal Relationship	
	Interpersonal	Intergroup
Categorical group	Positioning identity	Descriptive identity
Group of membership	Dyadic identity	Collective identity

to mentor, and does not work with people. However, when a person likes to think about himself or herself as a mentor, this identity provides a sense of self-esteem and can become salient. A person can consider himself or herself a mediator or practitioner but in reality never conduct any third-party mediation. He or she can speak about importance of this work and be proud of his or her (perceived) relationship with this category.

A *dyadic identity* develops when a person describes oneself in terms of a particular category and intensely engages in the corresponding interpersonal relations. For example, a woman will consider herself a mother and actively take care of and educate her children. She adopts all the values, beliefs, and norms associated with this position and aims to be a good mother. This identity will become her core identity and could be connected with ethnic, religious, or national identities, thus influencing her meaning of the mother identity. Thus, the meanings of being a "good mother" in different cultures vary and can even contradict one another in terms of controlling children, providing education, and so forth. A person can also acquire the identity of mentor or mediator-practitioner as a dyadic identity: he or she will actively participate in interactions connected with these positions, and the values and beliefs associated with them can become crucial for him or her.

A *descriptive identity* reflects one's identification with specific social categories without actual membership in a corresponding group. A person thinks and describes oneself in terms of group categories and considers them to be an important part of one's self-concept. However, he or she does not participate in group activities and does not share the group's beliefs, goals, and norms. Thus, one can consider oneself Swedish, but not observe customs or ethnic holidays and not share the goals and values of one's group.

A *collective identity* forms when a person identifies himself or herself with a group, belongs to this group, shares its beliefs and values, follows its norms and customs, and shows loyalty and deep attachment to its goals and expectations. Thus, a person can be a member of an ethnic, religious, or national group, share a common history or expectations, fight for ingroup goals, and thus perceive the world in terms of group relationships.

Each social identity will have different forms for different people. Thus, a person can have the *positioning identity* of a mentor or mediator but can also acquire it as a *dyadic identity:* he or she will actively participate in interactions connected with these positions, and the values and beliefs associated with them can become essential for him or her. The social identity "mother" can be a *dyadic identity,* but it would also become a *collective identity* if a woman participated in mothers' movements or organizations. Ethic, religious, and national identities can be *descriptive* or *collective* depending on the level of a person's involvement in a group.

Social identities can also change their form during a person's life. Thus, the identity "woman" can be first a *descriptive identity* for a person but can turn into a salient *dyadic identity* during a close dual relationship. Women can join women's organizations or clubs, thus making this identity a *collective identity.* Changes in one's identity can occur in reverse scenarios: *collective* ethnic identities can be converted into *descriptive* identities. For example, a person can have the salient *collective* identity "Russian" and share the beliefs, ideas, values, and traditions of his or her ethnic group. After emigration to another country, for example, America, he or she can adopt new American customs, traditions, beliefs, and values and speak English at his or her home. His or her children will not know the Russian language or Russian traditions. This person can still tell that he or she is Russian and from time to time remember some ethnic customs and traditions and celebrate holidays, but his or her identity will become *descriptive.*

Theories of social identities describe different types of identities. Thus, theories of personal social identity emphasize positioning and descriptive identities, those of role social identities study positioning and dyadic identities, and those of group social identities accentuate descriptive and collective social identities. These types of social identities influence the impact of identity on a person's behavior and attitudes. Dual and collective identities have a very significant effect on a person's values, beliefs, and positions. Descriptive and collective identities influence the perceptions and evaluations of the world in terms of group categories and intergroup relations. Therefore, the study of any social identity requires the detection and description of its type.

4.5. FORMS OF SOCIAL IDENTITY

The content of social identities can vary and can reflect different forms of social identity. Membership in social groups can include diverse components such as customs, traditions, cuisine, culture, values, beliefs, attitudes, stereotypes, history, norms, ideology, goals and aspirations, intentions, and activities. All these components can have different levels of importance for particular social identities; they can also be in different stages of development. Depending on their specificity, it is possible to describe three forms of social identity.

Some social identities are based on characteristics of the everyday life of a group. Such characteristics can include cuisine and diet; clothes; typical day routine; songs, music, and dancing; traditions and customs; and even holidays and ways of celebration. Values, beliefs, attitudes, and norms are also integrated within this identity, but they are perceived as essential or given and are never questioned. This knowledge is formed during the processes of early socialization within families and educational institutions. People can easily describe the specificity of their group and the differences from other groups by using these basic cultural characteristics. They can live "within" their social identity and follow all ingroup "recommendations and instructions," but never think deeply about the roots of their cultural traditions, ingroup's goals and intentions and its status and position within the society. This form of identity can be described as *cultural identity*.

Other social identities can include a reflective or advanced understanding of a group's past, present, and future. People can have a deep knowledge about the history of their ingroup and its relationship to outgroups, be aware of its current status and position, and recognize its future goals and perspectives. Such an identity also reflects an appreciation of the group's values and beliefs, an understanding of its roots and sources, as well as its role in society. Such components as cuisine, clothes, music, tradition, and customs can also be presented in this identity, but they all reflect the meaning and sense of the ingroup's main values and beliefs. This form of identity can be described as *reflected identity*.

Through intergroup comparisons of position, power, and status, a person can also understand ingroup identity within the framework of intergroup relations. In this case, the estimation of ingroups and outgroups is based on the positions and goals of both; traditions, customs, and cultural characteristics do not play an important role in this intergroup comparison. The values and beliefs of ingroups and outgroups are perceived in the context of intergroup interactions and contradictions. Such ideologization of identity results in the perception of competition among groups and the incompatibility of goals. The core aim of an ingroup is to increase its status or power, which leads to conflict intentions and a readiness to fight against outgroups. The perception of intergroup interaction is based on a "we-they" opposition; members of outgroups appear as adversaries. The main content and meaning of this identity are contradiction and competition among groups. Such an identity can be described as *mobilized identity*.

Consider religious identity. *Cultural forms* of this identity can reflect the behavior of people who follow the norms and traditions of religion—go to church, fast, pray before dinner at night—but never think about the meaning of their activities and do not understand the content of basic beliefs and treatises. People with *realized forms* of religious identity develop a sense of basic values and beliefs, understand the role of their religion in society, and know how to address the main challenges and problems of life on the basis of their religious faith. People with *mobilized forms* of religious identity perceive people from other confessions as nonbelievers and faithless and consider it their responsibility to teach or convert them to their religion. Thus, a woman can wear a scarf as an important symbol of her religious identity without knowing the meaning of this tradition or having wrong interpretations (*cultural form*). She also can understand the deep concept that a woman has to be "sacred and clean" (*realized form*). She can use the scarf to stress her distance from and opposition to other groups (*mobilized form*).

These three forms of social identity—cultural, reflected, and mobilized—can mirror the stages of identity development. First, people can have a *cultural form* of ethnic identity—that is, they can follow traditions and customs, celebrate ethnic holidays, eat ethnic food, and so forth. Then they can begin to question the meaning of this identity and try to understand their ethnic group's history and current position, thus developing a *realized form* of ethnic identity. If these people see that their group has a low status, they may blame other ethnic groups for discrimination and oppression against their ingroup. Looking for ways to change this situation, they will acquire a *mobilized form* of ethnic identity.

But in many cases, people can have one form of social identity without transitioning through another form. For example, a person can convert into a new religion and have a *realized form* of religious identity from the very beginning. A person can join a group that is in competition or conflict with an outgroup and immediately acquire a *mobilized* social identity, such as sport club fans. Each form of identity can vary by the level of salience; it can be a core identity or a local identity. People can also have different forms of their identities: for example, a person's identity system can include a *cultural* form of religious and regional identity, a *realized* form of ethnic identity, and a *mobilized* form of national and class identity. Forms of identity can and do influence the perceptions of situations and the behavior of people.

4.6. Collective Axiology

The concept of collective axiology is developed in the book *Identity, Morality, and Threat* (2006), co-edited by Dr. Rothbart and me. A collective axiology is a system of value commitments that offers moral guidance to maintain relations with those within, and outside, a group. It provides a sense of life and world, serves as a criterion for understanding actions and events, and regulates ingroup behaviors. With this criterion, individuals clarify group membership and relations with outgroups. "A collective axiology defines boundaries and relations among groups and establishes criteria for ingroup/outgroup membership. Through its collective axiology, a group traces its development from a sacred past, extracted from mythic episodes beyond the life of mortals, and seeks permanence" (Rothbart and Korostelina 2006: 4). It is a set of constructions that are used to validate, vindicate, rationalize, or legitimize actions, decisions, and policies. Such constructions function as instruments for making sense of episodes of conflict and serve to solidify groups.

A collective axiology includes three constructed forms: mythic narrative, sacred icons, and normative orders.

1. *Mythic narrative.* "Stories of the threatening Other gain potency through dissemination of shocking images, harrowing anecdotes, and accounts of violence. Over time, such stories solidify perceptions of the Other through seemingly fixed negativities that are grounded, presumably, in a common place of origin, a shared ancestry, or common flaws. Through

the power of such images, certain particularities of places, times, and actors become sacred to both storytellers and listeners" (Rothbart and Korostelina 2006: 37). The sacred episodes acquire archetypical meanings that shape group consciousness and contribute to the mythic narratives that color their perceptions of the Other.

2. *Iconic order.* Many images of enemy became deeply emotional and concentrated the whole pattern of characterizing others as dangerous. "Emerging from specific storylines about localized episodes, icons function as the graphic expressions of negativities. A particular episode, event, action, or encounter is privileged, venerated, and almost sanctified in this transition in the minds of the faithful. Certain impressions produce demonic images, adding to the religious significance of profane episodes. Viewed through such images, a stranger's actions function as *prototypes* of their unjust, immoral, uncivilized, or possibly inhuman character" (Rothbart and Korostelina 2006: 37–38).

3. *Normative order.* The normative order provides a basis for understanding the world in morally binary terms: good/evil, holy/disrespectful, sacred/profane, or virtuous/vicious. "To accept 'who we are,' it becomes necessary to define 'who we are not,' that is, 'who are the Others.' Such divisions are often contested and emotionally-charged. This duality of ingroup/outgroup identities develops value judgments about how the world should be organized" (Rothbart and Korostelina 2006: 40).

Two variables characterize the dynamics of collective axiology: the degree of collective generality and the degree of axiological balance.

1. *Collective generality.* The degree of collective generality "refers to the ways in which ingroup members categorize the Other, how they simplify, or not, their defining (essential) character" (Rothbart and Korostelina 2006: 45). The collective generality includes four main characteristics:

   (a) homogeneity of perceptions and behaviors of outgroup members,
   (b) long-term stability of their beliefs, attitudes, and actions,
   (c) resistance to change,
   (d) the scope or range of the outgroup category.

A high level of collective generality is connected with the viewing an outgroup as consistent, homogeneous, demonstrating fixed patterns of behaviors, committed to durable rigid beliefs and values, and widespread in the region or the whole world. A low degree of collective generality reflects the perception of the outgroup as differentiated, ready for transformation, exhibiting various kinds of behaviors, and relatively limited in scope.

The degree of collective generality can change over time, especially in the situation of strengthening intergroup tensions or violence. For example, escalation of conflict can lead to the perception of an enemy not as a small local group but as an entire race, ethnic group, nationality, or culture. The image of an outgroup can became more rigid, firm, and homogeneous. During violent conflicts, people tend to deny the diversity and competing priorities of an outgroup and its multicultural and political structure and to perceive it as a single "entity" with similar beliefs and attitudes and supporting common policies toward other groups.

2. *Axiological balance.* "Axiological balance refers to a kind of parallelism of virtues and vices attributes to groups. When applied to stories about the Other, a balanced axiology embeds positive and negative characteristics in group identities" (Rothbart and Korostelina 2006:46). Balanced axiology leads to the recognition of decency and morality as well as immorality and cruelty of both the Other and the ingroup. A high degree of axiological balance reflects recognition of one's own moral faults and failings, while a low degree of axiological balance is connected with the perception of an ingroup as morally pure and superior and an outgroup as evil and vicious. This tends to promote a "tunnel consciousness" and a diminished capacity for independent thought.

"In its extreme form, a low axiological balance is correlated to exaggeration, inflation, and fabrication of outgroup vices and ingroup glories. The 'Them/Us' duality seems fixed in the timeless social order. With a fabricated sense of its collective virtues, the ingroup promotes a sense of moral supremacy over the outgroup. Such an unbalanced depiction of group differences provides a ground for a struggle against criminal elements of the world" (Rothbart and Korostelina 2006: 46).

The range of axiological balance and collective generality is reflected in Figure 4.1. In this figure +I and −I represent positive and negative ingroup identities, respectively. The symbol ⇨ refers to a projection of characteristics to an outgroup. The "dotted" circles refer to a low degree of collective generality.

Two variables—axiological balance and collective generality—define collective axiology for each identity group. Quadrant 1 represents the pattern of *low* axiological balance and *high* collective generality. Such a pattern is familiar to cases of protracted conflict. A sacred ingroup requires loyalty and obedience. This collective axiology is often associated with extreme forms of nationalism, fascism, racism, and sectarianism. The narratives of ingroups and outgroups reflect the duality of perception in which the Others are portrayed as evil and vicious and ingroups are perceived as virtuous and moral. People are not able to recognize the Others' merits, understand their complexities, and assess their motivation, values, and behavior. "In the totalizing effect of protracted conflict, visions of evil tend to overpower visions of goodness. The retributive justice of 'an eye for an eye' can blind protagonists to exactly what a just world would look like. In many conflict settings, the symbols of negativities—the images of evil-doings of the other—are far more mesmerizing than images of ingroup virtues" (Rothbart and Korostelina 2006:48).

Quadrant 2 represents cases of *low* axiological balance and *low* generality. The ingroup views itself as morally pure, sacred, and glorified, while the

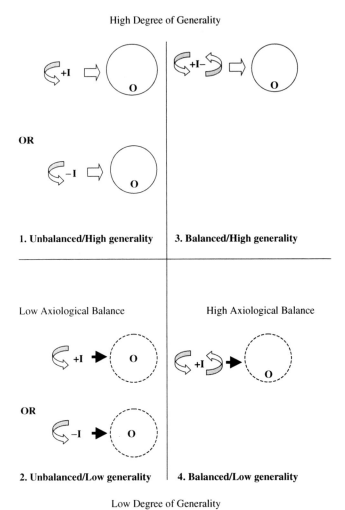

Figure 4.1   Types of collective axiology.

outgroup is characterized as exhibiting mixed values and virtues. Nevertheless, members of the ingroup can recognize the multiple voices of the outgroups, their ability to change, and the possibility of connection or collaboration with "the best" members of outgroups. They believe that particular policies and specially designed negotiations can produce changes in the Others. This kind of mixed attribution of values can be found in the patriotic sentiments of a nation's powerful social classes. For example, East Timoreans continue to struggle for ethnic identity as they seek to overcome the "totalizing" effects of Indonesian nationalism (see Tan 2006).

Quadrant 3 portrays a *high* degree of axiological balance and a *high* degree of collective generality. This collective axiology is connected with the attribution of positive and negative values to both ingroup and outgroup. Individuals are relatively free to criticize the ingroup and have some positive perceptions of the outgroup. However, they see the outgroup as homogenous, having similar beliefs and behaviors. The characteristics of the groups in Quadrant 3 are also evident in gender stereotyping as a major source of violence against women. Thus, Cheldelin (2006) shows that society produces and repeats through the media the stereotypes of women as sexual objects. The sexual violence against women is rooted in these rigid stereotypes, the perception of women as all alike, and discrimination.

Quadrant 4 represents groups with a balanced axiology and *low* generality. Both the ingroup and the outgroup identities are perceived as representing virtues and vices and moral and immoral behavior. The ingroup members are allowed to openly criticize the ingroup and respect outgroup members. Nevertheless, the support and loyalty to ingroup values in this quadrant are important, and ingroup identity is relatively salient. This collective axiology is found in liberal and humanistic movements, peacemakers, and human rights advocates. This is illustrated in the humanitarian ideals in the field of international relations (see Sterns 2006).

4.7. Locus of Self-Esteem

As I stressed above, outgroups are often evaluated less positively than ingroups. Such an evaluation often emerges through ingroup enhancement rather than through outgroup derogation (Brewer 1991, 1996, 2000). It is the result of social comparisons that lead to attributions of an ingroup's superiority and self-esteem, while outgroup derogation seems more likely to emerge in situations of conflict and when a group is under threat (Branscombe and Wann 1994; Canidu and Reggiori 2002; Jackson 2002). Nonetheless, these two processes are distinct, and one does not necessarily imply the presence of the other. A salient ingroup identity may lead to exaggerations of group differences and conflict among groups; research supports strong correlations between the salience of ingroup identity and intergroup hostility (Branscombe and Wann 1994; Grant and Brown 1995). Individuals, however, can also achieve a positive social identity and tolerance by encouraging positive ingroup stereotypes and self-esteem (Lalonde 1992; Mummendey and Schreiber 1984; Van Klippenberg 1978; Van Knippenberg and Van Oers 1984).

Thus, social identity provides self-esteem and a sense of dignity for ingroup members. If an ingroup has a high social and economic status, supremacy, and power, the ingroup members will be proud of their group and achieve high self-esteem without feeling the need to compare their group with other groups through negative estimations. Thus, the white Protestants in America have a high, powerful economic and social position within society. The members of this group are proud of their membership and have a high sense of self-esteem. Groups with rich cultures, famous artists, writers, scientists, and engineers can also provide self-esteem for their people, even if there is a lack of high status in society in the present day. For example, French minorities in many countries have a high self-esteem and are proud to be a part of French culture. Thus, some groups provide confidence on the basis of previous exceptional positions or roles throughout history. Another example is the Greeks, who have a high self-respect and are proud of their nation, even though it is now among the economically poorest countries in Europe. This sense of worth is based on the history of ancient Greece, its famous culture, and its great role in the cultural development of the world. Groups with very different cultural traditions and values can also deny comparisons with other groups and give opportunities for high self-esteem because of their uniqueness or exceptionality. For example, American Indians stress the exclusivity of their culture and traditions and are proud to be members of the ethnic group despite its low economic and social status. I suggest that all these identities have an *internal locus for self-esteem*. In these cases, ingroup members are satisfied with their positions, proud to be ingroup members, and have a high sense of confidence even if they do not make a favorable comparison between their groups and outgroups. Though they sometimes show discriminatory behaviour, they have few conflict intentions and do not consider fighting with other groups.

If groups have similar status and access to power and close cultures, their members need to use favorable comparisons with outgroups to increase their self-esteem. This comparison leads to the formation of negative stereotypes and attitudes toward outgroup members, perceptions of them as a "second sort" of people, prejudices, and blatant discrimination. If intergroup differences are small or insignificant, people will look for a different set of criteria for comparison that may help to pull apart two groups, or they will stress very diminutive differences (the phenomenon of minor differences; Volkan 1997). The need for positive comparison is even more important if groups have a low economic and social status, have a minority position in society, or lack the opportunity to promote, develop, or revive their culture. I suggest that identities in these groups have an *external locus of self-esteem* that usually creates a solid basis for conflict intentions and a readiness to fight with outgroups.

In some groups, people have both internal and external locus for self-esteem, so that some members are proud of their group and others search for favorable comparisons with outgroups as a source of their ingroup confidence. Other groups can impact the prevalence of one of the locus. Consequently, the following groups encourage an internal locus of self-esteem and peaceful attitudes toward outgroups:

(a) groups with a high economic and social position;
(b) groups with power and supremacy;
(c) groups with a rich culture;
(d) groups with a unique culture;
(e) groups with an exceptional position in history.

Members of groups with a low status or few opportunities to study and support their cultural heritage usually have an external locus of self-esteem and are ready for conflict with outgroups. The increasing awareness of one's own culture, famous artists, writers, scholars, and political leaders can increase ingroup confidence and self-respect as internal locus of self-esteem and can reduce conflict intentions and prejudice against outgroups, even if groups are in a minority or have an inferior status.

Study I. Identity Salience and the Perception of the Outgroup

Understanding the impact of identity salience on the readiness for conflict behavior requires the analysis of the influence of identity salience on the perception of other groups. My research aimed to compare the perceptions of the ethnic outgroup by people with and without salient social (ethnic) identities and to discover the effects of identity salience on the assessment and representation of the characteristics of and interaction with outgroup members. I propose that a salient social identity influences the perception and understanding of social situations reflected in stories about members of the outgroup, their behavior, and their characteristics. Such narratives reveal the knowledge, attitudes, and opinions of people who are socially determined and depend on the specificity of intergroup relations.

During this study, 100 Russians were asked to tell stories about interactions with another ethnic group, the Crimean Tatars. They also answered a short questionnaire on ethnic identity salience. The respondents were distributed into two groups of salient (43 persons) and nonsalient (57 persons) ethnic identity. All stories were examined using the discourse analysis method (Van Dijk 1997).

The analysis of the stories of people with salient ethnic identity showed the following structure of discourse:

Time: not used

Place of encounter

- Public transportation − 40%
- Market − 40%
- School − 10%
- Neighborhood − 10%

Conditions: riding public transportation, meetings with friends, shopping.

Participants

Outgroup

- Are rude, cruel, aggressive – 60%
- Steal – 30%
- Destroy, ruin – 27%
- Use cunning – 25%
- Are a bother – 23%
- Are insincere – 20%

- Are hidebound – 15%
- Are hospitable – 13%
- Are ready to help – 7%

Ingroup

- Offended
- Defended ethnic group
- Provoked by other group

Interaction

- Aggression – 45%
- Deception, fraud – 32%
- Harassment – 30%
- Theft – 15%

Consequences: negative attitudes, spite, resentment

The analysis of the stories of people with nonsalient ethnic identity showed the following structure of discourse:

Time: usual

Place of encounter

- Neighborhood – 35%
- Work, study – 25%
- Family, friends – 25%
- Shopping – 10%
- Street, transportation – 5%

Conditions: connected with work or community

Outgroup

- Are hospitable – 33%
- Are ready to help – 30%
- Are ready to understand – 27%
- Steal – 15%
- Use cunning – 12%
- Destroy, ruin – 10%
- Are a bother – 10%
- Are hidebound – 5%

Ingroup

- Good
- Tolerant
- Fair
- Victims
- Suffering

Interaction

- Friendship – 35%
- Cooperation – 35%
- Help – 20%
- Harassment – 15%
- Aggression – 12%
- Theft – 10%
- Deception, fraud – 5%

Consequences: positive or negative attitudes, readiness for cooperation, spite

The comparative analysis of the stories of people with salient and nonsalient ethnic identities and their interaction with the representatives of other ethnic groups reveals the following cognitive models of interethnic interaction for both groups:

1. The stories of people with salient ethnic identity were characterized by high similarity and related only to situations of interaction with strangers in public places. Those of people with nonsalient ethnic identity were more diverse and connected with the situations of everyday contact with neighbors, in the community and at workplace.
2. All stories of people with a salient ethnic identity were negative, while by contrast 60 percent of the stories of people with a nonsalient ethnic identity were positive (i.e., viewed the outgroup positively).
3. People with salient ethnic identities emphasized situations of insults in public places, while people with nonsalient ethnic identity described positive and negative acts of interaction in everyday life.
4. The stories of people with salient ethnic identity often used generalizations: in 45 percent of the cases, phrases such as "all the Tatars" were used. The stories of people with nonsalient ethnic identity had an individual character.
5. In the stories of people with salient ethnic identity, social actions were connected with negative emotional conditions, which involved rejection, intensity, and antagonism. They did not use positive emotions or describe outgroups or themselves negatively. The behavior of outgroup members in these stories was perceived as aggressive and antagonistic; the situations of intergroup interactions were described as depressing and tense. The attitudes of people with nonsalient ethnic identity were more diverse; they attributed both negative and positive actions to the Tatars and expected the same from them. In the situations that the people with nonsalient ethnic identity described, the Crimean Tatars quite often acted as the initiators of interactions and provided offers, help, and so forth.
6. People with salient ethnic identity attributed only negative emotions to outgroup members, especially anger and disgust. Those with nonsalient ethnic identity described various emotions, including interest, pleasure, and pleasant surprise.

7. People with salient ethnic identity perceived the outgroup as an absolutely strange group of people with minimal interaction. Those with nonsalient ethnic identity described Crimean Tatars as neighbors in society.

Study II. Salience of Identity and Structure of Consciousness

This study aimed to analyze the structure of consciousness of people with salient and nonsalient ethnic identity by examining the constructs of consciousness reflected in the perception and estimation of the other ethnic group. To study personal constructs, Kelly's repertory grid test (1955) was used.

Kelly suggests that people develop a set of personal constructs that they use to understand the world and the people in it. These constructs are bipolar (i.e., they have two ends), or are dichotomous, and vary from one person to another. To study a person's constructed system, Kelly developed a repertory grid. This idea originated when a therapist asked clients to think about people they knew and find words to describe them, providing the therapist with the main constructs. In the grid's modified version, respondents receive a list of constructs arranged in a grid. They are then asked to assess significant people or events by noting them on the grid. Certain constructs cluster together that show distinctive ways of understanding the world.

For the repertory grid in this study, I used a 15 × 7 matrix. I listed seven different roles in columns; each proposed the social position of people from other ethnic groups: neighbors, coworkers, community leaders, and so on. There were 100 respondents (50 Russians and 50 Crimean Tatars), with the age ranging from 20 to 40 years. The Crimean Tatars were asked to assess the Russians, and vice versa. The respondents were asked to identify the exact person for each social role and assess him or her using the 15 pairs of characteristics (constructs for evaluation of roles) presented in rows. They assessed each person by each characteristic using a five-point scale.

The grid offered to the Crimean Tatars is presented in Table 4.2.

The results of individual grids were summarized in two group grids by calculating means. The data were analyzed by correlation and factor analyses for groups with salient and nonsalient ethnic identities. This analysis provided an opportunity to find the structure of interconnections among

Table 4.2   Repertory Grid

	My Russian Neighbor	My Russian Coworker	Russian Teacher	Etc.
Moral/immoral				
Wise/shortsighted				
Responsible/irresponsible				
Interested/indifferent				
Etc.				

different criteria of estimations (constructs of consciousness) for people with salient and nonsalient ethnic identities.

The results showed that representatives of both ethnic groups with salient ethnic identity had strongly interconnected constructs of consciousness. The analysis revealed 67 significant correlations among the constructs, which means that the characteristics of people with salient ethnic identity that are used to assess representatives of other ethnic groups are interrelated. People with salient ethnic identity based their conclusions about the characteristics of persons belonging to another ethnicity on very firm assumptions that logically followed one another. While attributing one characteristic to a person of another ethnicity, people with salient ethnic identity automatically attributed him or her with a set of other connected personal characteristics. For example, if a person with a salient ethnic identity considered people of another ethnicity cruel, he or she immediately attributed them with short-sightedness and irresponsibility.

Figure 4.2 presents an example of the connections between constructs of consciousness for people with salient ethnic identity. All lines represent significant correlations.

The factor analysis found two main factors in the structure of consciousness of people with salient ethnic identity. The first factor included such characteristics as cleverness, kindness, wisdom, generosity, and moral inquisitiveness. The second factor included such characteristics as generosity, inquisitiveness, honor for traditions, morality, and responsibility. By attributing a person of another ethnicity as "malicious," people with salient ethnic identity simultaneously regarded this individual as silly, thoughtless, stingy, and adaptive. Having decided the person of the another ethnicity was careless, they automatically attributed him or her with characteristics such as nonsense, rage, levity, cowardice, and unscrupulousness.

The correlation analysis of the constructs of consciousness of people with nonsalient ethnic identity revealed only 15 correlations among the criteria of assessment. Therefore, the characteristics that people with nonsalient

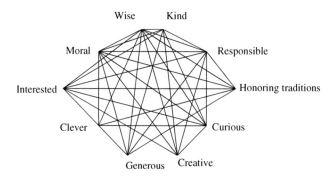

Figure 4.2 The connections between constructs of consciousness for people with salient ethnic identities.

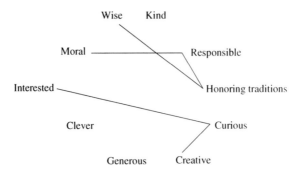

Figure 4.3 The connections between constructs of consciousness for people with nonsalient ethnic identities.

ethnic identity used to assess representatives of other ethnic groups were independent and represented different dimensions of judgment. People with nonsalient ethnic identity considered those of other ethnicities as possessing different characteristics and having unique personalities. They used a set of criteria to assess people of other ethnicities and considered each characteristic separately. While characterizing people of another ethnicity, people with nonsalient ethnic identity do not make generalized conclusions, but examine the others on each characteristic separately. For example, having decided that a person is clever, such people separately assess his or her kindness, creativity, wisdom, and so forth.

Figure 4.3 presents an example of the connections among the constructs of consciousness of people with nonsalient ethnic identity. All lines represent significant correlations.

Thus, salient identity leads to the perception of the world as rigidly connected and determined and does not allow for various interpretations. It reduces the ability to understand the world by various criteria and by using polymodal measures of assessment; it leads to the "tunnel consciousness," when people perceive representatives of other groups, situations, and activities in the narrow perspective of ethnic/religious/national identity. People with nonsalient social identity have a multidimensional approach to the assessment of the world, use different criteria, and consider both positive and negative sides of people and events. Using the metaphor of a color palette, one could say that people with salient social identity perceive the world in one color, while those with nonsalient social identity use multiple colors to paint reality.

Study III. Salience of Identity and Main Values

The main values attached to social identity reflect the meaning of this identity. Thus, the main values of an ethnic group characterize ethnic identity and reveal its sense and meaning. I propose that the values of people with salient ethnic identity will be more strongly connected or similar to the values of their ethnic groups than will be the values of people with nonsalient ethnic identity. I also propose that people with salient ethnic identity will assess other ethnic groups by attributing them with values opposite to the main values of their own ethnic groups. In other words, people with salient ethnic identity will deny the existence of their most important values among the representatives of a different ethnic group.

To verify these propositions, I conducted a study of values attached to two ethnic identities: Russian and Crimean Tatar. Research was conducted using the Rokeach Value Survey (RVS; Rokeach 1973), designed to measure an individual's perception of the relative weight attached to certain values as guiding principles in his or her life. It consists of two alphabetically ordered lists of 18 values. One list consists of terminal values, such as freedom, happiness, and a world at peace, which concern the "end state of existence." The second list contains instrumental values, such as ambition, helpfulness, and politeness, which deal with "modes of conduct." Each value is followed by a short defining phrase. I asked respondents to rank the terminal and instrumental values separately in terms of importance to themselves, to their ethnic groups, and to other ethnic groups (in their opinion). The most important value receives a rank of 1, the second most important value a rank of 2, and so forth. Finally, I calculated group medians of ranks for groups with salient and nonsalient ethnic identities.

To verify the first proposition, I compared the ranks of personal and group values for people with salient and nonsalient ethnic identity from both ethnic groups (Tables 4.3 and 4.4).

The analysis shows that people with salient ethnic identity from both ethnic groups perceive their values as very close to ingroup values. Many values in the "group list" have the same rank as those in the "personal list." People with salient ethnic identity also display a high level of consistency in their answers (or, a low dispersal of answers). This finding means that people with salient ethnic identities give the same significance to group values as they do to personal values. Independently of ethnic background, they consider group and personal values very similar and comparable; the structure of their value system depends on and is based on the group values structure. People with nonsalient ethnic identity place different importance on group values and personal values: some of their personal values are more essential than group values and some are less significant. Moreover, they display a high dispersal of answers, varying different ranks for values within the group. They possess their own value structure independently of the group value system.

The correlation analysis of interrelations between group values and personal values confirms this finding. It shows a significantly higher interrelation between group and personal values for people with salient ethnic identity than for those with nonsalient one.

The results also show that some values hold significant differences between group and individual ranks for both ethnic groups. Instrumental values such as obedience, forgivingness, and broad-mindedness and such

Table 4.3 Ranks of Personal and Group Instrumental Values

Instrumental Values	Crimean Tatars			Russians		
	Group Values	Individual Values		Group Values	Individual Values	
	Both Identities	Salient Identity	Nonsalient Identity	Both Identities	Salient Identity	Nonsalient Identity
Polite	1.5	1	3	4	4	2
Ambitious	8.5	9	7	16.5	17	15
Cheerful	4.5	5	8	7.5	7	10
Obedient	7.5	8	10	14	13.5	16
Independent	7	7	5	7	8	5
Clean	14.5	14.5	13	14.5	14	13.5
Intellectual	9	10	11	7	8	5.5
Responsible	6.5	6	5	5.5	5	4
Logical	14	14	12.5	13	13	11
Self-controlled	10	10	9	7.5	8	6
Courageous	11.5	12	14	9	9	7
Imaginative	11	10.5	11	7	7.5	6
Forgiving	11	12	8.5	8.5	9	4.5
Broad-minded	11	11	9	12	13	10.5
Honest	4.5	4.5	5	2	2	4
Capable	12.5	12	10	11	12	14
Loving	6	6	5	2.5	2	1.5
Helpful	2	2	3	6	6	6.5

Table 4.4 Ranks of Personal and Group Terminal Values

Terminal Values	Crimean Tatars			Russians		
	Group Values	Individual Values		Group Values	Individual Values	
	Both Identities	Salient Identity	Nonsalient Identity	Both Identities	Salient Identity	Nonsalient Identity
An exciting life	11	12	10	12	12	9
Wisdom	10.5	10	10	10	10.5	10
Happiness	1.5	3	1	2	2	1.5
A sense of accomplishment	8	8	7	6.5	7	4
Inner harmony	15	15.5	12	11	11	9
Mature love	4	4	3	4	4	4.5
Comfortable life	4.5	5	4	10	10	8
True friendship	6.5	6	7	6	6	5.5
Social recognition	12	12	15	15	15.5	17
Self-respect	12	13	8	11	10.5	6.5
National security	12	11	13	13.5	13	13
Salvation	13.5	14	15	10.5	10	12
Pleasure	10.5	10	9	16	16	14
Freedom	9	9	7	9	9	6
Family security	4.5	4	6	3	2	5
Equality	12.5	12	9	12	12	8
A world at peace	16	16	11	13	13.5	10

terminal values as inner harmony, social recognition, self-respect, freedom, equality, and world peace have significantly different ranks for people with salient and nonsalient ethnic identity. Analysis revealed several groups of divergent values:

1. Values connected with ingroup primacy: obedience, social recognition
2. Values connected with personal independence (social and cognitive): inner harmony, self-respect, broad-mindedness, freedom
3. Values connected with relations: forgivingness, equality, world peace

People with salient ethnic identity in this study consider obedience and social recognition as more important values than do people with nonsalient ethnic identity. Loyalty to the ingroup, primacy of ingroup norms, and following the rules and goals of the ingroup are important in interrelations with the ingroup. People with salient ethnic identity also expect social recognition and support from their groups, which is one of the main functions of social identity. For people with nonsalient ethnic identity, loyalty to ingroup and reciprocal ingroup recognition are less important values.

Values connected with personal independence are more essential in this study for people with nonsalient ethnic identity. These people value inner harmony, self-respect, and personal freedom and think it important to be broad-minded. Therefore, people with nonsalient ethnic identity possess personal worldviews and ways of life. Those with salient ethnic identity perceive these values as less significant, as they are more oriented to their groups and perceive the world in terms of group opinions. It is interesting that self-respect is more important for people with nonsalient ethnic identity than for those with salient one. The former believe that self-esteem leads to self-respect and inner harmony, while the latter stress that self-esteem is provided by social identity and close relations with the ethnic group.

For people with nonsalient ethnic identity in this study, values such as being forgiving, possessing equality, and living in the world in peace were more significant than for people with salient ethnic identity. One possible explanation of this finding is that the latter concentrate more on the happiness and well-being of their ethnic groups than on those of other groups. As previous research shows, they have more negative stereotypes and attitudes toward other groups and perceive a larger social distance between ingroups and outgroups. These patterns of behavior and consciousness lead to the perception that their ethnic groups occupy a special position in society—an ethnocentric view that assumes the dominance of ingroup goals and status.

Overall, this study revealed that people with salient ethnic identity maintain similar values with their ingroups and consider the values of ingroup primacy and interdependence as significant. People with nonsalient ethnic identity possess a personal, independent system of values and stress the importance of values connected with a personal worldview, style of life, and equality of people. They are readier to forgive others and more open to relationships with different people.

The analysis of values associated with other groups show that people with salient ethnic identity use their own most important values as a basis for the negative evaluation of other ethnic groups. The perception of "others" is not based on objective assessment of the others' values or an understanding of their value system. People with salient ethnic identity perceive members of other ethnic groups in terms of their own most important values and see them negatively. Thus, the main instrumental values for Crimean Tatars are civility (being polite) and helpfulness; they deny the existence of these values among Russians and believe them to be among the least important for Russians, even though Russians perceive themselves as polite and helpful. The main important instrumental values for Russians are honesty and love; they perceive Crimean Tatars as people who do not value honesty and love, while these values are the among significant ones for Crimean Tatars.

The analysis of stories about the ethnic groups in this chapter demonstrates that Crimean Tatars with a salient ethnic identity stress the perceived cruelty and impoliteness of Russians because these characteristics contradict the main values of Crimean Tatars. Russians with a salient ethnic identity accuse Crimean Tatars of dishonesty, since their main value is honesty. Therefore, my research shows that people with salient ethnic identity have strongly interconnected personal and ingroup values and use their most important values as the lens through which to blame and denigrate people from other ethnic groups. The subordination of individual values to ingroup values together with salient ethnic identity leads to nonobjective perceptions of outgroup members and the tendency to attribute them with a lack of the most important values of the ingroup. This devaluation provokes extremely negative attitudes and even violence toward outgroup members, who, presumably, neither regard nor respect the most important values of the ingroup.

Study IV. Components of the Meaning of Ethnic Identity

This study aims to analyze importance of the different components of the meaning of ethnic identity: language, history, culture, and religion/ideology. Respondents were asked to estimate the importance of each component on a five-point scale from "very important" to "not important." The results show that only 10 percent of Russians and 26 percent of Crimean Tatars consider language as the most important united factor for their ethnic identity. However, 45 percent of Crimean Tatars and 20 percent of Russians mention the significance of this factor. Interestingly, 55 percent of Russians believe that language is not an important factor of ethnic identity.

Shared history is deemed important by 75 percent of Crimean Tatars (40% consider it as very important and 35% as important) and 42 percent of Russians (8% consider it as very important and 34% as important factor).

Nearly 35 percent of Russians and 10 percent of Crimean Tatars regard this factor as not important.

National culture and traditions are considered as very important by 10 percent of Russians and 36 percent of Crimean Tatars; 40 percent of Russians and 32 percent of Crimean Tatars stress the importance of this factor, while 30 percent of Russians and 10 percent of Crimean Tatars deny its importance for common ethnic identity.

Shared religion and ideology are mentioned as very important by more than 60 percent of Crimean Tatars and only 8 percent of Russians. Nearly 20 percent of the representatives of both ethnic groups consider this factor as important; more than 60 percent of Russians and less than 8 percent of Crimean Tatars believe that it is not important for ethnic identity.

Thus, the representatives of both groups consider shared history as the most important component of the meaning of ethnic identity. For Crimean Tatars, the Muslim religion is also a very significant component of the meaning of ethnic identity. Research shows that language and culture are perceived as less important factors for common ethnic identity.

Study V. Analysis of the Meaning of Social Identity by Examining Interconnections with Attitudes and Stereotypes

This study aims to examine the meaning of ethnic, national, regional, and Soviet identities for two ethnic groups through the analysis of stereotypes and attitudes connected with each identity.

I conducted a correlation analysis between social identities and system of attitudes, stereotypes, and estimation of identity functions. Then I conducted correlation analyses within these variables for Russians and for Crimean Tatars.

Soviet Identity
For Russians, the following attitudes and stereotypes were the most significantly correlated with Soviet identity salience:

1. Deported ethnic groups must not have equal citizenship rights.
2. All Russians in Crimea must have dual citizenship of Ukraine and Russia.
3. Most Russians and Ukrainians in Crimea support the Russian policy even if it does not coincide with Ukrainian interests.
4. Most Ukrainians desire closer relations with NATO.
5. All Russians are ethnocentric.
6. The Crimean Tatars' language should not be made a state language.
7. All Russians are careless.
8. All Russians are fundamentalists.
9. The economic situation in Ukraine will improve.
10. Personal economic position will improve.
11. Turkey wants to help Crimea.

12. Russia wants to help Crimea.
13. The interests of Russia coincide with those of Crimea.
14. Russians in Crimea consider Crimea the territory of Russia.
15. Russians have a salient ethnic identity.

For Crimean Tatars, the following attitudes and stereotypes were the most significantly correlated with Soviet identity salience:

1. It is not important for us that representatives of other ethnic groups consider us as their compatriots.
2. All Crimean Tatars are ethnocentric.
3. Russia does not want to help Crimea.
4. Russians and Crimean Tartars have similar problems with unemployment.
5 Russian should not be made a state language.
6. The Crimean Tatars want to live in Crimea.
7. All Crimean Tatars are honest, polite, diligent, prudent, and fundamentalist.

An analysis of correlations shows that the Soviet identity among the Crimean Tatars and the Russians is associated with nationalistic tendencies. Thus, Russians with a salient Soviet identity have negative attitudes toward the Crimean Tatars and the realization of their rights in Crimea. The Crimean Tatars show less aggressiveness toward the Russians, but they are driven by strong, positive autostereotypes, which results in their refusing to interact with other ethnic groups. When commitment to principles emerges as one of the main autostereotypes, the Russians and the Crimean Tatars with a salient Soviet identity oppose granting rights to the representatives of other ethnic groups. These respondents stand for denying the national language status to languages of other ethnic groups. The Soviet identity of the Russians in Ukraine results in a dependant position, in which they expect help from other countries: Russia and Turkey. The Soviet identity among the Russians is also connected with ethnicity, strong orientation to Russia, and opposition to the West.

So, the Soviet identity is characterized by conflict behavior, nationalistic tendencies, and counteractions between the representatives of two ethnic minorities. The potential conflict is also connected with the Russians supporting Russian policies and nurturing a feeling of Russian citizenship.

National Identity

For Russians, the following attitudes and stereotypes were the most significantly correlated with national identity salience:

1. Russians in Crimea could not have a dual citizenship of Ukraine and Russia.
2. Russians have a salient Ukrainian national identity.

3. Common history is not important for ethnic groups.
4. A small number of Russians in Crimea consider themselves citizens of Russia.
5. Most Russians in the Crimea do not support policies of Russia if they do not coincide with the interests of Ukraine.
6. A small number of Russian in Crimea consider the republic a part of Russia.
7. Ukrainians do not want close relations with the NATO.
8. Russia does not want to help Crimea.
9. Russians are intolerant.
10. The Ukrainain identity provides social status, self-esteem, and recognition by group.
11. Ethnic identity provides group support.

For the Crimean Tatars, the following attitudes and stereotypes were the most significantly correlated with national identity salience:

1. Personal economic situation has worsened.
2. The Crimean Tatars have a strong ethnic identity.
3. Most Russians in Crimea consider it a part of Russia.
4. Russians want close relations with NATO.
5. Russia wants to return Crimea.
6. The interests of NATO do not coincide with those of Crimea.
7. The Crimean Tatars are diligent, prudent, and just.
8. Regional identity provides social status and personal safety.

The analysis of correlations shows that the national identity of Crimean Tatars and Russians is formed in opposition to orientation toward Russia and the West. Russians with salient national identity (as belonging to Ukrainian citizenship) deny they have any orientation to Russia, common Russian history, and they do not trust Russia. They see Ukraine as an independent state with its own history, which has not been connected with Russia and the West. Crimean Tatars attribute to Russians the aspiration to establish close relations with NATO and to return Crimea to Russia. The citizenship of Ukraine carries out the main function for Russians of enhancing their social status, self-esteem, and possibility for personal growth. Belonging to the Russian community in Crimea provides the function of increasing social status. National identity does not carry out the basic functions of identity for the Crimean Tatars, but helps them to defend their community in Crimea from the Russians. National identity among them is not a self-sufficient category but assists to create regional identity.

So, Russians with salient national identity perceive the citizens of Ukraine as an independent group, which is formed by denying connections with Russia and NATO and carries out the main functions of identity. For the Crimean Tatars, national identity is connected with opposition to the orientation of Crimean Russians toward Russia and NATO and is the frame for regional identity.

Regional Identity

For Russians, the following attitudes and stereotypes were the most significantly correlated with regional identity salience:

1. Language is a component of the meaning of identity.
2. Interests of Turkey do not coincide with those of Crimea.
3. Russians are polite and just.

For Crimean Tatars, the following attitudes and stereotypes were the most significantly correlated with regional identity salience:

1. The economic situation in Ukraine has become worse.
2. The Crimean Tatars are ready to perceive representatives of others ethnic group as compatriots.
3. The Crimean Tatars are proud of Crimea.
4. Religion is a component of the meaning of identity.
5. The Crimea must not be united with Turkey.
6. Only small number of Ukrainians in Crimea will support the policies of Russia.
7. Turkey wants to annex the Crimea.
8. The Crimean Tatars are honesty and diligent, and so are Russians.
9. Ethnic identity does not provide self-esteem.
10. Regional identity provides self-esteem and social status.
12. National identity provides self-esteem.

The formation of regional identity of representatives of both ethnic groups is based on the feeling of connection with Crimea and denying of connections with Turkey. It is interesting to note that attitudes toward Russia do not influence formation of regional identity of representatives of both ethnic groups. Regional identity of Russians is constructed on the basis of common language (Russian), which they use in Crimea. The Russians with salient regional identity consider that stereotypes of politeness and validity give them opportunity to unite around common ethnicity in formation of a regional identity. The Crimean Tatars stress the role of religion as a uniting factor, and their regional identity is characterized by tolerance toward representatives of other ethnic groups. The regional identity is the main identity for Crimean Tatars and helps them increase their self-esteem and social status.

So, the regional identity is characterized by ethnic tolerance and negative attitudes toward Turkey. The regional identity helps the Crimean Tatars to increase self-esteem and social status, and is directed against Russians. The Russians see Russian language as the unifying factor and the Crimean Tatars see religion as the basis for regional identity. The aspirations of representatives of both ethnic groups to become a unifying force for the formation of regional identity may thus lead to conflict.

Ethnic Identity

For Russians, the following attitudes and stereotypes were the most significantly correlated with ethnic identity salience:

1. The soviet identity is salient.
2. Most Russians in Crimea consider themselves as Soviet people.
3. Turkey wants to annex Crimea.
4. Political and economic interests of Turkey do not coincide with the interests of Crimea.
5. Russians are tolerant.

For Crimean Tatars, the following attitudes and stereotypes were the most significantly correlated with ethnic identity salience:

1. The personal economic situation will worsen.
2. It is important that representatives of others ethnic groups consider the Crimean Tatars their compatriots.
3. The Crimean Tatars consider representatives of other groups as compatriots.
4. Regional identity is salient.
5. Language is a component of the meaning of identity.
6. Religion is a component of the meaning of identity.
7. National identity is salient.
8. Crimea must be an independent republic.
9. Crimean Tatars will support the policy of Turkey, even if does not coincide with the interests of Crimea.
10. Turkey wants to help Crimea.
11. The Crimean Tatar language must have a national status.

The ethnic identity of Russians is characterized by a connection to the Soviet identity, feelings of Russian citizenship, and the attribution of threat to Turkey. Crimean Tatars oriented themselves around interrelations with Turkey and the independence of Crimea. Representatives of both ethnic groups give high value to their language receiving the national status in Crimea. Ethnic identity of Russians builds on their preference for the Soviet identity through the creation of "an enemy image" and is characterized by nationalistic tendencies with the autostereotype of arrogance. The ethnic identity of Crimean Tatars is characterized by tolerant attitudes toward other ethnic groups, but the line on interrelations with Turkey is precisely planed. So, ethnic identity appeared disputed, connected with orientation to the cross-purposes (e.g., state language and connection with Turkey).

Consequently, this research shows the importance of a system of stereotypes and negative attitudes toward other groups as factors, which influence identity formation. Soviet and ethnic identity among the Russians and Soviet identity among the Crimean Tatars are characterized by advanced systems of positive autostereotypes and negative heterostereotypes and by opposition to another group. Regional identity, as one of the most salient, is characterized by opposition to Turkey and advanced system of positive stereotypes toward all groups of Crimea. The national identity of Russians and Crimean Tatars is formed by the opposition to Russia and NATO, but the system of attitudes and stereotypes is not as advanced.

However, the basic statements of theory of social categorization are not relevant in case of ethnic identity. So, ethnic identity of Russians is not salient, but it is characterized by a well-developed system of positive auto-stereotypes, negative heterostereotypes, and opposition to other groups. Ethnic identity of Crimean Tatars is one of the most important identities, but it is characterized by tolerance and absence of negative autostereotypes. Perhaps, it may be explained in terms of interconnection of ethnic identity with Soviet identity among the Russians and association of ethnic identity with regional identity among the Crimean Tatars.

Nationalism may be analyzed as an elaborated concept embedding one's own nation into a set of nations and simultaneously differentiating one's nation from those nations. Soviet identity represents such an elaborated concept and leads to nationalistic tendencies. National and regional identity is characterized by undeveloped estimation of place of Ukraine and the Crimea in international relations, and such identities lead only to intense loyalty to the nation and do not create hostility toward other groups.

Study VI. Analysis of the Structure and Meaning of Social Identity by Examining Constructs of Consciousness

The aim of this study is to analyze the different meanings of social identity by examining the constructs of consciousness associated with social identities. Two methods were used during this study: repertory grid test of Kelly (1955) to study personal constructs (for the description of the method, see Chapter 3) and method of pair comparison between six identities.

For the repertory grid in this study, I used a 16×6 matrix, with six identities in the columns: national, regional, ethnic, religious, professional, and family; and 16 constructs for the evaluation of identities in the rows. The respondents assessed each identity by each construct using a seven-point scale.

One hundred respondents (50 Russians and 50 Crimean Tatars) from 20 to 40 years of age took part in this study. The data were analyzed by cluster, correlation, and factor analyses by ethnic groups and subgroups with prevailing identity. Cluster analysis reveals tree clusters for each ethnic group.

For Russians, the first cluster includes only one type of identity: national. This reflects unattached position of this identity in the system of social identities among Russians (that confirm the results of previous research). The assessment of this identity includes such constructs as *morality-immorality, friendliness-resentment, tolerance-biliousness,* and *principles–no principles* and is based on ideas of morality, principles, and tolerance. The second cluster consists of regional, ethnic, and religious identity, among which regional identity is the most significant component of the clusters. The constructs used for the estimation of such identities includes *friendliness/resentment, morality/ immorality, positive/negative, confidence/instability, tolerance/biliousness,* with morality and affiliation as the most important constructs. The third factor contains two identities—family and profession—that can be characterized as more personalized identities. They were described by the following constructs: *responsibility/irresponsibility, interest/indifference, fairness/improbity,* and *enterprise/inertness.*

For Crimean Tatars, the first cluster contains religious, ethnic, and family identities. It reflects the strong interconnection between these three identities and the role of the family in maintaining and developing the dyad of religious and ethnic identities. This cluster is connected with such constructs as *friendliness/resentment, interest/indifference, confidence/instability,* and *fairness/improbity.* The second factor includes professional identity only. This identity is a more personalized one and is not connected with other identities. It is assessed by the following constructs: *interest/indifference, responsibility/irresponsibility, competence/incompetence,* and *friendliness/resentment.* It was found that in comparison with Russians, Crimean Tatars did not characterize this identity by an activity. The third cluster consists of national and regional identities; it confirms previous findings that national identity to Crimean Tatars was viewed as a guarantee of security in the region. These identities are assessed by such constructs as *friendliness/resentment, positive/ negative, morality/immorality,* and *fairness/improbity.*

Constructs of Consciousness Connected with Prevailing Salient Identities

It was hypothesized that salient identity influences the structure of consciousness; accordingly, each prevailing salient identity is connected with specific constructs of consciousness. The pair comparison tests of social identity helped to identify five groups with different prevailing salient identity among Russians and four groups with different salient social identity among Crimean Tatars. The group with salient national identity was found only among Russians. For Russians, the major group was the group with prevailing salient professional identity, while Crimean Tatars' major group was the one with prevailing salient religious identity. The smallest groups were found for prevailing national and regional identities. Here I present several examples of the analysis of the structure and meaning of social identities with different prevailing identities.

Prevailing National Identity. Analysis reveals that 12 percent of Russians have a prevailing salient national identity.

A prevailing national identity in the structure of social identities among Russians is connected with regional identity and characterized by such constructs as *tolerance/biliousness, confidence/instability, cooperation/ competition,* and *friendliness/resentment.* The second group of identities includes religious and ethnic identities and is characterized by the constructs of *friendliness/resentment, sincerity/hypocrisy, confidence/instability,* and *interest/indifference.* The third group—family and professional identities—are assessed by *confidence/instability, friendliness/resentment, morality/immorality,* and *interest/indifference.* The most important characteristics for this system are friendly acceptance, morality, and interest. Russians with a prevalent national identity perceive their national affiliation as a result of belonging to Crimea and are ready to accept representatives of other ethnic groups.

Prevailing Ethnic Identity. A prevailing ethnic identity was found for 17 percent of Russians and 28 percent of Crimean Tatars. Analyses reveal three clusters for both ethnic groups.

For Russians with a prevailing ethnic identity, ethnic identity is connected with family and professional identities, which can be characterized as more personalized identity. It means that prevailing ethnic identity exists in the categorical form and does not reflect belonging to the ingroup. This group is characterized by the following constructs: *morality/immorality, positive/negative, interest/indifference,* and *responsibility/irresponsibility.* Regional identity is not connected with an ethnic one and is included in the dyad with national identity, which was assessed by the constructs of *morality/immorality, responsibility/irresponsibility, interest/indifference,* and *positive/negative.* Moreover, religious identity is not connected with a prevailing ethnic identity and is characterized by *sincerity/hypocrisy, positive/negative, friendliness/resentment,* and *cooperation/competition.* The main constructs of consciousness for Russians with prevailing ethnic identity are responsibility, morality, and assessment in terms of positive and negative.

The prevalent ethnic identity of Crimean Tatars is connected with religious identity and is assessed by the constructs of *confidence/instability, wisdom/shortsightedness, friendliness/resentment,* and *responsibility/irresponsibility.* Another important identity is the family identity, which provides confidence, defines morality, and is characterized by *confidence/instability, friendliness/resentment, morality/immorality,* and *responsibility/irresponsibility.* Professional, national, and regional identities can be characterized as instrumental identities that reflect belonging to secondary groups. They are assessed by such constructs as *friendliness/resentment, interest/indifference, wisdom/shortsightedness,* and *responsibility/irresponsibility.* The most important constructs of consciousness for Crimean Tatars with a prevailing ethnic identity are confidence, friendliness, and wisdom.

Prevailing Religious Identity. A prevailing religious identity was found for 16 percent of Russians and 38 percent of Crimean Tatars. Analyses reveal three clusters for both ethnic groups.

A prevailing religious identity among Russians constitutes the group of four identities and is connected with regional, family, and professional identities. This identity reflects everyday experience at home and work and has a moral rather than ideological meaning and is characterized by *confidence/instability, friendliness/resentment, competency/incompetence,* and *responsibility/irresponsibility.* National and ethnic identities have isolated positions. National identity is assessed by *confidence/instability, collaboration/competition, tolerance/biliousness,* and *wisdom/shortsightedness*. Ethnic identity is characterized by *confidence/instability, competence/incompetence, interest/indifference,* and *freedom/dependence*. The most important characteristics are confidence, competence, and responsibility.

For Crimean Tatars, a prevailing religious identity is interconnected with ethnic and family identities. This interconnection reflects strong ties between religious and ethnic identities and the role of the family in its preservation and development. It is characterized by such constructs as *fairness/improbity, confidence/instability, friendliness/resentment,* and *interest/indifference*. National and regional identities again develop a dyad assessed by such constructs as *fairness/improbity, interest/indifference, friendliness/resentment,* and *morality/immorality*. Professional identity has a single position and is characterized by *interest/indifference, friendliness/resentment, fairness/improbity,* and *responsibility/irresponsibility*. The most important characteristics are fairness, interests, and friendliness.

CONCLUSION

The studies presented in this chapter show the impact of salient identity on the structure of narratives about the others, the structure of consciousness, and value system. As shown, salient identity influenced the construction and content of stories about other ethnic groups. Stories of people with salient ethnic identity were characterized by high similarity, generalizations, and negative attitudes. People with salient ethnic identity perceived the outgroup as an absolutely strange and significantly different group, while keeping minimal interaction with it. The stories of people with nonsalient ethnic identity were more diverse, were positive, and had individual character. People with nonsalient ethnic identity described other ethnic groups as neighbors in society.

Salient identities led to the perception of the world as rigidly connected, determined, and not admitting various interpretations, which produced a "tunnel consciousness" when people perceived the representatives of other groups, situations, and activities through the narrow perspective of ethnic/religious/national identity. A nonsalient social identity was connected with a multidimensional approach to the assessment of the world, the use of different criteria, and both positive and negative sides of people and events.

Nonsalient ethnic identity influences the development of a personal independent value system connected with a personal worldview, lifestyle, and equality of people. Salient ethnic identities led to a high level of similarity between ingroups and personal values and to the significance of the values of ingroup primacy and interdependence. People with salient ethnic identity used the most important values to blame and slight people from other ethnic groups, devaluating them and attributing to them a lack of the most important ingroup values.

An analysis of the identity salience offers an explanation of people's perception and behavior but does not provide information about the content and sense of identity. The final three studies in this chapter show different methodological approaches to the meaning of social identity through an analysis of stereotypes, attitudes, and structures of consciousness. The results of these studies help us understand the motives and intentions of people with different identities and predict their behavior.

CHAPTER 5

DYNAMICS OF THE SYSTEM
OF SOCIAL IDENTITIES

5.1. THE DEVELOPMENT OF SOCIAL IDENTITY

The core social identities are formed within the consciousness of an individual person. Social identities are developed through an introspection of a person's place within the society and the larger world. Introspection leads to the creation of a hierarchical structure of social identities of varying salience. The progressive development of an identity system is a contradictory process in which new emergent identities can be incompatible with some preexisting identities or can challenge the hierarchical structure of the identity system. The joining of new groups, the formation of new outgroups, and changes in the status and power of ingroups and outgroups all lead to the reorganization of the identity system. The formation of new identities and the resulting contradictions between disparate identities cause changes in an individual's social behavior. The rise, development, and disappearance of any identity lead to changes within the whole system. During the first stage, the process of identity reconstruction affects the subsystem of short-term identities, but relationships within the overarching identity system are not fundamentally altered. During the second stage, major changes in multiple identity subsystems lead to critical changes in the entire identity system. The position of a new social identity within the system of social identities depends on its interconnections with other identities as components of the system and their places within it.

The process of the development of new identity can take several forms:

1. Newly developed identities can replace several (even the whole subsystem of) short-term identities without changing core identities. Thus, a new identity as a student at a particular university can become one of the core identities for an individual and replace the importance of a person's membership in a community club, a sports team, and so forth, without affecting one's ethnic, religious or national identity.

2. New social identities can be introduced into a subsystem of core identities without affecting it. For instance, individuals from a low-income family can receive stipends and get good education, which helps them earn a high salary and a prestigious position. While this new class identity (high middle-class) may eventually develop into a core identity, it will not shift the salience and positioning of national, ethnic, or religious identities within the subsystem of core identities. Being a member of the middle class will not alter the importance of ethnic, national, and religious identities.

3. New identities can be harmoniously integrated into the subsystem of core identities, modifying the hierarchy and salience of core identities and changing the interrelations among them. For example, if an individual decides to join a religious organization, his or her religious identity becomes more salient and develops into a core identity. A new religious identity can develop stronger interconnections with established ethnic identities and increase its salience. Thus, a Protestant religious identity can increase the salience of an English ethnic identity forming a new dyadic (English Protestant), which can become the most important self-identifier for a person and can decrease the salience of one's national identity. Moreover, if ethnic and national identities were strongly linked (Anglo-American) before the development of this new identity, new religious identities can destroy this connection, leaving national identity to adopt a singular position within the system of core identities.

4. New social identities can be in contradiction with core identities, thus leading to a conflict within the system of identities. For instance, if a country where one has lived most of one's life achieves independence from another country and assumes a new national identity, it might be different from a previously held ethnic identity. Before the independence of one's country, national and ethnic identities may have been harmoniously interconnected. For example, in Ukraine during the Soviet era, the Russians identified themselves as members of the Soviet people. Their national (Soviet) and ethnic (Russian) identities were not in contradiction. After independence, Ukraine began to develop a new national identity with a prevalent ethnic concept of national identity ("Ukraine is for people of Ukrainian ethnicity"). The new ethnic-national identity (Ukrainian) is at odds with the previously held salient ethnic identity (Russian). As a member of a new ethnic minority, a person must reconstruct a new national identity. The development of this national identity creates inconsistency in the subsystem of core social identities. Such contradictions can be resolved in different ways: (a) the established system of core social identities can resist change and prevent the development of a new national identity, which will result in ambivalence toward a new national ideal; (b) one can give up one's ethnic identity and identify oneself as a member of a nation; (c) the new dyadic ethnonational identities can be formatted and one will perceive oneself as Russian Ukrainian.

The development of an identity system is not based on the principle of "superposition": new identities cannot be added to other identities as new layers or strata. Instead, the appearance of a new identity or changes in the salience of existing identities lead to the differentiation of previously connected subsystems and integration of new, distinctly recognizable identities into the overarching system.

An identity system evolves by means of two basic processes: first, assimilation and accommodation (the restructuring of new components of the identity system); and second, estimation (the evaluation of the significance and value of new and old identities). One of the characteristic features of an identity system is the existence of mechanisms of competition between identities, which ends in the selection of the most stable identities, the rise of new identities, and the breaking of established patterns of behavior. The development mechanism of the identity system ensures the greatest possible initial variety of identities; within this context, important and insignificant elements are revaluated and irrelevant identities are discarded. The development of contradictions between identities, reciprocal strengthening or weakening among identities, and changes in the relationships between core and short-term identities can impact the salience of an identity. This process is most vigorous among adolescents who "try on" many different identities before selecting the core identities around which the whole system is organized (Phinney 1990). The same processes, albeit in more latent forms, takes place throughout an individual's life, especially during the periods of social change. When there is rapid social change and new information is introduced, people come to understand that their values, beliefs, and information are out of date. As a result, they do not know where to turn. They become alienated and unsure of how to resolve the problems associated with their identity.

5.2. The Development of Salient Identity

In specific situations, a salient identity develops into a dominant identity and influences an individual's worldview and perception. Below, I discuss three factors that lead to an increase in the salience of social identity. The first is the existence of a majority or prevalence of people relating to a specific social category, such as gender or class. Group categories relevant to this group must be a part of the person's system of social identities. For example, if class identity is not very important for individuals but is part of their system of identities, their class identity has the potential to become salient and even dominant. If individuals' national identity is not a significant identity while they are living in their own country, it can become a salient identity once these individuals are exposed to a foreign country in which they become a minority. Interestingly, even identities that go unnoticed can develop into salient identities. For example, a social psychologist colleague of mine went to Crimea, Ukraine, to conduct conflict resolution training. For several days, she lived in a situation in which everyone spoke Russian and Ukrainian, but no English. During this time, she realized that her "English-speaking" identity had become very salient and important for her in spite of the fact that she had never previously thought about herself in terms of this identity category.

The second factor that affects social identity salience is threatening or negative attitudes toward the ingroup. If an individual listens to negative remarks about the ingroup or faces negative attitudes toward it, his or her corresponding social identity becomes salient and significant. Usually, this identity has a situational and peripheral position in a person's hierarchy prior to exposure to anti-ingroup sentiments, but following that exposure, those negative sentiments can promote enhanced ingroup solidarity, loyalty, and subsequent negative attitudes toward the outgroup. For example, a regional (city) identity can be insignificant for some individuals, but if they experience negative remarks about their territory from inhabitants of other regions, they will be likely to defend their ingroup identities, values, and characteristics actively, and to feel more closeness with the ingroup. The more often individuals face such situations, the more salient their regional identity can become. For example, a friend who was born in an American state and moved to another told me that he never identified himself with his native state. But in his new environment, he faced jokes and remarks about his native place, which activated a feeling of affliction in him, prompting him to defend his ingroup. He realized after moving away from his native state that his regional identity was very important for him.

The third factor affecting social identity salience is a change in a person's goals and values on account of situational changes. Any type of activity can become significant for individuals when they attach a social identity to their activity, making it salient. For example, if a person begins to care for an ill parent and this activity becomes an important part of the person's life, his or her social identity as a son or daughter becomes salient and takes the dominant place in the identity system. Another example is when one's professional goals or career develops into a main activity. In this case, one's professional identity becomes salient and therefore the most dominant.

Although these factors affect the salience of social identities, any change in the social situation of an individual or ingroup will lead to the ascension of another identity's salience, necessitating restructuring within the system of identities. If one of the leading core identities becomes salient, changes are less considerable, because interconnections between core identities are more stable and stronger. But if a short-term identity becomes salient, a significant imbalance grows, and there must be restructuring efforts to return to a stable position. There is a possibility of an inverse process whereby a core identity can become a situational or short-term identity. For example, if an individual resides in the surroundings of ingroup members for a long time, the need for individuation can weaken the individual's ingroup identity. Changes in the system of personal goals and values can also decrease the importance of a goal as a result of the individual's loss of interest. In this case, the social identity connected with this goal or value can become less salient and move to the subsystem of situational and short-term identities. For example, one of my students told me that his sports team membership was very important to him and that his identity as a team member was salient. But when he took a great interest in the field of conflict resolution, he lost many connections with his team. He still met with his teammates from time to time, but his sports team identity became situational and then disappeared altogether.

Any change in the social situation or balance of power will lead to an increase in the salience of corresponding identity. This leads to a restructuring within the system of identities; if one of the core identities becomes salient, changes are less considerable because correlations between core identities are more stable and stronger. But if one of the short-term identities becomes salient, the resulting imbalance will grow exponentially until intensive restructuring efforts are made to restore the stability of the identity system. As identity theory demonstrates, the most numerous, authoritative, and powerful outgroup influences the development of salient identity. This asymmetry in the system leads to development and changes within the structure of identities. Research has shown that even disproportionate membership numbers among groups can increase the salience of identity. Children in an ethnic minority in their classrooms have strong ethnic identity. Those in families with more members of the opposite gender have strong gender identity (McGuire and Padawer-Singer 1976; McGuire et al. 1978).

As an evolving system, a system of social identities tends to become stable. It can have several stable positions and can move from one stable position to another. For example, a salient regional identity can reflect one stable position and a dyadic ethnoreligious identity can reflect another stable position for an individual or a community. In the context of regional development, a regional identity will become the dominant identity, and in the context of the nation, a dyadic relationship can assume primacy. Both positions of identity systems are stable and will not provoke any changes or contradictions within the system. But if the situation reinforces the other identity (e.g., religious identity in context of a religious dispute), a structural reconstruction within the system will occur; these changes will result in behavioral transformation and even conflict intentions.

5.3. Dynamics of the Social Identity System during Cultural Adaptation and Social Changes

In most theories, culture is described as a system of elements or components: basic worldview, values and norms, and material products of culture. These three factors are analyzed not as individual parts, but in the processes of interconnectivity and mutual influence. Thus, a basic worldview influences values and norms, which in turn affect cultural products. Conversely, changes in cultural products lead to the transformation of values and norms, and, further, of worldview. Such processes occur on an individual level and immediately affect a single person. But the person, in turn, influences the surrounding culture, which leads to the changes in culture on the whole.

Changes can be imperceptible or significant, quick or slow. The example of small changes can be alterations in one level of culture without an effect on other levels. Thus, new music trends can influence some segments of the young population. Significant changes are visible and influence the structure of the society as a whole during a short period of time. Examples of quick changes are historical dramatic revolutionary transformations: the end of the Third Reich, failure of communism in Eastern Europe, breakdown of British Empire or Soviet Union. In this situation, the values of the society change considerably in the short run. Slow changes appear over a long period of time. For example, the feminist movement reflects transformations of views, values, and attitudes during more than one century.

Cultural changes have a significant impact on the transformations of social identities system. Such transformations can often be described as a "cultural shock." Oberg (1960) explains cultural shock as an adjustment to a new culture following the loss of social and individual identity, identity crisis, and social discomfort. It can result in anxiety, irritability, depression, and psychosomatic disorders. Traditionally, it was characterized as a deep negative experience during contact with another culture, but during the last decades there was a tendency to analyze cultural shock as a phenomenon with a potential to change a person's as well as society's identity as a whole. Research shows that cultural shock has not only negative results, but it also leads to the acceptance of new values, attitudes, and promotion of personal growth.

Thus, Adler (1994) describes five stages in the process of cultural shock:

1. A person is situated in contact with another culture; he or she is excited and euphoric.
2. During the second stage, disintegration, cultural differences become more significant and lead to confusion, estrangement, and depression.
3. During the third stage, reintegration, the person rejects the other culture and finally makes a choice between regression (in early stages) and movement to a high level of adaptation.
4. The fourth stage, autonomy, is characterized by better understanding of the other culture, autonomy, and competency.
5. During the fifth stage, independence, a person analyzes cultural differences, improves cultural understanding, and demonstrates creative behavior in adapting to the new culture with a personal worldview.

Oberg (1960) proposes four stages of cultural adaptation:

1. The stage of "honeymoon" reflects sympathy and optimism.
2. During the second stage, a person feels animosity, has negative attitudes toward a new culture, and searches for contacts with people of his or her own culture.
3. The third stage is characterized by improved language skills and ability for orientation in the new culture.
4. The fourth stage consists of final adaptation to the new culture.

The process of adaptation is usually described as a U- or W-shaped line, both conditions reflecting cultural shock after returning to the country of native culture. All these stages describe the processes of cultural adaptations of emigrants or people who encounter new cultures within a framework of cultural exchange. All have positive expectations of and a readiness to adopt or understand new cultures into their worldview, but in many cases, cultural adoption is impeded by negative reactions of resistance and rejection. People who moved to another country (or even another region of their own country) for temporary work can immediately experience melancholy and depression, as they see no possibility of accommodating new cultures into their worldview. As a result, ethnic or religious identity becomes increasingly salient: they listen to ethnic music, strictly follow ethnic customs, and resist any contact with the new culture.

The process of cultural adaptation has a significant impact on a person's social identity. If individuals have positive expectations, they consciously or unconsciously suppress their social identity. Thus, ethnic, national, or religious identity is not important at the beginning and does not affect intergroup comparison, the estimation of outgroups, or a person's behavior: he or she is open to contacts and has positive attitudes toward outgroup members. However, social identity may unconsciously negatively influence the perception of outgroup members, resulting in the accumulation of feelings of dissatisfaction and irritability. Social identity again becomes salient and impacts the perception of intergroup differences and negative estimation of outgroups. Group boundaries become less permeable; social identities become increasingly salient and dominant in one's assessment of reality. Often the process of adaptation comes to an end during this stage: individuals can live in another culture, but may communicate only with ingroup members and read newspapers or watch TV programs in their native language. For example, many members of immigrant communities in America do not know English and cannot communicate with people from other groups.

However, if a new society requires the knowledge of its language or a person desires successful adaptation, he or she has to overcome the negative effects of salient social identity. In this case, individual identity becomes primary and suppresses one's social identity. The more salient original social identity is (especially among representatives of collectivistic cultures), the more complex the process of adaptation. The problems of adaptation are mitigated by the custom of collectivistic cultures to help new individuals by including them in an ingroup and supporting them during their first stage of acclimation. While the process of adaptation may be smoother for members of collectivistic cultures, collectivistic ingroups reinforce established social identity and retard the positive individual changes of acclimation to the new culture.

The results of intercultural contact are usually described by four types:

1. Genocide, that is, destruction of the outgroup;
2. Assimilation, that is, gradual voluntary or compulsory adoption of customs, beliefs, and norms of the dominant culture and total fusion into the dominant society;

3. Segregation, that is, development of separate groups within the society;
4. Integration, that is, preservation of the ingroup's cultural identity in association with common society.

A person can choose one of these ways. He or she can reject ingroup culture and adopt an outgroup culture ("turncoat"), totally decline other cultures ("chauvinist"), vacillate between two cultures while experiencing conflict of identity ("marginal"), or synthesize both cultures as a connecting link between them. Berry et al. (1989) consider that a person or ethnic group has four possible choices: assimilation, separatism, marginalization, and integration. Maintaining cultural identity and characteristics as well as relationships with other groups can be described as integration. Maintaining relationships with other groups while not maintaining cultural identity and characteristics can be called assimilation. Maintaining only cultural identity and characteristics can be described as separation. Marginalization results from the absence of connections with ingroup and outgroups.

Individuals can successfully integrate into a new culture if their newly developed social identities do not contradict their old social identities. If the process of formation of a new social identity is at odds with the preservation of old social identities, there are two ways of resolving this contradiction. In the first case, individuals will fight for and defend their social identity and experience negative attitudes toward a new culture. This form of behavior can be described as separation. In the second case, the old group identities, which do not reflect the new situation, will be destroyed and a new social identity will become salient. A person will be assimilated within the new group, become a member and adopt the values and norms of the new ingroup. Sometimes, the relationship between old and new social identities can be characterized as a relationship between categorical and membership identity. Thus, individuals can preserve their old identities as a categorical ones, while adopting a new identity as a membership identity: they will still describe themselves as Italian, but will become members of a new group (American) and adopt values, customs, and norms of the new ingroup. Or, they can maintain their membership and connections with the old ingroup and use the new social identity as a categorical identity: they can still speak Italian and preserve the old ingroup's customs and norms, but can also describe themselves as American. If the conflict between identities is complex and painful, individuals can reject any social membership identities and adopt a categorical identity. It helps them to maintain the complexity of their identity, but does not require a strong connection with groups.

The dynamic of the social identity system described above can be applied to the study of several processes: (a) the adaptation of an immigrant minority group within a new society; (b) the adaptation of a minority group in a new independent state; and (c) the adaptation of a new minority after regime change or revolution. There is a tendency to use knowledge and theories received in studies of the first type of adaptation process in the understanding and analysis of two other processes: minority adaptation to independence and regime change. Although these three processes have much in common, including stages and types of identity transformation, it is important to stress one significant difference. Most immigrants come to a new country for a better life; they make their choice to live in a new society and are ready to adopt new values and norms. Certainly, the process of their adaptation is influenced by the concept of national identity: it is easy to be integrated into a multicultural society than into an ethnically homogeneous nationalist society (the latter will encourage assimilation rather than integration). I will discuss concepts of national identity in Chapter 8.

Nevertheless, the position of minorities in a newly independent state or after a regime (social) change is very different from the position of immigrants. A particular group may live in the country for centuries and, before independence, constitute the majority as part of a larger state. During the creation of a new independent state, the group may be recategorized as a minority without language status, education in the new native language, and support for cultural development. Usually it is not the immigrants' choice; they just happen to live in that part of the new independent state. Sometimes it is hard and painful for them to accept their new reality, and the process of adaptation becomes very complicated. Newly independent states typically provide ethnonational ideas of national identity and require the assimilation of "new" minorities rather than their integration. Moreover, the idea of "justice" and "revenge" results in discriminative actions toward the language and the rights of the former dominant group and even genocides and mass killings.

After the collapse of the Soviet Union, the Russians who lived in other republics, such as Ukraine, the Baltic, and Central Asia, became citizens of newly independent states. Their status as representatives of the "Big Brother," the Russian ethnic group, changed, so that they became a minority. While during the Soviet period, the Russian language was the common official language for all 15 republics, and every person had an opportunity to receive education in Russian and use it at work, the new independent states removed Russian as their official state language. In Ukraine, the Russians found that as an ethnic minority they had to adapt to a new domestic reality—they needed to study and speak Ukrainian or face problems such as access to well-paying jobs and professional advancement. The situation was more complicated in the Baltic states, where many Russians were even denied citizenship in countries where they had lived for decades.

Study I. The Structure and Meaning of the System of Social Identities

The following study was conducted using specially designed survey in different towns and villages in Crimea several times during 1998–2001. The sample was stratified by location, number of resettlements, and rural/urban status. The participants were Russians (235) and Crimean Tatars (216) and were equally distributed across these locations. Of them, 43 percent were male and 57 percent female; 37 percent were between 20 and 30 years old, 31 percent between 30 and 45, 16 percent between 45 and 60, and 14 percent above 60; 55 percent were residents of towns and 45 percent lived in villages. Participation was voluntary, and the respondents were provided with a questionnaire and selected answers from a list.

To study the structure of the system of social identities, correlation and factor analyses were conducted. The following variables were included: the salience of social identity and the functions and components of meaning of social identity.

As the results show, the most important correlations for the group of Crimean Tatars are religion and history as components of the meaning of identity, as well as ethnic and regional identity. The analysis shows that for Crimean Tatars the most important idea is the unification around ingroup religion and history on the basis of interconnected ethnic and regional identity (the idea of the indigenous people in Crimea). The dyad "ethnic-regional identity" is a core identity for Crimean Tatars. The most important components in the meaning of this identity are shared religion and shared history. The formation of such identity leads to the increase in self-esteem, social status, and recognition by group. National identity is a developing one and provides social status for regional identity: Crimean Tatars consider that their belonging to the Ukrainian nation can improve their position in Crimea. At the same time, they are concerned that their religion will not have enough recognition within the Ukrainian nation (negative interrelations between religion and social status and personal safety provided by national identity).

The correlation analysis for the Russian group shows two possible groups of interconnections. In the first, all components of the meaning of regional identity are interconnected and create complex connotation of this identity: the Russians in Crimea identify with Russian historical and cultural roots, language, and specific history (Crimea belonged to Russia before its transfer to Ukraine in 1954). The history of the ethnic group has negative connections with four functions provided by national identity: the Russians consider that as Ukrainian citizens they will have no opportunities to increase self-esteem, improve social status, and receive personal safety and ingroup support. Thus, belonging to the Ukrainian nation contradicts the very history of the Russian ethnic group in Crimea.

As analysis of the second group shows, the ethnic identity of the Russians is connected with the Soviet identity, which, in turn negatively correlates with the national identity. Thus, the Russians still (in 2002) felt themselves as Soviet Russians—the dominant ethnic group in the former Soviet Union. This identity is incompatible with the new Ukrainian national identity: the Russians could not perceive themselves as citizens of Ukraine.

Consequently, the system of social identities of Crimean Tatars is strongly interconnected and characterized by the strong dyad "ethnoregional identity" on the basis of a common religion and history (the indigenous people). National identity is still developing; it helps to preserve regional identity. However, there is a concern that Islam would not be fully accepted by the Ukrainian state. The system of social identities among the Russians contains two groups of interconnected elements. The first reflects the importance of regional identity, which contradicts national identity; the second shows the existence of "soviet-ethnic" dyad of identities, which is incompatible with the new Ukrainian national identity. So the system of social identities among the Crimean Tatars is balanced with the new national identity harmoniously entering the system; for the Russians, strong contradictions between the new national identity and ethnic and regional identities can lead to conflicts within the system.

PART III

SOCIAL IDENTITY AND CONFLICT

CHAPTER 6

THE FACTORS THAT INFLUENCE
CONFLICT DYNAMICS

6.1. INTERGROUP PREJUDICE

Cognitive social psychologists suggest that cognitive processes, including cognitive prejudice, underlie the judgments and behaviors not only at personal and interpersonal levels, but also at the intergroup level (Mackie and Hamilton 1993a). In cognitive processes, situations are estimated both in terms of personal and ingroup consequences (Mackie and Hamilton 1993b). Many social psychologists using cognitive approaches in studying relationships between majority and minority place emphasis on the processes of stereotypization and prejudice.

Intergroup prejudice has been analyzed within frameworks suggested by two theories: the theory of social identity (Tajfel and Turner 1979) and realistic conflict theory (Sherif 1953, 1966). Each theory has different explanations of positive evaluations of ingroups and negative evaluations of outgroups. The theory of social identity suggests that the need to acquire high social status and a positive identity through membership in socially prestigious groups is the basis for the formation of intergroup prejudice (Brown 2000; Huddy and Virtanen 1995; Jackson et al. 1996; Tajfel and Turner, 1979; Taylor et al. 1987; Wright, Taylor, and Moghaddam, 1990). This basic need leads to the formation of positive stereotypes to compensate for the low social status of one's own ingroup (Lalonde 1992; Mummendey and Otten 1998; Van Knippenberg 1978; Van Knippenberg and Van Oers 1984). The social identity theory describes different ways of achieving a positive social identity (Brown 2000; Tajfel and Turner, 1979): the theory accentuates the impact of status and self-esteem on stereotypes, attitudes and prejudice and provides explanations of a person's behavior in situations of increasing status through the collective action or intergroup migration.

The realistic conflict theory posits that the basis of intergroup prejudice lies in the defense and achievement of realistic ingroup interests (Blumer 1958; Bobo 1999; Bobo and Hutchings 1996; Hardin 1995; Sherif 1966). The theory stresses that the realization of ingroup interests depends on the context of intergroup relations and studies the impact of different contexts on the satisfaction of ingroup interests. It is important to note that the basic premises of this theory do not require that an actual competition over resources exists. Rather, it is the perception of competition that leads to conflict and intergroup hostility. The theory also stresses that prejudices are assumed to occur at the group level rather than at the individual level. Although many scholars stress the differences between these theories (see Duckitt and Mphuthing 1998), both theories provide explanations of a person's needs and behaviors; a person tends to satisfy either his or her needs in self-esteem and material resources. Moreover, both theories stress that intergroup prejudices become stronger when the goals and interests of groups are in opposition (Jackson 1993).

Prejudice has been commonly defined as a negative attitude, or as "antipathy based on faulty and inflexible generalization. It may be felt or expressed. It may be directed toward a group as a whole or toward an individual because he is a member of that group" (Allport 1954, 9). As an attitude, prejudice has three components: cognitive (thoughts and beliefs about other groups), affective (feelings and emotions), and conative (e.g., behavioral predisposition and intended actions) (Esses, Haddock, and Zanna 1993; Zanna and Rempel 1988). Nevertheless, some scholars note that attitudes do not necessarily have all three aspects and can be formed primarily or exclusively on the basis of only one component (Eagly and Chaiken 1988). Each component can have a different level of development and can define the structure and nature of prejudices. In addition, theories of stereotypes, prejudice, and discrimination posit a wide range of relations between and among these concepts (Stephan and Stephan 2004).

Usually stereotypes reflect physical and psychological features of ingroup and outgroup members (Taylor and Brown 1988). Stereotypes have been analyzed as widely shared ideas about characteristics of members of different outgroups (Esses et al. 1993), features that characterize the majority (Katz and Braly 1933), typical representatives of outgroups and ingroups (Brigham 1971), or characteristics of one group in comparison with other (McCauley and Stitt 1978).

The consequences of stereotypization become apparent not only in the estimation of reality, but also in personal behavior. First of all, stereotypes influence the perception of other people and the estimation of their behavior. Most stereotypes are inaccurate and lead to several kinds of biases and prejudices (Allport 1954; Fiske and Taylor 1991). Because of the selectivity of perceptions, people do not notice when facts are not in concurrence with their stereotypes. It is very difficult to change negative images: the negative behavior of others against whom we are biased is usually interpreted as a result of favorable events or recondite negative motivation.

Personal stereotypes are made apparent in most of an individual's actions: they reflect a person's social position. Stereotypes lead to explanations of events in ways that further strengthen the positive views about the ingroup and negative views about the outgroup (Crocker and Luhtanen 1990). Pettigrew (1979) defined predispositions as involving a tendency to make internal attributions for successes of the ingroup and external attributions for ingroup's failure and to make internal attributions for outgroup's failure and external attributions for outgroup's success the fundamental attribution error. Hewstone (1989) reviewed many studies documenting the fundamental attribution error and found that this error leads to increased conflict between groups. The greater the perceived difference in the typical characteristics of the ingroup and the outgroup, the greater the predisposition to hostility (Oakes 1987; Turner et al. 1994).

Though definitions of stereotypes may vary, most of scholars agree that stereotypes are attributed not to separate individual people, but the entire group (Augoustinos, Ahrens, and Innes 1994; Devine 1989). Often, social groups are perceived not only as social categories, but as organized entities with shared goals, histories and ideas about the future. In assessing outgroups, together with stereotypical characteristics, one must take into account their common aims and intentions. The influence of perceptions about outgroup goals on stereotypes has been analyzed in several experiments (Blumer 1958; Kofta 1985), which found that prejudice is not a set of individual attitudes toward outgroup members, but is a result of estimations of the outgroup's position. The attribution of goals is based on an estimation of the actions of outgroups in the context of their position in society based on several criteria. For ethnic and national groups, the set of criteria can include: the relative size of a group; social statuses and economic and political power; cultural development; memories about group history and intergroup relations; and the interconnection with other groups (Hagendoorn et al. 1996). Thus, Hungarians in modern Slovakia can be characterized as a small national minority concentrated in the south near the border with Hungary, with little control over economic and political systems formerly dominated by Hungary. These characteristics provoke the Slovaks to perceive the Hungarians as disloyal and aspiring to join Hungary. Similarly, Ukrainian Russians are also perceived as disloyal to Ukraine. The attribution of goals explains the perception of other groups as a threat to the existing ingroup. Stereotypes about previously dominant minorities can reflect attributed intentions to rule and dictate again (as in "good former days") and to betray the country as agents of their foreign motherland.

Ingroup members also share symbolic beliefs—the confidence that outgroups infringe upon or maintain important values and norms (Esses et al. 1993). Symbolic beliefs consist of a variety of ideas and values, including perceptions of the place of outgroups in the society and their role in its development, as well as ideas about the best organization of the society. According to Esses and colleagues (1993), prejudices or negative attitudes toward other groups are influenced not by ethnocultural characteristics, but rather, by perceived differences in such beliefs.

Most studies on social identity provide evidence of a relationship between the salience of identity and attitudes toward outgroups. In fact, research has demonstrated that strong identification with racial and ethnic groups among South Africans influences their desire for group solidarity, their antipathy toward outgroups, their fear of threat, and their feelings of intolerance (Gibson and Gouwa 1999). There is also an echo effect: the intention of a national minority to become autonomous or independent will provoke a corresponding and opposed nationalistic reaction among the indigenous majority (Hagendoorn, et al. 2000). Other research results confirm the role of subjective group membership in shaping political attitudes and behavior (Conover 1988; Miller, et al. 1981); and yet more research reveals strong correlations between ingroup identification and outgroup hostility (Branscombe and Wann 1994; Grant and Brown 1995). Studies show that negative stereotypes can be reinforced not only by ingroup members attributing antagonistic goals to outgroup members, but by ingroup members attributing goals to themselves based on the assumption that outgroups may become hostile to these shared goals (Hagendoorn et al. 1996). Experimental research conducted on the impact of personal and national identity on prejudice against immigrants in Holland demonstrated an insignificant effect (Hagendoorn et al. 1996). However, it was shown that respondents with a less salient national identity, in experimental condition of stressing Dutch identity, demonstrated an increase in anxiety regarding new immigrants.

Whether there is a causal relationship between them is still open to debate. Two main theories about intergroup relations and ethnocentrism—social identity theory and realistic conflict theory—provide opposing explanations for the interrelation between identity and attitudes. The realistic conflict theory considers the conflict of interests between groups and negative interrelations as an initial cause for the strengthening of social identity. It proposes that prejudice and discrimination are often based on conflicts of interests between groups (Levine and Campbell 1972); intergroup attitudes and behaviors reflect group interests, and are based, at least in part, on the nature and the compatibility of group goals. When group goals are compatible, positive relations are likely to exist, whereas when group goals are incompatible, conflict and negative intergroup attitudes and behavior are likely to result. The theory of social identity suggests that a strong identification with the ingroup leads to negative attitudes toward any and all outgroups. The study by Duckitt and Mphuthing (1998) shows that black African identification has a significant impact on their attitudes toward African whites. However, longitudinal analyses show a causal link between attitudes and identification.

Core identities of individuals and groups are connected with stable attitudes and result in a higher readiness for conflict. Attitudes connected with *short-term* identities are less stable and tend to change very quickly. Perhaps the stability of attitudes can serve as an index for core identities. As research shows, group members who respond more rapidly to traits that are characteristic of both themselves and their ingroup have much stronger group identities (Smith and Henry 1996).

The stability of attitudes connected with core identities assists in the preservation of a dynamic balance in the system of identities. If one of the situational identities becomes salient, corresponding attitudes become stronger and frequently take an extreme meaning in one's value system. A study involving role-play scenarios simulating negotiations between representatives of the Crimean Tatars and Russians showed that new ingroup members have more extreme attitudes than old members. Those playing the role of the Crimean Tatars (but not ethnically Crimean Tatars) had more extreme points of view and stances than real Crimean Tatars (Druckman and Korostelina 2001). This proved that developed attitudes and stereotypes can be the criteria of core positions and salience of identity. The more developed the system of positive autostereotypes (about the ingroup), negative heterostereotypes (about the outgroup) and stable attitudes, the more salient and stable the corresponding identity will be.

6.2. Readiness for Conflict

Prejudice is usually measured using standardized scales that contain statements about attributes of the group, feelings about the group, and support for policies that affect the group (Dovidio et al. 1996). Other special methods measure single components of prejudice. Thus, many scholars consider stereotypes to be cognitive components of prejudice and measure them by asking respondents to provide descriptions of the members of a group or by rating the extent to which specific traits are associated with the group. The affective component of prejudice contains different emotions, such as dislike, hate, discomfort, and anxiety, which interact with cognitive components and lead to negative intergroup perceptions (Hyers and Swim 1998). Emotions are measured by simply asking participants to indicate the level to which they experience a range of emotions.

Psychological research findings provide sufficient empirical information about both stereotypes and emotions, but shed considerably less light on the conative component of prejudice. Although discrimination is described as a separate phenomenon, research results can be used to understand the behavioral elements of prejudice. Thus, discrimination means denying equal treatment (Allport 1954) or favoring the position of one's own group at the expense of other groups. Discrimination has been measured in terms of failure to help, self-disclosure, seating distances, and nonverbal behavior (Dovidio and Gaertner 2004). Some studies show the distinction between intergroup discrimination that is based on ingroup favoritism, and discrimination that involves aggression and derogation (Levin and Sidanius 1999; Struch and Schwartz 1989). However, there is almost no research on behavioral intentions related to the readiness for conflict with another group as part of the conative component of prejudice. The readiness for conflict with another group with the aim of ingroup dominance over outgroups or at defending ingroup status and goals is an extreme consequence of intergroup prejudice. It is therefore important to extend research on prejudice to include intentions to fight with another group, because these intentions reflect the conflict potential resulting from these intergroup relations.

As I discussed in Chapter 4 the salience of social identity is connected with the *primacy of the ingroup,* or the belief in the supremacy of ingroup goals and values over personal goals and values. The primacy of the ingroup identity contains several components: (1) predominance of ingroup goals over personal goals, (2) the readiness to forget all internal ingroup conflicts in situations of threat to the ingroup, and (3) the readiness to unite against outgroups. The higher the level of ingroup primacy for ingroup members, the higher their willingness to disregard their own goals and values and follow the modes of behavior required by the ingroup.

Ingroup primacy can increase or decrease the influence of identity salience on conflict behaviors of ingroup members. Some groups require a high level of ingroup primacy as a condition of group membership, while other groups provide opportunities for maintaining a balance between personal and ingroup values and goals. If high ingroup primacy is obligatory to membership, a salient ingroup identity will lead directly to intergroup prejudice and conflict behavior. If high ingroup primacy is not required for membership, ingroup members with salient identities can rethink and revise their attitudes toward the outgroup and their readiness for conflict behavior based on their personal experience. This freedom to rethink will reduce the impact of identity salience on intergroup prejudice.

A relevant question was discussed by Hagendoorn, Linsen, and Tumanov (2001), who suggested studying the willingness of ingroup members to put their own interests and safety at risk in order to contribute to the realization of ingroup goals and general opposition to all outgroup goals. They stressed that the willingness to fight for goals aiming at the dominance of the ingroup over outgroups is an extreme consequence of intergroup bias and discrimination. I suggest that readiness for conflict can have two main components: a willingness to defend ingroup goals, safety, values, and ideals; and a willingness to fight against outgroup goals.

The readiness for conflict is interconnected with cognitive and affective components of prejudice, and it reflects the conflict potential resulting from intergroup perceptions. Negative stereotypes, beliefs, feelings, and emotions reinforce this readiness. However, on the basis of cognitive dissonance theory (Festinger 1957), one can expect that the readiness for conflict will reshape negative stereotypes and feelings. According to this theory, there is a tendency for individuals to seek consistency among their cognitions (i.e., beliefs, opinions). When behavior intentions and stereotypes are inconsistent, something must change to eliminate the dissonance. In the case of a discrepancy between stereotypes and behavior, it is most likely that the stereotypes will be changed to accommodate the behavior. Therefore, if people have high conflict intentions, their stereotypes and attitudes almost certainly will become more negative and extreme to avoid dissonance.

6.3. RELATIVE DEPRIVATION

Intergroup comparisons also lead to the estimation of the economic and social position of the ingroup in the context of a relative assessment of the ingroup and outgroup. Research shows that perceptions of deprivation or disadvantage are usually based on comparisons rather than the estimation of the ingroup position alone. There is a range of definitions of relative deprivation, and it has been viewed in terms of deprivation relative to a number of standards of comparison: a feeling of offense resulting from perceptions of positions based on comparisons between the actual status and expectations (Davis 1959; Runciman 1966); actors' "perception of discrepancy between their value expectations and their value capabilities" (Gurr 1970:24) or a perception that the ingroup has less than it deserved in comparison to others.

Research during World War II demonstrated that soldiers in units with high promotion rates had more complaints about the promotion system than those in units with fewer promotions: the soldiers who had not been promoted felt deprived comparing themselves with promoted soldiers despite higher opportunities for promotion (Stouffer et al. 1949). Similarly, black soldiers in southern states with strong discrimination had higher morale than black soldiers in the less racist northern states: they compared themselves to fellow civilians who received small wages. The perception of possible loss or expectations of decreasing status can also influence the rise of relative deprivation. In India, young people from upper castes committed suicide in protest against a government decision to open more jobs to the members of low castes, the perception of losing high positions resulting in deep feelings of deprivation (Brewer 2003). In Fiji, higher demographic growth rate among Indians led to fears among Fijian leaders that they were becoming a minority in their land and provoked strong discriminatory and inegalitarian measures introduced by military regime (Eriksen 2001).

People can compare their ingroup with similar groups or with advantaged outgroups; the outcomes of the later comparisons are called fraternal deprivation (Runciman 1966). As a result of fraternal deprivation, members of the disadvantaged groups will perceive more discrimination on the level of group identity rather than on that of individual identity (Crosby 1984), and will more strongly desire for social change (Kawakami and Dion 1993; Walker and Pettigrew 1984).

The idea of relative deprivation has been used either to measure fairness, inequality, or social justice, or to explain grievances, social hostility, and aggression. Thus, Gurr (1970) stresses that deprivation occurs when people feel that they cannot improve their condition under the current state of affairs; if one feels able to achieve more, one perceives the situation as just and will not feel deprived. According to Gurr, when people get frustrated they have "an innate disposition" to lash out at the source of their frustration in direct proportion to the intensity of their frustration. Political violence occurs when a period of simultaneous rising value expectations and rising value capabilities suddenly meet with a period of rapidly declining capabilities without a similar decline in expectations. This situation is often found in states under simultaneous ideological and systemic change; people feel that their position and status can and will decrease and worsen. Relative deprivation will provoke social activity if people recognize that a higher standard of living exists and that they will have the opportunity and ability to personally achieve that higher standard of living. Thus, Gurr (1970) notes that political violence results from the frustrations of relative deprivation only in situation of normative and utilitarian justifications for violence.

Social identity and feelings of relative deprivation are interconnected and can strengthen each other. Members of the ingroup with a more salient social identity will compare their group with other groups and perceive more relative deprivation. Possibly, this impact of social identity on relative deprivation can be moderated by *locus of self-esteem:* members of groups with external locus of self-esteem use more comparisons and feel a stronger sense of deprivation. Relative deprivation, in turn, impacts the salience of social identity by increasing ingroup solidarity.

6.4. MAJORITY-MINORITY POSITION AND CONFLICT INTENTIONS

Most of the groups in the social world can be described in the dichotomous terms of majority and minority. "Minority" is a term usually defined as a group with smaller numbers of members in comparison with numerically larger groups (Brewer 1991, 2003; Moscovici and Paicheler 1978; Simon 1992) or as a group with relatively low status and power in comparison with the majority (Tajfel 1981). The definition of majority or minority is not stable, but contextual and reflects the relationship between these two groups. Demographic changes, migration, changes in borders and the independence of a nation-state can provoke an interchange of places between groups: former minority groups can become a majority, and vice versa.

Research shows that identification among minority groups is stronger than among majority groups (Kinket and Verkuyten 1997; Perreault and Bourhis 1999; Van Oudenhove and Eisses 1998; Verkuyten and Masson 1995), possibly because minority groups are more insecure (Gerard and Hoyt 1974; Mullen et al. 1992; Sachdev and Bourhis 1984). Minority groups experience a stronger collective self, they have more elaborated positive or negative self-stereotypes, and they focus on group-level information (Ellemers et al. 1999; Simon 1992; Simon and Hamilton 1994). They perceive more ingroup homogeneity and ingroup similarity than majority group members (Brewer and Weber 1994). Moreover, the interrelations between salient identity and bias are different for majority and minority groups: the ingroup identity of majority group members is primarily provoked by perceptions of intergroup conflict, while minority group members have salient ingroup identity for a variety of reasons (Jackson 2002; Verkuyten and Masson 1995).

The main idea of Tajfel's theory (Tajfel 1974; Tajfel and Turner 1986) is that people strive for a positive social identity. Since social identity develops as a result of membership in groups, a positive social identity is an outcome of favorable social comparisons between the ingroup and outgroups. Tajfel suggests that members of minority groups have difficulties in achieving positive social identity since minorities often have worse social status in comparison with the majority group. Therefore, membership in the minority group usually does not contribute to the self-esteem and dignity of a person (Turner et al. 1984). In some cases, people can have a negative individual identity and even self-hatred. This was the case for many African Americans in America before desegregation laws; Haitians in the Dominican Republic have low self-esteem as a result of discrimination and the absence of basic legal and human rights. If the group is unable to satisfy esteem needs, individuals have several options (Tajfel 1978): (a) a person can try to change the structure of group (social change); (b) seek new criteria of comparison that can increase ingroup dignity and, thus, strengthen social (social creative) potential, or (c) leave/decline the ingroup in order to join a "better" group (social mobility).

If strong ingroup identification contributes to ingroup bias (Brewer and Miller 1984; Deaux 1996; Perreoult and Bourhis 1999), then minority groups appear to be more prone to bias. Research shows that ingroup bias is stronger among social or numerical minority groups than among majority groups (Brewer and Weber 1994; Ellemers et al. 1999; Simon and Hamilton 1994). In particular, members of low-status minority groups show the largest amount of discriminatory behavior (Espinoza and Garza 1985; Otten et al. 1996). The reasons for the stronger ingroup bias of minority groups are their concerns about social identity (Gerard and Hoyt 1974; Mullen et al. 1992), and the compensation of perceived insecurity (Sachdev and Bourhis 1984). Minority groups often are low status groups; therefore, they need a greater amount of group support than majority groups and are highly motivated to improve the fate of the ingroup (Mummendey and Otten 1998). However, the evidence is not conclusive. Mullen, Brown, and Smith (1992) report that ingroup bias is weaker among low-status groups. Another study stresses that a stronger sense of collective self among minority groups is connected with the high status of the minority group (Ellemers et al. 1992). Some studies show that stronger ingroup identity does not lead to more ingroup bias in the same way for majority groups as for minority groups. Under conditions of perceived intergroup conflict or outgroup threat, ingroup bias may be stronger among majority group members than among minorities. This suggests that the relationship between identity and bias is contingent on the position of the groups (numerical, social majority, or minority).

As research shows, members of minority groups who perceive their status relationship as unstable and unfair have a less developed ingroup identity

(Brown 2000; Jackson 2002; Verkuyten and Masson 1995). Tajfel (1984) describes three possible positions of minorities within stratified societies:

1. If social systems are perceived as legitimate and stable and do not have any perspectives for changes or alternatives (like feudalism), the minority accepts their dependence on the majority.
2. If the minority perceives the system as illegitimate, it will develop new alternatives to the system. Society loses its stability and the state uses terror and oppression tactics to hold the system together.
3. If relations between the minority and majority are perceived as illegitimate and the system is unstable, members of the minority group attempt to change their low status. They will also redefine and reinterpret the characteristics of their group and, consequently, transform their identity into positive one.

Thus, minority group members are more socially mobile and ready for transformation. Political goals of minorities are connected with the changes in social and political situations; as a result of such transformations, they can gain more than they stand to lose. They support ingroup goals more actively than members of the majority group and more aggressively oppose outgroup goals.

Gurr and Harff (1994) identified four key causal factors that can lead to of ethnic violence in multiethnic societies (see also Crighton and MacIver 1991; Rothchild 1991). First, there is an external affinity problem: for example, Russians are minority in Ukraine, but a majority in Crimea. Second, the salience of ethnic identity, as well as negative stereotypes, increases the possibility of ethnic tensions. Third, all ethnic groups have to experience ethnic domination (e.g., in Ukraine, the Russians were the dominant group during USSR administration; the Ukrainians became a dominant group after the Ukrainian independence in 1991; and Crimean Tatars had their autonomy before deportation). Last factor is competition in ethnic outbidding. Tilly (1994) characterized these factors in terms of ethnic secessionist and autonomist movements. Also, as was argued by Tilly (1978) and Horowitz (1985), the smaller the size of domestic ethnic groups, the higher possibility for conflict. Moreover, transnational affinities (Lake and Rothchild 1998) of ethnic group with strong neighbor of the same ethnicity also can increase the likelihood of conflict.

6.5. Intergroup Boundaries

Nevertheless, according to Tajfel (1984), many ethnic minorities and their members who disagree with their low status prefer assimilation with the majority instead of redefining their identity. They choose membership in the highest status outgroup, and use social mobility as a way of improving social identity (Ellemers, Wilke, and Van Knippenberg 1993). Therefore, in such systems, ethnic conflicts are usually connected with the opportunity for minorities to assimilate or deal with the level of the perceived permeability of social borders. Permeability reflects the degree of ability of ingroup members to shift their social identity by moving from one group to another.

However, permeability impacts the mobility of minority and majority group members differently. As research shows, if group boundaries are permeable, members of low status groups show less salient identities and ingroup preference while members of high-status groups strengthen their identification with the ingroup (Ellemers, Spears, and Doosje 1997). Manipulating permeability can help increase or decrease social mobility. While minority groups can decrease the level of permeability to stop this assimilation, majority groups too can close their boundaries to prevent the formation of an association with the minority (Hutnik 1991).

Permeability influences the ability of ingroup members to be included in new groups or the possibilities for the formation of common identities. The more group membership is evident and obvious for others, the greater possibility that members of this group will be perceived and estimated in terms of their ingroup and will be less welcome to join other groups. Thus, Western Germans differ in their readiness to perceive Eastern Germans as fellow compatriots as well as showing a great variation in their expectations about the changes in identity for Eastern Germans. In contrast, Eastern Germans, who perceive regional boundaries as more permeable, easily adopt the new Western identity and identify themselves with Germany as a whole.

If the situation becomes complicated as a result of differences in economic and political positions, it can lead to conflict between groups. Kriesberg (2003) describes the impact of the clarity of group boundaries in reinforcing the willingness of group members to fight for power and resources. The clear recognition of intergroup differences and socially defined categories leads to the mobilization of group members and increasing conflict. This conflict can result in hostility and violence if structural changes are not set up. However, Fenton (2004) showed that boundaries of differences not always lead to the serious conflict.

Taylor and McKirnan (1984) further developed social identity theory by introducing five stages of social transformation for any established, stratified society with low status minorities. They analyzed the development of competition and conflict between majority and minority groups, and showed the critical role of causal attributions and social comparisons in all stages of this societal transformation. They described five stages of changes in society:

1. *Strictly stratified intergroup relations.* In societies where feudal and caste structures or slavery exist, the majority defines the stratification between the groups. The minority group is forced to believe that they deserve their low status and are responsible for their position. The social comparison with the majority group often leads to lower self-esteem and fosters the development of self-hate within minority group.
2. *The emergence of an individualistic social ideology.* Social, political, or economic processes, such as industrialization, urbanization, growth of

capitalism, spread of literacy, and modernization can lead to the development of individualistic ideologies. At this stage, minorities consider the social structure illegitimate. Minority members begin to make social comparisons on the basis of individual ability and merit; and stratifications that do not reflect individual differences are considered improper. This is the first stage of the ingroup conflict.

3. *Social mobility.* During this stage, highly qualified, better-educated minority members will attempt to join the majority group and try to assimilate either completely or partially. Individual strategies always precede collective actions. Members of minorities make interpersonal comparisons and develop strategies for themselves and for their families, not the whole group. The majority usually accepts these highly qualified members of the minority group, both because their desire to assimilate is seen as proof of the majority group's superiority and because the encouragement of this assimilation process brings some stability to society. Other members of the minority also see the possibilities for assimilation and search for successful ways to move up.

4. *Consciousness raising.* Some highly qualified members of the minority, for various reasons, can be unsuccessful in assimilating with the majority, or will not be accepted by it. The less qualified members of the minority understand the low probability of assimilation and improvement of their status. Thus, the highly qualified, nonassimilated minority members will provoke the rise of ingroup consciousness and stress the necessity of changes in the stratification not only on the individual level, but also at the group level. Self-hate is replaced with pride and ethnocentrism. The minority group now attributes the responsibility for its low status to the dominant group.

5. *Competitive intergroup relations.* Consciousness raising is followed by collective action as the minority group begins to struggle with the system in to secure social justice. The majority group strives to preserve the social order and blame the minority group for inciting conflict. But if such ideological arguments do not reduce the majority-minority conflict, the majority group may either use violence and suppression or begin to negotiate with the minority group to create mutually acceptable social norms.

6.6. OUTGROUP THREAT

The understanding of outgroup threat requires a clear definition of the terms "danger" and "threat." The term "danger" refers to a situation of possible harm or conditions of being susceptible to harm or injury. It stresses the possibility of some event or action without reference to source or agent. The term "threat" always points to something that is a source of danger and declares an intention of or a determination to inflict harm on others. It stresses the potential of activities of the source of danger and the ability or intent of a threat agent to adversely affect a specific target. Thus, if danger describes a situation, threat shows the vector of intention from the source to its target; it always stresses the cause of harm. Consequently, outgroup threat reflects negative or aggressive intentions toward the ingroup. It can be real or perceived, but always affects the behavior of ingroup members (for a more in-depth analysis, see Harre 2006).

Studies show that outgroup threats increase as the perceived competition between groups for resources rises, since groups in conflict determine that they have more to gain from competition than collaboration. Realistic conflict theory stresses that intergroup prejudices become stronger when the goals and interests of the groups are in opposition (Blumer 1958; Bobo 1999; Bobo and Hutchings 1996; Hardin 1995; Sherif 1966). It has also been suggested that outgroup threats lead to more hostility toward the outgroup, which helps justify the conflict and the unfavorable treatment of outgroup members. Situations of competition, proximity, and contact increase intergroup hostility rather than decreasing it (LeVine and Campbell 1972). Considerable research evidence supports these premises (e.g., Brewer 2000; Brown 2000; LeVine and Campbell 1972; Sherif 1966; Sherif and Sherif 1953; Taylor and Moghaddam 1994). A series of studies by Stephan, working with several others (Stephan, Ybarra, and Bachman 1999; Stephan et al. 1998), has posited several types of perceived threats to predict attitudes toward immigrants. Assessments of realistic threat included perceived job loss, social assistance, and redirection to immigrants. The results showed that realistic threats are strong predictors of unfavorable attitudes toward immigrants in three locations within the United States (Florida, New Mexico, and Hawaii) (Stephan, Ybarra, and Bachman 1999) and also in Spain (Stephan et al. 1998). Research suggests that a homogeneous outgroup is perceived as more threatening than a heterogeneous outgroup (Corneille et al. 2001) because such groups are perceived as more able to mobilize for collective action.

As already discussed, members of the ingroup perceive outgroup not only in terms of stereotypes, but attribute goals to outgroup as well. This leads to a perceived threat to the well-being and position of the ingroup. The attribution of negative rather than positive attitudes and goals has been described in attribution theory as being a fundamental attribution error: the tendency among people to overemphasize dispositional, or personality-based, explanations for behaviors observed in others, while underemphasizing the role and power of situational influences on the same behavior (Heider 1958; Jones and Harris 1967; Ross 1977; Ross et al. 1977). In the situation of perceived competition between groups, all actions of an outgroup are interpreted in terms of their harmful and aggressive motivation and goals, and possible threat to an ingroup.

Volkan (1997) also explains the tendency to attribute negative characteristics and goals to outgroups. According to his theory, members of an ingroup experience problems with the integration of negative and positive features of their group image. Since people have a need for positive identity (Tajfel 1984), they tend to internalize the positive characteristics of their group, but externalize and project onto outgroups the negative characteristics of their ingroup. People can believe that the ingroup does not have enough power because the outgroup is immoral, aggressive, and has defeated the ingroup in battle. These projections 'coalesce' in the form of negative reservoirs that characterize outgroups and chosen traumas that stress an outgroup's negative intentions toward the ingroup.

Thus, the perception of an outgroup as a threat is mostly based on the attribution of negative goals to outgroups through the interpretation of current intergroup relations. Usually, the ingroup tends to perceive the outgroup as a threat in several contexts of intergroup relations:

(a) Unequal economical, cultural or political positions of ethnic groups (Gellner 1994);
(b) Different citizenship of ethnic groups (Brubaker 1996);
(c) Memories of the former domination of the outgroup and attribution of the desire for its revival (Gurr and Harff 1994);
(d) A perceived weaker or worse position in comparison with the outgroup (Gurr 1970, 1993);
(e) Limiting of the socioeconomic opportunities of the ingroup by outgroups (Gellner 1994);
(f) Political extremism, violence, and nationalism of outgroups (Hagendoorn et al. 1996).

Changes in intergroup positions have an even stronger impact on the perception of outgroup threat. Among triggering factors are: (a) changes in the demography of groups (including asymmetrical birth rates, the politics of natalism, or baby boom); (b) economic competition; (c) new territorial claims of outgroups; (d) new barriers to upward mobility, economic competition, and the rise of outgroup educational levels and mobility; and (e) intentions to change the existing intergroup positions.

In Crimea, Ukraine, the return of the Crimean Tatars, who were accused of collaborating with the German army and deported to Central Asia in 1944, created tensions with the Russians. Russians feared that the repatriation and a subsequent growth in their population would make Crimean Tatars a numerical majority, and that this would reinforce their claim on the foundation of an autonomous Crimean Tatar Republic (Korostelina 2000a, 2003; Sasse 2002; Shevel 2000). Russians also feared that Islamic fundamentalism would take root among Crimean Tatars. However, Crimea was an autonomous republic of the Russian Federation and even though it had been transferred to the Ukrainian Soviet Socialist Republic in 1954, it had historically experienced strong ties with Russia. After Ukrainian independence in 1991, the local Russian majority group was concerned with its minority position in Ukraine and advocated closer relations with Russia and incorporation in the Russian Federation. This activity increased the perception of the threat posed by Crimean Tatars who blamed Russia for deportation and did not want to live within its borders.

Hagendoorn and colleagues (2000) describe the violent conflict between Azeris and Armenians in Nagorno Karabach in the former Soviet Union in the 1980s as having been aroused by the fear of Azeri population growth, economic competition between Armenians and Azeris, historical enmity between the two groups, and feelings of relative deprivation by the Armenians in Nagorno Karabach in comparison to Armenians in Armenia. The Armenians were afraid to lose their titular status in Nagorno Karabach and their autonomy within Azerbaijan.

Thus, the perception and behavior of ingroup members becomes complicated under the conditions of outgroup threat. This threat may increase or decrease the readiness for conflict among ingroup members and their willingness to fight for ingroup goals in opposition to outgroups' goals. First, the change in the readiness for conflict under threats depends on the importance of interests and goals for the ingroup. If interests and goals are vital and critical for the ingroup, an outgroup threat will increase the ingroup's readiness for conflict. But if the goals of the ingroup are not particularly significant for its well-being, the readiness for conflict decreases under the threat from outgroups. Secondly, majority or minority positions can also influence the changes in ingroup conflict intentions under the conditions of threat. If the minority group has a worthy position and fewer interests to lose, threat will only strengthen their readiness for conflict. The majority group can be more ready for compromise in situations of fighting for its own goals than in situations of opposition to minority goals. Therefore, it is more important to prevent the changes in social structure and the realization of outgroup goals.

6.7. Security Dilemma

In situations of competition between groups, such factors as information failure, credible commitments, and the security dilemma can reshape social identities and provoke identity conflict (Lake and Rothchild 1998). The first two elements, information failure and credible commitment, are connected with the problem of uncertainty and, consequently, so are the elements of the security dilemma.

The security dilemma was first analyzed by Herz (1950) as a situation in which people, knowing that they require the assistance of other people in order to survive, are faced with a dilemma because they know there is a possibility of being killed by these same people; therefore, they must choose social interaction to survive even in the face of potential threat to their lives. The dilemma arises from uncertainty, mutual suspicion, and fear among people regarding the others' intentions toward them. In reality, the intention to harm others may not exist at all, but the fear will lead them to view all others with suspicion. This fear can lead to violent actions. Herz (1950) stresses that "it is one of the tragic implications of the security dilemma that mutual fear of what initially may never have existed may subsequently bring about exactly that which is feared most."

The security dilemma has traditionally been used to explain the interactions of states in the anarchical international system. The role of the security dilemma was analyzed on the level of international relations, including the Cold War (Collins 1997; Jervis 1976, 1978; Spear 1996; Wheeler and Booth 1992), as a source of ethnic conflicts (Posen 1993; Snyder and Jervis 1999), and the rise of nationalism (Van Evera 1999). But the very essence of the security dilemma provides the opportunity to analyze its role in identity conflicts. The dilemma arises as a result of the zero-sum game perception: interpretations of any gain by an outgroup is seen as an ingroup loss. Intergroup comparison typically leads people to see competition with other groups as a struggle for status that provides self-esteem, pride, and a sense of dignity. Groups often perceive that the outgroup gain is automatically ingroup loss, and vice versa. Emotion-laden status competition leads to the increase of the perception of threat.

In situations based on a lack of information, ingroup members tend to use their beliefs and stereotypes as a basis for forecasting outgroup behavior. These beliefs can be formed through historical experience and include chosen traumas and glories. These beliefs can also be the result of favorable comparisons, prejudice, and attribution errors, where outgroups are perceived as cunning, artful, cruel, mean, and aggressive. The salient mobilized identity strengthens this perception of the outgroup as a homogeneous evil. As previously mentioned, perceived external threats produce feelings of insecurity among ingroup members who perceive the ingroup as targets of this threat, and this leads to the ingroup taking actions against all outgroups. These actions are, in turn, perceived by outgroups as threatening, and their counteractions will develop a new turn in the spiral of conflict and violence.

6.8. INGROUP SUPPORT

The readiness for conflict also depends on the support from ingroup members. Ingroup support reflects the expectation that all members of the outgroup maintain the same goals and aspirations, a common perception of the outgroup, and similar intent to change the current social situation. It reduces the fear of social disapproval and of evaluation and increases ingroup loyalty. Support from outgroup members increases the level of participation in decision-making processes and collective actions of ingroups.

If more ingroup members are willing to fight with outgroups, the likelihood of success will increase and therefore the readiness for conflict will increase. Thus, ingroup support will increase the willingness to fight for one's goals and against the goals of any outgroup. According to the 'false consensus effect' (Ross, Greene, and House 1977), the estimation of ingroup support for violent action differs among majority and minority groups. Research on conservative biases shows that individuals tend to overestimate the number of people having attitudes similar to their own (Granberg 1987; Holtz and Miller 1985; Wilder 1984). This effect is found to be stronger among members of low-status and minority groups (Mullen 1983; Wetzel and Walton 1985). Minority group members overestimate ingroup consensus on relevant standpoints and underestimate majority group support for the same standpoints (Sanders and Mullen 1983). False consensus is reinforced if individuals perceive their interests to be threatened (Crano 1983; Suls and Wan 1987).

CHAPTER 7

THE DYNAMICS OF IDENTITY CONFLICT

7.1. THE CONCEPT OF IDENTITY CONFLICT

The prevalent view of identity conflicts stresses the difference between conflicts of interest and those of identity. Many scholars and experts describe conflict as being identity-based because it deals with basic needs and values. Such identity conflicts are categorized by existential needs, values, safety, dignity, and control over destiny and are rooted in complex and multidimensional psychological, historical, and cultural factors. Among the existing needs are participation, consistency, security, recognition, and distributive justice. The frustration of these basic needs along with a denial of human rights leads to social conflicts (Fisher 1997). Such conflicts arise when identity groups perceive that they are oppressed and victimized through a denial of recognition, security, and equity. Burton (1987, 1990) calls such conflicts "deep-rooted conflicts" and points out that they rest on underlying needs that cannot be compromised: interest and position in these conflicts are not negotiable.

Azar (1990) suggests that such protracted social conflicts are not based on the competition around economics and power issues, but are provoked by the denial of the elements necessary for the development of all people, and whose pursuit is therefore a compelling need. He stresses that such conflicts "distinct from traditional disputes over territory, economic recourses, or East-West rivalry . . . revolve around questions of communal identity" (1991:93) and are "characterized by [a] blurred demarcation between internal and external sources and actors" (1990:6). Azar points out four main factors that influence the reinforcement of protracted social conflicts: (1) communal content that rests on the identity of racial, religious, ethnic, and other groups and reflects the level of responsiveness of major "communal groups" to the needs of other group in the society; (2) deprivation of human needs that are ontological and nonnegotiable, including security, development, political access, and identity; (3) governance and state role including "incompetent, parochial, fragile, and authoritarian governments that fail to satisfy basic human needs" (1990:10) complicated by rapid population growth and limited resources; and (4) the impact of international system, including economic dependency and political-military linkages, on weak and developing states. He stress the importance of group identity development and mobilization as well as formation of political goals of autonomy, secession, access to power, and resources in the dynamic of protracted social conflicts.

Rothman (1997) further develops the concept of identity-based conflict and stresses that these "conflicts have high stakes for all parties involved. Their intensity often is destructive, as each side seeks to avoid or subdue the others . . . They are deeply rooted in the underlying individual human needs and values that together constitute people's social identities, particularly in the context of group affiliations, loyalties, and solidarity" (1997:6). The dynamics of such conflicts are based on a group's history, psychological and cultural factors, and values and beliefs. However, as Rothman points out, the differences between identity and interest conflicts are not precise and cannot be clearly defined in practice: "All identity conflicts contain interest conflicts; not all interest conflicts contain identity conflicts" (1997:11). Furthermore, many ignored or unresolved interest-based conflicts can be developed into identity conflicts, including the issues of dignity, identity, pride, and group loyalty.

In his conceptualization of the social conflict, Kriesberg (2003) does not distinguish between interest-based and identity-based conflicts and describes four components that may generate social conflict: strong group identities, grievances, goals to reduce these grievances by changing other parties, and belief in the possibility of such change. People who share the same identity belief have the same fate and interest and think that they experience similar deprivation and aggravation caused by other groups. They establish common goals of changing the social situation and reinforce ingroup support and loyalty to achieve their aims. Kriesberg also emphasizes the importance of the characteristics of the groups involved in conflict. First, it is vital how a group defines itself and which political ideologies and religions constitute its self-image: "The self conception as special beings provides justification for destructive militancy against others who are necessarily less valuable" (2003:11). Second, leaders can mobilize constituencies and strengthen their group loyalty to deal with adversaries. The third important factor is clarity of group boundaries. The clear recognition of intergroup differences and socially defined categories reinforces the willingness of group members to fight for power and resources. Fourth, the degree of ingroup differences defines the probability of the perceptions of internal threat and others as enemies.

Numerous studies on the dynamics and sources of identity conflicts profoundly explored the fundamental question, Do ethnic and national identities cause political conflict, or do they arise out of political conflict? The primordial approach stresses that a salient social identity provokes conflict intentions and leads to violence; the instrumentalist suggests the importance of economic and political factors that influence identity salience and inflame conflict. Despite these two approaches, I support the idea that social identities should be understood neither as sources nor as consequences of conflict but as a form of consciousness that entirely changes the dynamic and structure of conflict. As shall be stressed, social identity itself, including a very salient one, never causes or initiates conflict. Strong social identities, or feelings of belonging to a specific group (ethnic, national, religious, regional), have existed for centuries, yet have rarely resulted in conflict. Consequently, social identities themselves do not arise as a result of conflict among groups, but they do have the potential to become more salient and mobilized. Once a social identity gets involved in interest-based or instrumental conflict, it changes the nature of political or economic conflict in particular ways, making it protracted and deep-rooted.

7.2. THE FOUR C MODEL OF IDENTITY-BASED CONFLICT

To describe the dynamic of identity conflict, I have proposed a *Four C model* that illustrates four stages: comparison, competition, confrontation, and counteraction. The model is presented in the following scheme:

Comparison
(We-They perception and favorable intergroup comparison)

Competition
(Instrumental conflicts of interest among counterpoised interactive communities)

Confrontation
(The ideologization of social identities; transformation of conflicts of interest into moral confrontations between the virtuous Us and the demonized Other)

Counteraction
(Discrimination, violence, genocide)

Comparison

Members of counterpoised interactive communities have peacefully coexisted for centuries, while holding multiple and cross-cutting identities. They perceive themselves as members of different groups: ethnic, religious, national, regional, urban or rural, local community, professional union, and so on. Some identities can be more salient; others can be interconnected and bound into groups (dyads, triads) of identities. Interpersonal social identities (positioning or dyad identity) can be important or even prevail in the system of social identities, especially in individualistic societies. People can perceive themselves as members of categorical groups or groups of membership and have, accordingly, descriptive or collective identities. These identities can have different forms: cultural, reflective, or mobilized. Thus, in interactive communities, people have multiple identities characterized by different forms, types, and levels of salience.

Nevertheless, even in peaceful and cooperative communities, ingroup members have some negative perceptions of outgroup members, such as derisive and degrading stereotypes, an underestimation of and irony toward the outgroup culture, and the attribution of unacceptable or inadmissible behavior to the outgroup members. Thus, each European nation has negative stereotypes and anecdotes about other nations, even about those with whom they have coexisted without war or conflict for centuries. In Italy, inhabitants of the South and North attribute negative stereotypes to one another; Catalans and Andalusians in Spain perceive each other in derisive terms (Ros, Huici, and Gomez 2000).

Several factors influence the unfavorable perception of outgroups. First, in homogenous societies with negligible cultural diversity, people cannot fully satisfy their need for differentiation (Brewer 2000, 2003) and tend to develop loyalties to smaller groups based on regional location or ethnicity. If distinctions among groups are not significant, people tend to shape these regional or ethnic identities by stressing minor differences (Volkan 1997). Second, since a positive social identity is the outcome of favorable social comparisons made between an ingroup and other social groups, ingroup members tend to evaluate outgroups negatively. Thus, certain negative stereotypes, biases, and prejudice against outgroup members can exist within a community. Third, even in situations of economic and social equality, relative assessments of ingroups and outgroups lead to the underestimation of the economic and social position of ingroups and the perception of relative deprivation or disadvantage and negative attitudes toward outgroups.

Fourth, an asymmetrical status leads to the negative estimation of outgroups. In stratified societies with economic and political inequality, minority groups and groups with a low status experience a stronger collective sense of self and more ingroup homogeneity. Their concerns about social identity, self-esteem, sense of dignity, and the compensation of perceived insecurity leads to a stronger ingroup bias and negative perception of outgroups. If a community's history contains wars, violence, or conflicts among particular groups, the identities of these groups are more likely to be salient, collective, and mobilized than other social identities within an identity system. Thus, the history of an intergroup conflict is also a powerful factor in negative outgroup perceptions.

The process of the reproduction of ingroup identity (e.g., the socialization of children, or accommodation to the changes in intergroup relations) also forms a basis for the "positive We–negative They" perception. Parents and educational institutes influence ingroup socialization by telling children fairy tales and stories about heroes and events that contain chosen glories, ingroup pride, positive symbols, and positive memories. Since an ingroup identity is developed and reformulated on the social border of a group in the process of intergroup interaction (Barth 1969), the negative characters ("bad guys") often represent the entire outgroup and reflect the projected negative feelings of shame, loss, and defeat. In these narratives, the ingroup becomes a source of collective pride and self-esteem, while the outgroup is described as a source of threat and aggressiveness.

Parents also use ingroup prototypes (Turner et al. 1994) to shape their children's personalities by teaching them about positive and negative things, behaviors, and values. The prototypes of social groups serve as sources of the homogeneity of attitudes, opinions, and behavior of the members of these groups and provide measures for the estimation and perception of situations. Such prototypes reflect certain values, beliefs, and glories and are perceived as very favorable, thus influencing the "content" and meaning of ingroup morality. The need for certainty in subjectively important domains leads to the ascribing of meaning to identity and a search for agreement with similar people, or ingroup members. This consensus reinforces confidentiality and strengthens narratives. Because of the positive content of prototypes, ingroup members, who are prototypical, are estimated as having a positive morality, while outgroup members, who are less so, are estimated as having the wrong morality or are even accused of being vicious. Such a sense of morality would help children to socialize in their groups and to be successful as group members. Thus, this social self-concept includes memories of the ingroup and serves as a basis for negative estimation of other groups.

Consequently, certain negative perceptions of outgroups exist even in the context of peaceful cooperative communities. Inequality and a history of conflictual relationships can reshape these unfavorable images. Nevertheless, common and cross-cutting identities, intermarriages, and a culture of peaceful coexistence help to maintain stability and balance within an identity system.

Competition

Conflicts of interest typically arise between two or more groups that share or have intentions to share resources or power. Conflict can involve issues regarding the use or control of land, water, and information; access to property or resources; and the sharing of power or political influence. Usually, such conflict occurs among groups that coexist on a common territory or in a common community and often have different statuses: minority and majority, advantaged and disadvantaged, and so forth. As discussed above, minority groups and groups with a low status have more salient identities and prejudices against outgroups. In situations of competition or perceived or experienced conflict with outgroups, a threat will strengthen this negative evaluation and influence the attribution of such stereotypes as aggressiveness, anger, and antagonism.

Confrontation

Conflicts of interest will lead to the polarization of communities and increase of the importance of one social category that (a) best describes adversary groups, (b) was used in previous conflict situations, and or (c) is more obvious or useful for people. Leaders of the groups fighting over power and resources employ social identity to mobilize group members for the struggle. The leaders and elite present their economic and political interests as ingroup ones. Social identity is used as a tool to increase group loyalty and readiness to fight for these "group interests." The leaders employ collective traumas and glories (Volkan 1997) to increase the salience of identity. Thus, in Northern Ireland, where every Sunday neighbors attend churches, the most evident category is a religious one. The conflict that began as a fight for independence and control over economic and political issues turned into religious one on the basis of historically conflictual and the most noticeable category for the groups. In Bosnia, conflicts over employment, welfare, and political influence were categorized as ethnic rather than regional or class based. Despite a closer relationship among ethnic groups than between regional groups (urban, country-based) in prewar Bosnia, a new powerful categorization—religious— developed boundaries between Serbs, Slovaks, and Bosniaks.

Even if most group members have multiple identities, competition and relative deprivation can make conflict more intense and generate situations where individuals tend to choose one identity over others. Members of different groups with multiple identities feel that their sense of security, identity, and moral authority has been disrupted by conflict and look for a strong single identity that employs ideological myths to provide new security, certainty, and moral authority. One salient identity can replace the entire complex of core identities and influence one's perception of the world. This dominant identity has a form of mobilized collective identity and contains ideologies and attributed intentions. In a politicized field of intergroup relations, negative evaluations of outgroups lead to taking positions about ingroup goals in relation to those of outgroups, and hence to defining outgroups as opponents or enemies and to attributing aggressive intentions to them.

Consider the conflict in Senegal over Casamance. Casamance is mostly separated from the rest of Senegal (administered by the French) by Gambia, which was colonized by the British Empire (for a more in-depth analysis, see Sy 2006). Casamance also differs from the rest of Senegal by climate: Senegal is dry, with the rainy season of only three months, while Casamance is green and has enough rains. Many historians stress that Casamance has been a part of Senegal long before the colonial era and peacefully coexists with the rest of the Senegalese nation and people. Other scholars show that until the early years of the twentieth century, Casamance was involved in many insurgencies and forms of resistance against the French control, while most of the Senegalese nation was relatively peaceful. Because of the perceived "rebellious" nature of the populations in the region, many Senegalese, explaining the cause of the current crisis in Casamance, label the province a "rebellious" one. The Senegalese stress ethnic and cultural differences that may cause potential conflict and refer to any member of the Diola, an ethnic group in Casamance, as a "rebel," regardless of whether she or he is or is not a member or supporter of the secessionist movement. In reality, the same distinctness could be applied to all other ethnic groups that had evolved as separate political entities before merging into one Senegalese nation: the Bassari in the extreme southeast, the Pulaar in the north, and the Wolof in the west central part of the country. These ethnic differences influence the negative views about one another, but never produced violence, until the Casamance conflict. The attribution of goals, positions, and political labels such as "rebellious" resulted in the overemphasizing of the distinctness of the Casamance and Diola identities, played an important role in developing ethnic and regional identities, and served as a cause of violent conflict in the region.

Several factors can play an important role in the process of reshaping social identity:

1. States categorize their peoples into ethnic, regional, or religious groups. The politics and ideologies of states toward these groups influence the content and meaning of these identities and can also influence conflicts among them.
2. Elites and leaders play a crucial role in the process of identity formation, transforming cultural and realized identities into mobilized ones. Leaders invoke social movements and define the movements' aims and targets. Through terrorist acts and bloodshed, these leaders strengthen the walls dividing social groups, thus intensifying mistrust among them.
3. International interventions estimate situations in terms of "ethnic conflict," "indigenous rights," the "right of self-determination," and so forth, and apply these concepts in specific local conditions.
4. The media, including modern information technology such as the Internet, e-books, and so on, creates the ideas of belonging and confrontation, reshapes the meaning of membership in groups and intergroup boundaries, and mobilizes support and loyalty toward them.

Finally, only one social identity prevails and replaces the entire complex of multiple identities. This contradictory identity has a form of mobilized collective identity and contains ideologies and attributed intentions. Moreover, the meaning of this identity transforms from a multilateral mode (which includes ingroup traditions and values, characteristics of ingroup members, ingroup ideology, and interrelations with outgroups) to a mode with prevailing threat-narratives about outgroups. Such identity can be described as a *dominant* identity (see Chapter 4) and leads to the perception of the world in terms of positive We–negative They. The greater the perceived difference between the typical characteristics of the ingroup and the outgroup, the greater the disposition to hostility (Oakes 1987; Turner et al. 1994). Fighting with the outgroup becomes the main goal and condition of ingroup survival.

Counteractions

Once a society has become divided into antagonistic groups, social identities become a cause of confrontation among groups competing not just for material advantage, but also for the defense of their security, beliefs, values, and worldview that serve as the basis for ingroup identity. Following behavioral intentions can vary from negotiation and collective voice to violent conflict. In particular, intergroup situations in which the power and status relations are unstable, unclear, or considered illegitimate will provoke defensive or aggressive ingroup actions.

Violence is interconnected with the changes in people's morality or moral concepts. Why are people who consider themselves moral ready to kill others? How does conflict promote a complete revision of moral concepts and ideas and lead to changes in identities? Possible explanations lie in the collective axiology (see Chapter 4): a set of constructions that is used to validate, vindicate, rationalize, or legitimize actions, decisions, and policies. Such constructions function as instruments for making sense of episodes of conflict and serve to solidify a group (Rothbart and Korostelina 2006). Collective axiology includes three components: mythic narrative, sacred icons, and teleomorphic models. Mythic narratives stress the perceptions of a threatening "they" through shocking images, stunning anecdotes, and accounts of violence that can generate fear, terror, and panic. Through narratives and icons that present a concentrated threat and negative images of others, ideas about remote acts of violence are shaped. A teleomorphic model is constructed in a binary form, leading to the perception of a fair "us" and the inhuman "them"; sacredness, good, and virtue are characteristics of the ingroup, and profanity, evil, and vice are those of outgroups. A constructed "we-they" duality produces a normative dichotomy, as if the stories exhibit a boundary crossing between what is true and what "ought" to be true. The collective axiology of intergroup relations and ingroup identity justifies hostility against outgroups. These myths are easily discernible in the national media, school curricula, official government documents and speeches, popular literature and history, and so on. Violence and hostility, in their turn, affect the strengthening of collective axiology and the transformation of social identities.

Consequently, the Four C Model of identity-based conflict provides a basis for the systemic analysis of conflict dynamics that includes economic, political, social, and psychological factors. Ethnic and religious groups living in multicultural communities develop intergroup stereotypes and beliefs. These beliefs can be formed through historical experience and include chosen traumas and glories. They can also be the result of favorable comparisons, prejudice, and attribution errors, where outgroups are perceived as cunning, artful, cruel, mean, and aggressive. In situations of competition for power or resources, group leaders use these stereotypes and beliefs as well as chosen traumas and glories, selected histories, and ingroup loyalties as tools of group mobilization. These employed identities are connected to economic and political interests, and they reinforce negative perceptions of outgroup members, attributing aggressive goals to them. The perceived external threat, especially in the circumstance of a lack of information, strengthens these feelings of insecurity among ingroup members. The ingroup identity becomes more salient and mobilized, and finally dominant, influencing the development of the dual "positive We–negative They" perception. In the narratives of ingroup members, the outgroup is devalued and dehumanized and turned into a homogenous evil. It becomes moral and honorable to take actions against the outgroup and totally destroy it. These actions are in turn perceived by the outgroup as threatening, resulting in the development of counteractions and causing a new turn in the spiral of conflict and violence.

The Zapatista Revolution in Mexico is a great example of the dynamic of identity conflict (for a more in-depth analyses, see Carrigan 1995 and Jung 2003). A further example is the long-time indigenous and peasant people of Chiapas, who have had a negative and conflictual relationship with the government. Chiapas is the eighth-largest state in Mexico. It has the richest natural resources, including oil, natural gas, and hydroelectric power. In addition, it is the largest producer of coffee and the second-largest producer of beef, corn, bananas, honey, melons, avocados, and cocoa. The population of this state never had control over these resources and was under the rule of the Spanish, French, and caudillo landowners and the Mexican state. Moreover, the state's indigenous and peasant communities live below the poverty line, without basic educational and health services. During the1970s, cattlemen from outside the state took over the lands of the communities and forced them into the jungle.

The indigenous and peasant communities did not have a common identity; they were separated from each other despite the fact that many of the tribes were of Mayan descent. In the1970s, the Catholic bishop Don Samuel Ruiz Garcia encouraged the development of a common, shared identity by showing similarities between the Bible story of the Jewish escape from slavery in Egypt and the escape of the indigenous and peasant people into the Lancandona jungle. He reinforced a sense of self-esteem and developed a positive common image of indigenous and peasant people on the basis of their ancestral traditions and culture in opposition to the caudillos and the government as the negative outgroup. This new identity was created as a class identity of peasant against wealthy people and landowners. Simultaneously, a new common identity also adopted the meaning of "indigenous people" on the basis of the increasing importance of this political category and the international recognition of indigenous rights in 1977. After the fall of the communist regimes, a class categorization became less salient and the "indigenous" component of the meaning of a common identity prevailed.

The new salient identity led to the development of ingroups' aims and aspirations to increase their social status and change their position. The arrival of the Zapatista National Liberation Army and the continued threat from the cattlemen increased the salience of the new identity. The continued loss of lands and lack of recognition of basic needs led to frustrations and subsequently negative attitudes toward the Mexican government. The membership in a strong community and military group enhanced the readiness to fight for land and sentiments of self-determination. In 1994, the new land policy of President Salinas and expansion of NAFTA created a new threat to the indigenous and peasant identity and reshaped the goals of the Zapatistas. The situation was perceived within the context of –the "We-They" duality. The latent conflict steadily transformed into low-scale warfare.

Thus, the mobilization of identities can arise as a result of the existence of vital incompatible interests (economic recourses) and the collective perception of new, fresh possibilities (e.g., the possibility of establishing a new autonomic republic after the collapse of the state). Identity conflicts become a new, complex form of competition over interests inside the state and on an international level.

Study I. The Primacy of the Ingroup and Readiness for Conflict Behavior

As I mentioned above, the primacy of the ingroup—the feeling of supremacy of ingroup goals and values over personal ones—can reduce or increase the influence of identity salience on conflict behavior of ingroup members. I propose that feelings of ingroup primacy play a less important role if social identities are salient and have a strong impact on the readiness for conflict behavior. If social identity is less salient and has less influence on the readiness for conflict behavior, feelings of ingroup primacy contribute to an increase in the readiness to fight.

The study was conducted using a specially designed survey in different towns and villages of Crimea during September 2001, just after the events of September 11. The sample was stratified by location, number of resettlements, and rural-urban status. The participants were Russians (257) and Crimean Tatars (257), who were equally distributed across these locations. Of them, 41 percent were male and 59 percent were female; 38 percent were between 20 and 30 years old, 32 percent between 30 and 45, 18 percent between 45 and 60, and 12 percent above 60; and 58 percent were residents of towns and 43 percent lived in villages. Participation was voluntary. The respondents were provided with a questionnaire and selected answers from a list.

Feelings of ingroup primacy were measured by several questions regarding (1) the predominance of ingroup goals over personal goals, (2) the readiness to forget all internal ingroup conflicts in a situation of threat, and (3) the readiness to unite against outgroups. The higher the level of the feeling of ingroup primacy for members, the higher their willingness to disregard their own goals and values and follow ways of behavior required by a collective ingroup identity.

The results of the study confirm my proposition that the feeling of ingroup primacy is higher among Crimean Tatars than among Russians (see Table 7.1).

The Crimean Tatars, as distinct from Russians, are highly confident that the existence of enemy unites ingroups against outgroups, that ingroup members have to forget all internal ingroup conflicts in a situation of treat to ingroups, and that ingroup goals (ethnic and religious) are more important than personal goals. The most significant difference was found for the predominance of the goals of religious groups over personal goals.

I conducted a correlation analysis to study the impact of the feeling of ingroup primacy on the readiness to defend the ingroup's safety, norms, and values. The results show that for Crimean Tatars, the readiness to defend their ethnic group's safety is connected with the supremacy of the ethnic group's goals ($r(256) = .140$; $p < .05$); the readiness to defend their religious group's safety is connected with the supremacy of the religious group's goals ($r(255) = .144$; $p < .05$); the readiness to defend their ethnic group's norms and values is connected with the necessity of ingroup unity in a situation of threat ($r(256) = .140$; $p < .05$). The readiness to defend the religious group's norms and values is connected with the attitude that the existence of an enemy unites ingroups against outgroups ($r(256) = .122$; $p < .05$), the necessity of ingroup unity in a situation of threat ($r(256) = .147$; $p < .05$), the supremacy of the ethnic group's goals ($r(255) = .249$; $p < .001$), and the supremacy of the religious group's goals ($r(255) = .244$; $p < .001$).

For Russians, the readiness to defend their ethnic group's safety is connected with the attitude that the existence of an enemy unites ingroups against outgroups ($r(255) = .145$; $p < .05$), the necessity of ingroup unity in a situation of threat ($r(256) = .244$; $p < .001$), the supremacy of the ethnic group's goals ($r(256) = .186$; $p < .005$), and the supremacy of the religious group's goals ($r(255) = .229$; $p < .001$). The readiness to defend

Table 7.1 The Mean of the Feeling of Ingroup Primacy among Russians and Crimean Tatars

Ingroup Supremacy	Russians	Crimean Tatars	t Test
Enemy as uniting factor for ingroup	2.4591	2.8794	3.115*
Ingroup unity in situation of threat	2.9336	3.1829	2.115**
Goals of ethnic group more important than personal	1.6770	2.2461	5.285*
Goals of religious group more important than personal	1.5117	2.1176	5.567*

Note: *$p < .001$; **$p < .005$.

their religious group's safety is connected with the attitude that the existence of an enemy unites ingroups against outgroups ($r(255) = .141; p < .05$) and the supremacy of the religious group's goals ($r(255) = .256; p < .001$). The readiness to defend the norms and values of their ethnic group is connected with the attitude that the existence of an enemy unites ingroups against outgroups ($r(255) = .170; p < .05$), the necessity of ingroup unity in a situation of threat ($r(256) = .317; p < .001$), the supremacy of the ethnic group's goals ($r(255) = .167; p < .05$), and the supremacy of the religious group's goals ($r(255) = .255; p < .001$). The readiness to defend the religious group's norms and values is connected with the necessity of ingroup unity in a situation of threat ($r(256) = .200; p < .001$) and the supremacy of the religious group's goals ($r(255) = .243; p < .001$).

Thus, the feeling of ingroup primacy has a higher impact on the readiness to defend safety, norms, and values of religious and ethnic groups among Russians than among Crimean Tatars. For Crimean Tatars, only the readiness to defend the religious group's norms and values is connected with all parameters of the feeling of ingroup primacy. The results confirm our proposition that ingroup supremacy is higher among Crimean Tatars than among Russians. It was also found that the feeling of ingroup primacy has a higher influence on the readiness to defend an ingroup's norms, values, and safety than does the feeling of identity. I proposed that the ingroup primacy plays a less important role if social identity is salient and has a strong impact on the readiness for conflict behavior; if social identity is less salient and has less influence on this readiness, the feeling of ingroup primacy contributes to an increase in the readiness.

A partially saturated general linear model (GLM) was used to simultaneously test this proposition for two groups: with a low level of social identity salience (211 respondents) and with a high level of this salience (203 respondents). For the first group (with less salient ethnic and religious identities), the feeling of ingroup primacy has main effects on the readiness to defend the ethnic group's safety ($F(1,210) = 14.532; p < .001$), the religious group's safety ($F(1,209) = 19.122; p < .001$), the ethnic group's norms and values of ($F(1,210) = 12.752; p < .001$), and the religious group's norms and values ($F(1,208) = 8.712; p < .01$). Religious identity has a main effect only on the readiness to defend the religious group's safety ($F(1,209) = 8.438; p < .01$).

For the second group (with a salient social identity), ethnic and religious identities both have main effects on the readiness to defend the ethnic group's safety ($F(1,202) = 24.235; p < .001$; and $F(1,202) = 17.534; p < .001$, accordingly), the religious group's safety ($F(1,201) = 8.015; p < .05$; and $F(1,201 = 40.414; p < .001$, accordingly), the ethnic group's norms and values ($F(1,202) = 19.650; p < .001$; and $F(1,02) = 11.772; p < .01$, accordingly), and the religious group's norms and values ($F(1,203) = 9.812; p < .01$; and $F(1,202) = 26.794; p < .001$, accordingly). The feeling of ingroup primacy has a main effect only on the readiness to defend the religious group's norms and values ($F(1,203) - 18.549; p < .001$).

Thus, for ingroup members with a low level of social identity salience, the feeling of ingroup primacy has an impact on the readiness to defend safety, values, and norms of ethnic and religious groups. Only religious identity influenced the readiness to defend the religious group's safety. For ingroup members with a high level of social identity salience, ethnic and religious identities influence the readiness to defend the safety, values, and norms of ethnic and religious groups. The feeling of ingroup primacy has an impact on only the readiness to defend the religious group's norms and values. Ingroup members with a salient social identity have stronger feelings of ingroup primacy; however, these feelings do not play an important role in influencing the readiness for conflict behavior. It is the salient social identity that leads to the readiness for conflict. For ingroup members with a less salient social identity, ingroup primacy has stronger impact on the readiness for conflict behavior. In other words, people with a low level of social identity salience show the readiness for conflict behavior only if they feel that the ingroup goals and values are more important than personal ones and believe that the existence of an enemy unites ingroups against outgroups. For people with a salient ethnic identity, the readiness for conflict is a result of identity salience; ingroup supremacy is derived from identity salience and does not have a direct impact on the readiness for conflict behavior.

Study II. The Readiness for Conflict Behavior: The Effects of Social Identity Salience and Ingroup Interests

Studies of intergroup relations show that categorization and competition over scarce resources are important determinants of intergroup discrimination. Social identity theory and realistic conflict theory clearly focus on different motives for intergroup bias and discrimination: social identity on the one hand and interests on the other. As I have already stressed, social identity theory argues that the need to maintain a positive social identity leads to favoring an ingroup, evaluations, intergroup bias, and stereotypes. Realistic conflict theory argues that intergroup bias and intergroup discrimination develop on the basis of incompatible interests of groups. But some resent research show that individuals may combine and balance the needs for both belonging to high-status groups and defending material interests.

This study was conducted in collaboration with Drs. Louk Hagendoorn and Edwin Poppe, my colleagues from the European Research Center on Migration and Ethnic Relation at Utrecht University, the Netherlands. On the basis of social identity theory, we predicted that group members who more strongly identify with their group would show a higher readiness for conflict behavior (i.e., they support ingroup goals and oppose outgroup goals). On the basis of realistic conflict theory, we predicted that the interests would determine the readiness for conflict, including support for ingroup goals and opposition to outgroup goals. The question was, Which determinants work under what conditions, and do they work together, separately, or sequentially?

In this sense it is relevant to find out which of these two determinants, ingroup identity or ingroup interests, is more important for the readiness to fight and thereby provoke violent intergroup conflict. To study this question, we have developed the following hypotheses:

1. (a) A salient ingroup identity leads to a higher readiness for conflict behavior.
   (b) Strong ingroup interests lead to a higher readiness for conflict behavior.
2. A salient ingroup identity and ingroup interests can have different effects on the endorsement of ingroup goals and opposition to outgroup goals.

Data Collection

The study was conducted in May–October 2001 in towns and villages in the Crimea varying in rural-urban setting and number of Tatar resettlements. The participants were Russians (505) and Crimean Tatars (578) and were equally distributed across these locations. Of them, 42 percent were male and 58 percent were female; 39 percent were between 20 and 30 years old, 31 percent between 30 and 45, 20 percent between 45 and 60, and 10 percent above 60; and 55 percent were residents of towns and 45 percent of villages. Participation was voluntary.

Results

The Effect of Ingroup Identification on Taking Position. Crimean Tatars identify more strongly with their ethnic group ($M = 0.68$ on a scale of 0 to 1) than Russians ($M = 0.49$; $F(1,892) = 147.40$; $p < .001$). A majority of Russians agree that Crimea should become a part of Russia ($M = 0.67$), while a majority of Crimean Tatars oppose it ($M = 0.75$ after recoding). Most Crimean Tatars agree with the cultural autonomy of Crimean Tatars ($M = 0.69$), while Russians oppose it ($M = 0.66$). Overall, the support for ingroup goals does not differ significantly between the groups ($F(1,812) = .830$; n.s.), but Crimean Tatars are more opposed to the outgroup goals than are Russians ($F(1,815) = 5.66$; $p < .05$).

The hypothesis that a salient ingroup identity leads to more endorsement of ingroup goals and stronger opposition to outgroup goals was tested in two ways. The participants were divided, firstly, into those with a weakly and strongly salient ethnic identity, and, secondly, into whose who answered the questions about their conflict intentions from their personal standpoint (personal identity) and whose who answered them from the standpoint of an ingroup member (social identity).

The ANOVA of the support for the ingroup's goal shows a main effect of the salience of ethnic identity and an interaction effect of ethnic groups and salience of ethnic identity (see Table 7.1). A highly salient ethnic identity reinforces the support for ingroup goals. A simple slope analysis shows that this effect is stronger for Crimean Tatars ($F(1,684) = 14.61$; $p < .001$) than for Russians ($F(1,684) = 0.23$; n.s.). There is no significant effect of identity

Table 7.2 Russians and Crimean Tatars with Low or High Salience of Ethnic Identity Taking Position about Ingroup and Outgroup Goals under the Condition of Primed Personal and Social Identity

In/Outgroup Goals	Russians		Crimean Tatars	
	Low Salience of Ethnic Identity	High Salience of Ethnic Identity	Low Salience of Ethnic Identity	High Salience of Ethnic Identity
Support ingroup goal	0.64	0.68	0.65	0.72
Oppose outgroup goal	0.86	0.90	0.63	0.76

conditions on ingroup goals and no significant interaction effect of identity condition and the salience of ethnic identity.

The ANOVA of opposition to the outgroup's goal shows main effects of ethnic groups, the salience of ethnic identity, and identity conditions and an interaction effect of ethnic groups and identity conditions. The main effects show that Russians are opposed less to the outgroup goal than are Crimean Tatars, that a salient identity leads to more opposition, and that a primed social identity moderates opposition (see Table 7.2). The interaction effect shows that the priming of social identity reduces the Russians' opposition to Tatar autonomy ($F(1,687) = 193.24$; $p < .001$), but there is no significant effect for Crimean Tatars' opposition to Crimea becoming a part of Russia ($F(1,687) = 2.47$; $p > .05$, n.s.).

The results confirm the expectation that ingroup identification leads to more endorsement for ingroup goals. In particular, strongly identifying Crimean Tatars endorses Crimean Tatar cultural autonomy. Similarly, a strong ethnic identity reinforces the opposition to outgroup goals. However, there is no effect for the priming of social identity on the endorsement of ingroup goals, which is in contradiction to hypothesis 1. And the priming of social identity reduces the opposition to outgroup goals, in particular among Russians.

The Effect of Loyalty and Interest-Related Factors. The question whether interest- or identity-related factors are more important in determining the readiness for conflict behavior (the fight for ingroup goals against outgroup goals) can be answered by analyzing the results of experiment 1. The salience of identity reflects the loyalty that group members feel toward the ingroup, because it contributes to their self-esteem and social status. The interests for which ingroup members are willing to fight are represented by the ingroup goals. Outgroup threat affects the calculation of possible risks and successes in trying to realize the interests reflected in these goals. Interests were measured as a score above (interests) or below (no interest) the midpoint of the scale measuring the support for the ingroup and opposition to the outgroup goal in experiment 1.

Table 7.3   Russians' and Crimean Tatars' Readiness to Fight for the Ingroup Goal and against the Outgroup Goal Depending on Interests and Ingroup Identity

In/Outgroup Goals	Russians		Crimean Tatars	
	No Interest	Interest	No Interest	Interest
Ingroup goal				
Low salience of ethnic identity	0.39	0.63	0.53	0.6
High salience of ethnic identity	0.58	0.74	0.64	0.67
Outgroup goal				
Low salience of ethnic identity	0.45	0.59	0.46	0.59
High salience of ethnic identity	0.59	0.58	0.45	0.6

The ANOVA of ingroup goals shows an additive model in which both interests and the salience of identity equally contribute to the willingness to fight (see Table 7.3.). The results show that the readiness to fight for ingroup goals is lower among Crimean Tatars and especially among Russians who have a nonsalient social identity and attach less value to the realization of ingroup goals.

The ANOVA of the willingness to fight against outgroup goals shows that only interests determine the willingness to fight and no other factors have a significant effect. The conclusion is that identity and interests together determine the willingness to fight for ingroup goals, while the willingness to fight against outgroup goals is determined only by interests.

It appears that Crimean Tatars with a salient ethnic identity support the goal of Tatar cultural autonomy more than those with a less salient ethnic identity, and that Russians with a salient ethnic identity are more strongly in favor of Crimea becoming a part of Russia than those with a less salient ethnic identity. Russians and Tatars with a salient ethnic identity show more opposition toward each other's goals than those with a less salient ethnic identity. In other words, a salient social identity reinforces the support for the group goals, but more strongly among the minority than among the majority, as was expected.

Results show that explanations derived from social identity theory and realistic conflict theory are not necessarily competitive, but should be combined to understand the dynamics of group-intergroup evaluations, discrimination, and conflict. Group members on the one hand react on the basis of salient ingroup identity and on the other hand on the basis of interests. The analysis showed that both identity and interests, specifically the salience of identity and the attachment to the ingroup interests, contribute to the readiness of Russians to fight for Crimean incorporation in Russia and the readiness of Crimean Tatars to fight for autonomy. However, the readiness to fight against the outgroup goals is only an effect of interest, reflected in the attachment to the ingroup goals. Therefore, the salience of identity contributes only to the readiness to fight for ingroup goals and does not influence the readiness to fight against outgroup goals. So, the assumption of social identity theory that salient ingroup identity leads to intergroup conflict is only partly correct and cannot be extended to fighting against outgroups.

Study III. The Readiness for Conflict Behavior: The Model of Determination

Several factors that influence the readiness for conflict behavior and the dynamic of identity conflict were described above. First, power relations between contesting groups are a factor influencing intergroup bias and discrimination: social identity is stronger among minority groups than among majority groups, and minority group members often are highly motivated to improve the fate of their ingroups. Second, the readiness for conflict behavior is reinforced by the outgroup threat. Third, the readiness to fight for ingroup goals and against outgroup goals also depends on the support from ingroup members. If more ingroup members are willing to fight for the goal, the likelihood of success, and therefore the willingness to fight, will increase. Thus, the readiness for conflict behavior is a function of ingroup identity, the value attached to the goals, and calculations of risk considering ingroup support, outgroup threat, and potential gains and damages based on ingroup status position. On the basis of previous research, I propose the following model of interconnections among social identity, ingroup support, outgroup threat, ingroup interests, minority/majority position, and readiness for conflict behavior (Figure 7.1). In this model, the main factors determining the readiness for conflict behavior are ingroup identity and ingroup interests. The additional factors affecting this readiness—outgroup threat and ingroup support—have aspects that are related to ingroup identity as well as common interests. The outgroup threat of violent opposition is a threat to the ingroup's material interests, but is also a threat to its status. The question is whether this factor further contributes to the explanation of the readiness for conflict behavior in

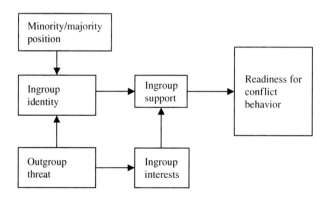

Figure 7.1 The model of determination of the readiness for conflict behavior.

addition to the support for the ingroup goals. A salient social identity leads to an overestimation of the potential ingroup support for violent action; ingroup support can also increase the readiness to fight if the possibility of success is evaluated. The question is whether the expected ingroup support for violent action contributes to the readiness to fight for ingroup goals in addition to ingroup identity.

In this study the focus is on the effect of ethnic identity, endorsement of the ingroup goal, majority or minority position, perceived outgroup threat, and ingroup support on the readiness to fight for ingroup and against outgroup goals.

The following are the hypotheses:

1. Perceived outgroup threat increases the readiness to fight for ingroup and against outgroup goals among the minority group but moderates this readiness among the majority.
2. (a) Perceived ingroup support reinforces the readiness to fight for ingroup and against outgroup goals, but is stronger among the minority than among the majority.
   (b) The members of the minority group perceive more ingroup support for fighting for ingroup goals than do members of the majority group.

Data Collection

The study was conducted in May–October 2001 in towns and villages in Crimea, and it varied in rural-urban setting and the number of Tatar resettlements. The participants were Russians (505) and Crimean Tatars (578) and were equally distributed across these locations. Of them, 42 percent were male and 58 percent were female; 39 percent were between 20 and 30 years old, 31 percent between 30 and 45, 20 percent between 45 and 60, and 10 percent above 60; and 55 percent were residents of towns and 45 percent were residents of villages. Participation was voluntary.

The participants filled out the questionnaire in about 20 minutes.

The Threat and Ingroup Support Experiment

In this experiment the intention to fight for ingroup and against outgroup goals was measured under the presence or absence of outgroup threat. The participants were asked to indicate their personal intention to fight, as well as to indicate their estimation whether ingroup members were willing to fight. The no-threat versions for personal intentions to fight were (for Russians): "If Russia wants to have back the Crimea, would you be prepared to actively fight for [for Crimean Tatars, "against"] this?" and "If Crimean Tatars receive cultural autonomy, would you be prepared to actively fight against [Crimean Tatars, "for"] this?" The threat versions for Russians were: "If Tatars in Crimea massively resist the desire of Russia to have back the Crimea, would you be prepared to actively fight for this?" and "If Tatars in Crimea massively support the desire of Crimean Tatars to receive cultural autonomy, would you be prepared to actively fight against this?" The threat versions for Crimean Tatars were: "If Russians in Crimea massively support the desire of Russia to have back the Crimea, would you be prepared to actively fight against this?" and "If Russians in the Crimea massively resist desire of Crimean Tatars to receive cultural autonomy, would you be prepared to actively fight for this?" The questions have to be answered on a scale of 1 (No) through 2 (Yes, I would protest) to 3 (Yes, I will fight actively). All the answering scales of the dependent variables in the experiments were transformed into values between 0 and 1.

Results
The Effect of Outgroup Threat on the Willingness to Fight. The results show that outgroup threat has an interaction effect on the willingness of ethnic groups to fight for ingroup goals (see Table 7.4). Outgroup threat (massive outgroup opposition to ingroup goals) reinforces the readiness to fight for cultural autonomy among Crimean Tatars, but moderates the willingness of Russians to fight for the incorporation of Crimea in Russia. This is what was expected in hypothesis 1. The analysis of the willingness to fight against outgroup goals shows a main effect of outgroup threat (see Table 7.4). Outgroup threat reinforces the willingness to fight against outgroup goals among Crimean Tatars as well as among Russians, which differs from what was expected from Russians in hypothesis 1, namely, moderation. Including the salience of ethnic identity in the ANOVA shows that a highly salient ethnic identity reinforces this effect ($F(1,873) = 4.98; p < .05$). People with a salient ethnic identity in a situation of threat are more ready to fight against outgroup goals than are people with a nonsalient ethnic identity.

The Effect of Ingroup Support on the Willingness to Fight. Ingroup support reinforces the willingness to fight for ingroup goals and against outgroup goals among both Russians and Crimean Tatars (for the main effect of ingroup support, see Table 7.5). This was expected in hypothesis 2, but the expectation that the effect of ingroup support is stronger among Crimean Tatars is not confirmed. The effect of ingroup support is reduced if outgroup threat is present (see the interaction effects in Table 7.5), except for the Russians' willingness to fight against Tatar autonomy. The moderating effect of outgroup threat on Russians' willingness to fight for ingroup goals is still visible, but not significant.

Table 7.4 Russians' and Crimean Tatars' Intention to Fight for the Ingroup Goal and against the Outgroup Goal under Absence and Presence of Outgroup Threat

In/Outgroup Goals	Russians		Crimean Tatars	
	No Threat	Threat	No Threat	Threat
Fight for ingroup goal	0.58	0.53	0.53	0.67
Oppose outgroup goal	0.49	0.52	0.45	0.53

Table 7.5   Russians' and Crimean Tatars' Willingness to Fight if the Ingroup Massively Supports the Ingroup Goal or Opposes the Outgroup Goal, in Combination with Absence or Presence of Outgroup Threat

In/Outgroup Goals	Russians		Crimean Tatars	
	No Ingroup Support	Ingroup Support	No Ingroup Support	Ingroup Support
Ingroup goal				
No threat	0.39	0.76	0.29	0.69
Threat	0.42	0.70	0.53	0.75
Outgroup goal				
No threat	0.34	0.62	0.34	0.54
Threat	0.40	0.71	0.45	0.60

False Consensus. It is expected that Crimean Tatars overestimate the convergence between their own standpoints and those other ingroup members. The results show that the ingroup willingness to fight is estimated higher by Crimean Tatars ($M = 0.67$) than by Russians ($M = 0.64$). Under outgroup threat the estimation rises among Tatars ($M = 0.75$) and decreases among Russians ($M = 0.56$). The ANOVA shows a main effect of ethnic groups ($F(1,1053) = 21.62; p < 0.001$) and an interaction of ethnic groups by outgroup threat ($F(1,1053) = 21.62; p < .001$). This confirms that the false consensus effect is significantly stronger among Crimean Tatars than among Russians, as was expected (hypothesis 2b). Crimean Tatars expect more ingroup members to be willing to fight for Tatar autonomy if many Russians oppose it, while Russians expect that the support from the ingroup will be drastically reduced if there is a massive Tatar opposition to Russian claims on the incorporation of Crimea. In sum, while Crimean Tatars believe that a massive opposition from the Russian majority will incite even more ingroup members to fight for cultural autonomy, Russians believe that a massive opposition from Crimean Tatars will moderate the readiness to fight for Russian incorporation of Crimea among Russians.

The last question is whether ingroup support contributes to the willingness to fight in addition to identification and interests. The analysis shows that both the salience of identity and ingroup support have a significant effect on the willingness to fight for ingroup goals, while ingroup support alone has a significant effect on the willingness to fight against outgroup goals (see Table 7.6).

The results make clear that identity and interests determine how minority and majority group members decide on their behavioral intentions for achieving ingroup goals and preventing the realization of outgroup goals. Outgroup threat contributes to the willingness to fight in proportion to the ingroup interests, and ingroup support contributes to it in proportion to both interests and loyalty. Ingroup members consider the readiness of

Table 7.6 Russians' and Crimean Tatars' Willingness to Fight for the Ingroup Goal and against the Outgroup Goal Depending on Ingroup Support and Ingroup Identification

In/Outgroup Goals	Russians		Crimean Tatars	
	No Ingroup Support	Ingroup Support	No Ingroup Support	Ingroup Support
Ingroup goal				
Low salience of ethnic identity	0.40	0.67	0.40	0.64
High salience of ethnic identity	0.47	0.83	0.44	0.76
Outgroup goal				
Low salience of ethnic identity	0.39	0.66	0.31	0.58
High salience of ethnic identity	0.43	0.71	0.43	0.58

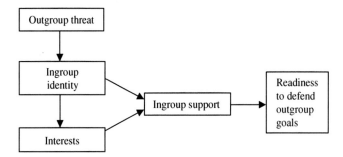

Figure 7.2 The model of determination of the readiness to defend ingroup goals.

ingroup members to fight important only if they attach much value to the ingroup's interests and identity.

The hypothesis that the readiness of the minority to fight for autonomy becomes only stronger if the majority massively opposes Tatar autonomy, while the majority moderates the willingness to fight for ingroup goals if the minority massively opposes it (hypothesis 1), was confirmed. The interpretation is that the minority has much to gain and little to lose, while the majority has much to lose and less to gain by its insistence. The expectation that ingroup support reinforces the readiness for conflict behavior (to fight for ingroup goals and against outgroup goals (hypothesis 2) was confirmed.

Thus, analysis shows that ingroup identity, ingroup support, and outgroup threat and interest have an impact on for the readiness to fight for ingroup goals. In this case, the basic model will have a specific structure (see Figure 7.2).

However, the readiness to oppose outgroup goals is connected only with ingroup interests. The basic model for the readiness to fight against outgroup goals is presented in Figure 7.3. Outgroup threat does not have

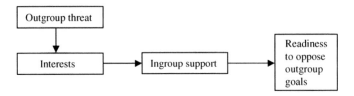

Figure 7.3   The model of determination of the readiness to oppose outgroup goals.

a strong influence on the readiness; ingroup support increases the effect of interests on the readiness.

Study IV. Comparative Analysis of the Impact of Actuality and Type of Identity on Conflict Behavior

In his writing on ethnic conflict, Horowitz (1985) distinguishes between "hard" and "soft" approaches to ethnic identities. The hard approach views ethnic groups as firmly bounded, durable communities inclined to ethnocentrism, hostility to outsiders, and passionate conflict. The soft approach considers ethnicity as a social construct within which solidarity is based on material rewards and conflict behavior is based on calculation. Evidence for the former approach comes from a case-study literature that emphasizes the importance of identity in virulent internal conflicts or civil wars (e.g., Gellner 1994; Zartman 1995). Support for the latter approach comes largely from studies in social psychology, which show that ingroup-favoring biases indicative of group identity develop quickly in temporary groups formed with strangers assigned to work on laboratory tasks. Further, broader literatures on such topics as communication and persuasion, influence, and attitude change demonstrate behavior, thoughts, and feelings. An implication of these studies is that group identities are dynamic in the sense of being sensitive to changes in incentive structures or role expectations; they are largely constructed.

Although a lively debate has ensued on this issue, there is virtually no empirical research designed to compare the approaches. Such an evaluation would consist of comparing at least two cases of ethnic conflict, one where the disputing groups are composed of relatively permanent, life-long members or representatives, and the other where group membership is "assigned," recruited for incentives, or developed in relation to specific tasks. The cases would be compared on various indicators of conflict intensity, including its duration, escalation, and intransigence and the results of attempts to negotiate termination. This is the kind of comparison entertained in the proposed project. The results would provide clarification for the plausibility of alternative sources of ethnic group identity. The conflict chosen for this project is the dispute between the ethnic minority, Crimean Tartars, and the ethnic majority, Russians, living on the Crimean peninsula in the Ukraine.

This study was conducted in collaboration with Prof. Daniel Druckman, my colleague at George Mason University. The aim of this experimental design was to examine if actual historical (ethnic) identities would produce different results than the situational identities simulated in a role play. In this experimental design, there were several competing hypotheses, including the following:

1. Actuality of the group identity influences conflict behavior.
2. The type of group identity (ethnic-historical identity vs. situational identity) has an important influence on conflict behavior.

This experiment was designed in the form of a negotiation between two individuals. Ten pairs of participants represented each of the experimental groups. To test these hypotheses, four issues were negotiated. Each session (role-play simulation and the real case) took nearly 50 minutes, and on each issue the participants were given four alternative choices in addition to the one that they could choose on their own (open ended). The issues were displayed on a scale ranging from one side's desired position to the other's desired outcome, the position in between reflecting varying degrees of compromise.

Independent Variables
The actuality of group identity (actual vs. nonactual) and type of identity (situational vs. historical) are presented in Table 7.7.

1. *Ethnic/Actual Identity.* In this condition, historical (ethnic) identities were recalled by involving representatives of two different ethnic groups in a discussion of the issues within an ethnic context. The participants also were informed that the results of these negotiations would be used in implementing new ethnic policies (actuality of identity).
2. *Ethnic/Nonactual Identity.* Representatives of two different ethnic groups discussed and negotiated ethnic issues without stressing the implementation of the ethnic policy.
3. *Situational/Actual Identity.* This condition represented a role play of opposing ethnic identities. Russian role players were assigned randomly to either a Crimean Tatar or a Russian role. The participants were also informed that the results of these negotiations would be used in implementing new ethnic policies (actuality of identity).
4. *Situational/Nonactual Identity.* Russian role players were assigned randomly to either a Crimean Tatar or a Russian role and negotiated ethnic issues without stressing the implementation of the ethnic policy.

Table 7.7   Independent Variables in the 2 × 2 Experiment

Types of Identity	Actuality	
	Actual	Nonactual
Historic (ethnic)	1	2
Situational	3	4

Dependent Variables

1. *Negotiation Outcomes.* The measurement included number of issues resolved willingness to compromise from initial positions (to see how far they move from their initial position), time taken for resolution, the pattern of resolution as symmetrical or asymmetrical.
2. *Postnegotiation Perception.* A small questionnaire was used that probed the participants' perceptions of the negotiation situation (opposing negotiator, etc.).

The participants of this simulation negotiated on the following issues:

1. Development of the Crimean Tatars' autonomy
   - Total autonomy
   - Multiethnic republic with three languages
   - Crimean Tatars' language as official in Crimea
   - No autonomy
   - No decision
2. Status of indigenous people for Crimean Tatars
   - Status that gives them more rights than for other people
   - Status with equal rights with other people
   - Status of deported people that gives them the right to receive citizenship during the year after return to Crimea
   - No right
   - No decision
3. Affirmative actions for Crimean Tatar students
   - Entry to a university without examination
   - Additional points
   - Additional points only in special cases
   - No action
   - No decision
4. Elections for Crimean Tatars
   - More representatives in Parliament than other minorities
   - Only one more representative in Parliament than other minorities
   - Representatives pro rata their population
   - No representatives
   - No decision

Questionnaire

1. Which emotions do you have during negotiation? 1 negative, 5 positive
2. Which emotions do you have now? 1 negative, 5 positive
3. Was another party aggressive during negotiation? 1 yes, 5 no
4. Did you feel the pressure? 1yes, 5 no
5. Was the other party ready to have contact with you? 1 no, 5 yes
6. Was another party ready to listen to you? 1 no, 5 yes

7. Was another party willing to reach a joint decision? 1 no, 5 yes
8. Are you contented with the process of negotiation? 1 no, 5 yes
9. Are you contented with the results of negotiation? 1 no, 5 yes
10. Are you ready to negotiate with this party again? 1 no, 5 yes

Results

Analysis of Decisions. The analysis of decisions in four experimental groups shows the following:

Group 1: Ethnic actual identity
    Issue 1. 45% – total autonomy
    Issue 2. 90% – equal rights
    Issue 3. 90% – no affirmative actions
    Issue 4. 85% – equal representation

Group 2: Ethnic nonactual identity
    Issue 1. 80% – Multiethnic republic with 3 languages
    Issue 2. 90% – equal rights
    Issue 3. 85% – no affirmative actions
    Issue 4. 55% – Specific affirmative actions for Crimean Tatars

Group 3: Situational actual identity
    Issue 1. 65% – Multiethnic republic with 3 languages
    Issue 2. 90% – equal rights
    Issue 3. 80% – affirmative actions for Crimean Tatar students
    Issue 4. 35% – specific affirmative actions for Crimean Tatars

Group 4: Situational nonactual identity
    Issue 1. 25% – no autonomy
    Issue 2. 95% – equal rights
    Issue 3. 90% – no affirmative actions
    Issue 4. 65% – equal representation

1. The decisions of participants in groups with ethnic identity are similar regardless of the actuality of identity.
2. The actuality of identity influences the differences in decisions between groups with situational identity.
3. The type of identity influences the differences between groups with actual identity.

Analysis of Indexes. An ANOVA of emotions during negotiation shows the main effect of the type ($F = 27.532$; $p < .001$) and actuality ($F = 8.078$; $p < .01$) of identity, as well as the interaction of the two ($F = 13.814$; $p < .001$). More positive emotions were connected with ethnic identity and actual identity; the most positive emotions were expressed in the condition of ethnic actual identity. Fewer positive emotions were connected with situational actual identity.

An ANOVA of emotions after negotiations shows the interaction effect of actuality and type of identity ($F = 3.004$; $p < .05$). The participants showed more positive emotions after negotiations in the condition of ethnic identity, especially actual ethnic identity. They expressed the most negative emotions after negotiation in the condition of situational actual identity.

The ANOVA of aggression from another participant shows the main effects of identity type ($F = 29.470$; $p < .001$) and actuality ($F = 34.087$; $p < .001$). More aggression was perceived from other participants in the conditions of ethnic nonactual and situational nonactual identities. They perceived less aggressiveness in the condition of actual identity.

The ANOVA of pressure from another side shows the main effect of identity type ($F = 14.535$; $p < .001$). The highest pressure from other participants was experienced in the conditions of situational nonactual and situational actual identities. The participants showed less aggressiveness in the condition of ethnic identity.

The ANOVA of the readiness of another participant for contact shows the main effect of actuality ($F = 36.735$; $p < .001$). This readiness was perceived as highest in the conditions of ethnic actual and situational actual identities. Thus, the participants showed the most readiness for contact in the condition of actual identity.

The ANOVA of the readiness of another side to listen shows the main effect of identity type ($F = 64.742$; $p < .001$) and actuality ($F = 24.849$; $p < .001$) and an interaction of the two ($F = 22.365$; $p < .001$). The strongest readiness to listen was connected with the conditions of ethnic and actual identities. The least readiness to listen was shown in the condition of situational, not actual, identity.

The ANOVA of willingness to find a collaborative decision shows the main effect of identity type ($F = 4.595$; $p < .05$) and actuality ($F = 38.175$; $p < .001$) and an interaction of the two ($F = 5.740$; $p < .05$). The highest willingness to find a collaborative decision was connected with ethnic and actual identities; it was shown in the condition of ethnic actual identity.

The ANOVA of satisfaction with negotiation shows the main effect of identity type ($F = 26.152$; $p < .001$) and actuality ($F = 131.383$; $p < .001$) and an interaction of the two ($F = 33.864$; $p < .001$). The highest satisfaction with negotiation is connected with the conditions of ethnic and actual identities and was shown in the condition of ethnic actual identity.

Similar to the estimation of the negotiation process, the highest satisfaction with decisions was perceived in the conditions of situational actual and ethnic actual identities. The ANOVA of satisfaction with decisions shows the main effect of actuality ($F = 5.074$; $p < .05$). The biggest satisfaction with decisions is connected with the condition of actual identity.

The ANOVA of the readiness to participate in negotiation again shows the main effect of identity type ($F = 12.455$; $p<.001$) and actuality ($F = 10.383$; $p<.005$) and an interaction of the two ($F = 10.382$; $p < .005$). The highest readiness to participate in negotiation again is connected with the conditions of ethnic and actual identities and was shown in the condition of ethnic actual identity.

Thus, negotiations in the condition of ethnic nonactual identity are characterized by middle levels of expressed emotions, feelings of pressure from another side, a readiness to listen, and a readiness to participate in negotiation again (Figure 7.4.).

Negotiations in the condition of ethnic actual identity are characterized by positive emotions, the absence of feeling of pressure and aggression from another side, a readiness for contact and to listen, satisfaction in decisions and negotiation, and a readiness to participate in negotiation again.

Negotiations in the condition of situational nonactual identity are characterized by feeling of pressure and aggression from another side, the absence

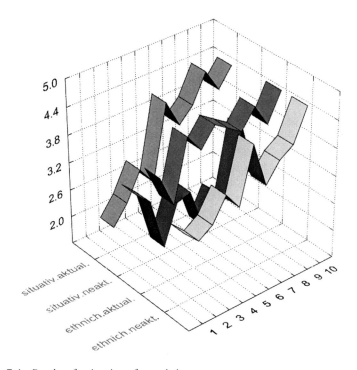

Figure 7.4   Results of estimation of negotiations:
1. Emotions during negotiation;
2. Emotions after negotiation;
3. Estimation of aggression from another side;
4. Estimation of pressure from another side;
5. Readiness of another side for contact;
6. Readiness of another side to listen;
7. Willingness to find collaborative decision;
8. Satisfaction by process of negotiation;
9. Satisfaction by decisions;
10. Readiness to participate in negotiation again.

of readiness to listen and of contact, low satisfaction in decisions, and the absence of readiness to participate in negotiation again.

Negotiations in the condition of situational actual identity are characterized by negative emotions and feelings of pressure and aggression from another side, but also by a readiness to listen and for contact, satisfaction with decisions and negotiation, and a readiness to participate in negotiation again.

Conclusion

1. More decisions were proposed in the condition of ethnic nonactual identity than situational actual identity.
2. The participants had more collaborative decisions in the condition of ethnic identity than situational identity. So, situational identity leads to conflict behavior.
3. The most effective and comfortable negotiations were conducted in the condition of actual ethnic identity. Negotiations in the condition of actual situational identity were estimated as effective, but not very comfortable. Negotiations in the condition of situational nonactual identity were estimated more negatively.
4. The type of identity influences emotions during negotiations, feelings of pressure and aggression from another side, the readiness to listen, the satisfaction with negotiation, the willingness to find collaborative decision, and the readiness to participate in negotiation again.
5. The actuality of identity influences emotions during negotiations, feelings of aggression from another side, the readiness for contact and to listen, the satisfaction with negotiation and decisions, the willingness to find collaborative decision, and the readiness to participate in negotiation again.
6. The interaction of type and actuality influences emotions during and after negotiations, the readiness to listen, the willingness to find collaborative decision, the satisfaction with negotiation, and the readiness to participate in negotiation again.

Thus, the results show that situational identity determines more conflicts than ethnic identity. Several possible interpretations for this effect come to mind. One hypothesis—that of responsibility—assumes that in the condition of situational identity, participants try to win using every method; the implications are not important for them. In the condition of ethnic identity, participants view tasks in the context of real social situations in which activities or actions of groups can evoke conflict, so they show a more tolerant behavior.

Another hypothesis—that of attribution—assumes that participants attribute negative features to other groups, such as aggressiveness, antagonism, and cunning. While playing their roles, the participants demonstrated projected behavior and stressed negative stereotypes in their performance.

Examples of these two hypotheses can be found in experimental social psychology. Zimbardo's (1972) "prison experiment" is a wonderful example of the hypothesis of attribution, while the experiments of Stanley Milgram (1983) provide good examples of the hypothesis of responsibility. Future research will compare these competing hypotheses.

Study V. The Influence of Identity Salience on the Perception of Foreign Conflicts

Social identity (belonging to an ingroup) influences not only sympathy toward ingroup members but also the shared interests, solidarity with the actions of ingroup members, and support of their aims. People can feel ingroup solidarity not only with ingroup members who live in a particular region but also with those from other countries. Thus, salient ethnic or religious identities can enhance feelings of commonality with ingroup members living internationally.

Ethnic conflict, which arises in other countries or between foreign countries, always attracts attention of the inhabitants of other regions characterized by ethnic tensions. The strongest reaction toward foreign ethnic or religious conflict appears in regions characterized by similar ethnic or religious composition. The perception of foreign conflicts is connected with attitudes toward conflict in one's own country and with opinions about possible ways of resolving it. The proposition is that people experiencing a higher salience of ingroup identity see clearer connections between conflict in their own region and foreign conflict and show stronger support for goals and actions of ingroup members in that other conflict.

Hypothesis: A salient ingroup identity influences the development of attitudes and stereotypes toward foreign conflict and the perception of interconnections between situations in own region and region of conflict.

To verify this hypothesis, two studies were conducted: "The Perception of Conflict in Kosovo" (summer 1999) and "Response to Terrorist Attacks in United States on September 11, 2001" (September 2001).

Study V.I. The Perception of Conflict in Kosovo
The study was conducted using a specially designed survey in different towns and villages of Crimea during the summer of 1999. The sample was stratified by location, number of resettlements, and rural-urban status. The participants were Russians (164) and Crimean Tatars (157) and were equally distributed across these locations. Of them, 45 percent were male and 55 percent were female; 25 percent were between 20 and 30 years old, 42 percent between 30 and 45, 21 percent between 45 and 60, and 12 percent above 60; and 54 percent were residents of towns and 46 percent of villages. Participation was voluntary. The respondents were provided with a questionnaire and were asked to select answers from a list.

Results. The results show that representatives of both ethnic groups with a salient ethnic identity have stronger opinions about conflict in Kosovo and draw clearer parallels between the situation in Kosovo and that in Crimea.

The most developed attitudes and stereotypes of Russians and Crimean Tatars with salient ethnic identity are presented below.

Russians

Attitudes toward conflict in Kosovo. Their attitudes toward Kosovo were positive, while those toward the decision to bomb Yugoslavia were negative.

Attitudes toward Western Europe and NATO. They considered that Western Europe and NATO intended to control all of Europe and planed to divide Eastern European countries to increase their own power.

Attitudes toward Eastern Europe. They agreed that Eastern European countries lost their power and influence; however, they felt that Russia still had influence on world politics.

Ethnic conception. They did not support the Serbs' efforts to evict Kosovars and considered equal rights for Serbs and Kosovars. They stressed that Serbia had to belong to all ethnic groups that lived in the country.

Attitudes toward military actions. They considered evictions of Kosovars inadmissible; however, they decried third-party intervention in this situation.

Attitudes toward situation in Crimea. They completely disagreed that Crimea could become a Crimean Tatar autonomy, but supported equal rights for Crimean Tatars.

Autostereotypes. They perceived Slavs as kind, patient, and intelligent and rejected egoism, aggressiveness, and arrogance as characteristics of ingroup members.

Stereotypes toward Muslims. They perceived Muslims as egoistic, aggressive, arrogant, and intolerant, but stressed their intelligence and guile.

Stereotypes toward Western European people. They described them as egoistic, artful, kind, and tolerant.

Crimean Tatars

Attitudes toward conflict situation in Kosovo. Their attitudes toward peacekeeping forces were positive.

Attitudes toward Western Europe and NATO. They disagreed that the termination of bombing in Kosovo was a victory of Milosevic and perceived military intervention as a way to restore the autonomy of Kosovars. Similar to Russians, they believed that Western Europe and NATO intended to control all Europe, but also believed that Western Europe/NATO wanted to retain existing boundaries to avoid ethnic conflicts.

Attitudes toward Eastern Europe. They agreed that people in Eastern European countries felt that their life was a mistake and had no purpose.

Ethnic conception. They completely disagreed that Kosovars should be evicted as foreigners and believed in equal rights for Serbs and Kosovars. They strongly supported the restoration of Kosovars' autonomy and opposed the idea of Serbia belonging to the Serbs. They stressed that Serbia had to belong to all ethnic groups that lived in the country.

Attitudes toward military actions. They totally agreed that the Liberation Army had to fight for the independence of Kosovo. They considered the evictions of Kosovars inadmissible; however, they supported third-party intervention in this situation.

Attitudes toward situation in Crimea. They fully supported equal rights for Crimean Tatars and agreed that Crimea could become a Crimean Tatar autonomy.

Autostereotypes. They perceived Muslims as kind, patient, and intelligent and rejected egoism, aggressiveness, guile, and arrogance as characteristics of ingroup members.

Stereotypes toward Slavs. They perceived Slavs as egoistic, aggressive, arrogant, and guile, but stressed their intelligence and tolerance.

Stereotypes toward Western European people. They described them as egoistic, aggressive, artful, and very arrogant and intelligent and rejected such characteristics as kindness and tolerance.

Comparative Analysis

1. Russians with a salient ethnic identity had clearer attitudes toward Serbia and bombing by NATO. They had very negative opinion about bombing, but their view of NATO military force was ambivalent. Crimean Tatars with a salient ethnic identity supported NATO military force and had neutral attitudes toward Serbia and bombing. Both groups had opaque attitudes toward Milosevic.

2. Crimean Tatars with a salient ethnic identity hoped that military forces would help to restore autonomy in Kosovo.

3. The representatives of both ethnic groups with a salient ethnic identity believed that Western Europe and NATO wanted to control Europe, but disagreed about motivation: Russians suggested that Western Europe and NATO planned to divide Eastern European countries to increase own power, while Crimean Tatars believed that they wanted to retain existing boundaries to avoid ethnic conflicts.

4. Russians with a salient ethnic identity agreed that Eastern European countries had lost their power and influence; however, they believed that Russia still had an influence on world politics. Crimean Tatars with a salient ethnic identity perceived the situation on a personal level and agreed that people in Eastern European countries felt that their life was a mistake and had no purpose.

5. Crimean Tatars with a salient ethnic identity had stronger attitudes toward the rights of Kosovars in Kosovo and autonomy and firmly denied an ethnic conception of Serbia.

6. Crimean Tatars with a salient ethnic identity supported the right to fight for the independence of Kosovo.

7. Opinions about military intervention differed significantly: Russians with a salient ethnic identity denied any military intervention, while Crimean

Tatars with a salient ethnic identity considered that military intervention could help to defend rights of minorities.

8. Crimean Tatars with a salient ethnic identity had stronger attitudes toward equality of rights in Crimea. The views about the future of Crimea were different: Russians with a salient ethnic identity rejected the idea of cultural autonomy for Crimean Tatars, while Crimean Tatars with a salient ethnic identity strongly supported this idea. Russians supported close relations between Russia and Crimea, while Crimean Tatars strongly opposed this possibility.

A factor analysis was conducted to study the structure of attitudes and stereotypes for the representatives of both ethnic groups with a salient ethnic identity. The analysis revealed two factors for Russians.

The first factor can be described as the "ethnic conception of a country": the idea that only an ethnic majority can live in a country and have all rights. The positive pole of the factor includes the following attitudes:

1. Serbia has the right to expel the Kosovars from Kosova because they are a foreign people in Serbia.
2. It was right that Serbia canceled the cultural autonomy of Kosova within Serbia, because Kosova is a holy, historical ground for the Serbs.
3. Serbia belongs to the Serbs.
4. Muslims are a threat to the European Civilization.
5. Muslims cannot not live in Europe.

The negative pole of the factor contains the following attitudes:

1. The Kosovars should have equal citizenship in Serbia as the Serbs.
2. Serbia belongs to all the people who have been living there for years, including the Kosovars.
3. Muslims have the right to live in Europe and have autonomies.
4. Crimean Tatars have to have equal rights with Russians.
5. It is unacceptable that 1 million Kosovars are driven out of Kosovo with violence.
6. It is unjust that Serbia canceled the cultural autonomy of Kosovo within Serbia.

This conception is connected with the perception of threat from Muslims and the denial of equal rights to Crimean Tatars. The acceptance of equality of rights is connected with the inadmissibility of aggression.

The second factor reflects the attitudes toward Western Europe. The positive pole of the factor includes the following attitudes:

1. Military intervention should be supported.
2. The West and NATO do not want to change the existing borders of East European countries, because that would evoke much ethnic conflict.

3. The Kosovar Liberation Army has the right to fight for an independent Kosovo.
4. The Slavs are aggressive, arrogant, and selfish.

The negative pole of the factor includes the following attitudes:

1. The West and NATO want to control Europe and the world.
2. The West and NATO want to divide the Eastern European countries to improve their own dominant power.
3. Milosevic should be supported.
4. Serbia should be supported.
5. Military intervention in a sovereign country is unacceptable, even if human rights of minority groups are violated.
6. Now Yugoslavia is subordinate to Western Europe.

The Russians support the actions of NATO and a liberation army, even if they perceive the Slavs as characteristically arrogant, aggressive, and egotistic. In this case they blame the Serbs for injustice and aggressive actions. The other pole of the factor shows feelings of threat from Western Europe and NATO, denial of the possibility of an intervention in a sovereign country, and sympathy for Milosevic.

The first factor for Crimean Tatars is also connected with ethnic conflict in Kosovo. The positive pole of the factor contains the following attitudes:

1. The Kosovar Liberation Army has the right to fight for an independent Kosovo.
2. The Kosovars should have equal citizenship in Serbia as the Serbs.
3. Crimea has to be a Crimean Tatar autonomy.
4. Military intervention will help to restore the Kosovars' autonomy.
5. It is unacceptable that 1 million Kosovars are driven out of Kosovo with violence.
6. Military intervention in a sovereign country is acceptable if the United Nation is too powerless to prevent the violation of the human rights of minority groups.
7. Western Europeans are arrogant.

The negative pole of the factor contains the following attitudes:

1. It was right that Serbia canceled the cultural autonomy of Kosovo within Serbia, because Kosovo is a holy, historical ground for the Serbs.
2. Muslims are aggressive, arrogant, and artful.
3. Western Europeans are kind and tolerant.

The Crimean Tatars draw a parallel between the situations in Kosovo and Crimea. They support equal rights and autonomy in Kosovo and Crimea and accept military intervention as a method for establishing or restoring autonomy. Stereotypes play an important role in this factor.

The second factor reflects the age divide within the Crimean Tatars' group. The positive pole of the factor includes the following:

1. Milosevic must be supported.
2. Military intervention in a sovereign country is unacceptable even if human rights of minority groups are violated.
3. The West and NATO want to divide the Eastern European countries to improve their own dominant power.
4. The West and NATO want to control Europe and the world.
5. The Slavs are tolerant and intelligent.

The negative pole of the factor includes the following:

1. The age of respondents: the attitudes of older people.
2. Muslim people have the right to live in Europe and have autonomies.
3. The West and NATO do not want to change the existing borders of East European countries, because that would evoke much ethnic conflict.
4. Military intervention in a sovereign country is acceptable if the United Nations is too powerless to prevent the violation of the human rights of minority groups.
5. Military intervention will help to restore the Kosovars' autonomy.
6. Milosevic is an enemy of the European civilization.

Elder people hope that Western Europe will help to restore autonomy in Kosovo and support all activities of NATO. Younger people are oriented toward collaboration with the Slavs and consider that the West and NATO want to control Europe and the world.

Thus, the study revealed two main factors: opinion about conflict in Kosovo and attitudes toward Western Europe and NATO. The first factor is connected with the denial or support for equal rights of all ethnic minorities, in that both ethnic groups draw a parallel between situations in Kosovo and Crimea. However, this factor had specificity for both groups: for Russians with a salient ethnic identity, it reflects an ethnic conception of a country but a rejection of aggressive actions, while Crimean Tatars a with salient ethnic identity connect the restoration of autonomy in Kosovo with the establishment of autonomy in Crimea and support any military action for these purposes.

The second factor also has significant differences for the two groups. While for Russians with a salient ethnic identity, condemnation of NATO activities and support for Milosevic is connected with a high estimation of the Slavic ingroup, Crimean Tatars with a salient ethnic identity have contradictory orientations for collaboration with either the Slavs or Western Europe. Accordingly, they either support Milosevic or blame him.

Study V.II. Response for Terrorists Attacks on September 11, 2001
The study was conducted using a specially designed survey in different towns and villages of Crimea during September 2001, just after the events of September 11. The sample was stratified by location, number of resettlements, and rural-urban status. The participants were Russians (257) and Crimean Tatars (257) distributed across these locations in equal proportions. Of them, 41 percent are male and 59 percent are female; 38 percent are between 20 and 30 years old, 32 percent between 30 and 45, 18 percent between 45 and 60, and 12 percent above 60; 58 percent are residents of towns and 43 percent those of villages. Participation was voluntary. The respondents were provided with a questionnaire and were asked to select answers from a list.

The proposition that the system of stereotypes and attitudes toward conflict situation in a foreign country could be verified by the following experimental hypotheses about the results of factor analysis within the system of stereotypes and attitudes:

1. The number of factors with the Eigen value higher than 1 will be higher for people with a salient ethnic identity.
2. Factors will explain a higher percentage of the total variance for people with a salient ethnic identity.

These hypotheses were verified during factor analysis by the principal component method using Oblimin rotation with Kaiser normalization.

The study reveals two factors with the Eigen value higher than 1 for the group with a nonsalient ethnic identity (205 respondents) and three factors with the Eigen value higher than 1 for the group with a salient ethnic identity (309 respondents). The factors for the group with a nonsalient ethnic identity explain 51 percent of the total variance, while those for the group with a salient ethnic identity explain 68 percent of the total variance.

Thus, a salient ingroup identity influences the development of attitudes and stereotypes toward foreign conflict and perception of interconnections between situations in one's own region and region of conflict. People with salient ethnic and religious identity have a more developed system of attitudes and stereotypes toward conflict in a foreign country.

CONCLUSION

The Four C model presented in the chapter illustrates the four stages of identity-based conflict: comparison, competition, confrontation, and counteraction. It is acknowledged that counterpoised interactive communities can peacefully coexist for centuries, while holding multiple and cross-cutting identities. Nevertheless, even in peaceful and cooperative communities, the process of reproducing ingroup identity (e.g., the socialization of children, or accommodation to the changes in intergroup relations) is the basis for the perception of "positive We–negative They." This is influenced by factors such as unfavorable perceptions of the outgroup, the tendency to evaluate the outgroup negatively, relative deprivation or disadvantage, asymmetrical status, and the history of conflict with the outgroup. In situations of competition, perceived or real conflict, a threat strengthens this negative evaluation and influences the attribution of such stereotypes as aggressiveness, anger, and antagonism. The perception of an outgroup as a threat is mostly based on the attribution of negative goals to outgroups through the interpretation of current intergroup relations. Such factors as information failure, credible commitments, and the security dilemma can reshape social identities, provoke identity conflict, and generate situations where individuals tend to choose one identity over others. These dominant identities take the form of mobilized collective identity and contain ideologies and attributed intentions. In a politicized field of intergroup relations, the ingroups position themselves positively as they define outgroups as opponents or enemies and attribute aggressive intentions to them. Fighting with outgroups is viewed as necessary for ingroup survival.

The five studies in this chapter explored the impact of different factors on the readiness for conflict behavior and assessed models of determination. The studies I have included show that feelings of ingroup primacy have an impact on the readiness to defend safety, values, and norms of ethnic and religious groups for ingroup members with a low level of social identity salience. For ingroup members with a high level of social identity salience, the readiness to fight is influenced by ethnic and religious identities. Study II shows that both the salience of identity and the attachment to an ingroup's interests contribute to the readiness of ingroup members to fight for their goals; however, the readiness to fight against outgroup goals is only an effect of interest. The salience of identity contributes only to the readiness to fight for ingroup goals and does not influence the readiness to fight against outgroup goals.

Study III explained that ingroup identity, ingroup support, and outgroup threat, and interests have a significant impact on the readiness to fight for ingroup goals. Nevertheless, the readiness to oppose outgroup goals is connected only with ingroup interests. The specially designed experimental study IV showed that situational, rather than ethnic, identity determines more conflicts. This study also discusses several possible interpretations for this effect. Study V revealed that a salient ingroup identity influences the development of attitudes and stereotypes toward foreign conflicts. This also impacts the perceptions of interconnections between situations in one's own region and a region of conflict.

CHAPTER 8

FORMATION OF NATIONAL IDENTITY AND
CONFLICT INTENTIONS OF MINORITIES

8.1. NATIONAL IDENTITY

In social science, national identity is viewed as a part of an individual's social identity and as a collective phenomenon that unites people into a national groups. "Insofar as a group of people have come to see themselves as constituting a unique, identifiable entity with a claim to continuity over time, to unity across geographical distance, and to the right to various forms of self-expression, we can say that they have acquired a sense of national identity. National identity is the group definition of itself as a group—its conception of its enduring characteristics and basic values; its strengths and weaknesses; its hopes and fears; its reputation and conditions of existence; its institutions and traditions; and its past history, current purposes, and future prospects" (Kelman 2001: 191).

Anthony D. Smith (1991, 1994) defines national identity as a product of both (1) ethnic history and identity of the continuity, religious and belief system and (2) dominant ideology and conscious manipulation, including commemoration, ideology, and symbolism. Smith stresses the importance of the third dimension—the "need for community"—a sociopsychological mechanism that serves a fundamental role in the formation of national identity. Membership in the nation is based not on similarities among people, but on their feelings of strong attachment to the nation and solidarity with other members of their nation.

Anderson (1991) approaches national identity as a sociocognitive concept and stresses the constructed nature of culture and the role of capitalism and broader social forces in developing and shaping national identity. "It is *imagined* because the members of even the smallest nation will never know most of their fellow-members, meet them, or even hear of them, yet in the minds of each lives the image of their communion" (Anderson 1991: 5).

The author stresses that people in different regions of the country feel a connection to people they have never met because they imagine their kinship and association with other members of the national group. This feeling of comradeship and fraternity is deep and, despite its imaginative nature, national identity leads to the willingness to sacrifice oneself in order to defend the nation.

Kelman (1997a, 2001) develops this approach and points out that the dual process of social construction of identity involves discovery and creation of common elements. "The social construction of identity implies a degree of arbitrariness and flexibility in the way the identity is compromised (which elements are admitted into it and which omitted from it), and in what its boundaries are (who is included and who is excluded)" (Kelman 2001: 194). These elements—priorities and boundaries—can have different definitions depending on political, economic, and religious goals of leaders and elites. According to Kelman (2001), national identity is constantly reconstructed to serve several functions: (1) to provide a sense of uniqueness and unity as well as a sense of belonging to group members, (2) to develop positive self-image, (3) to offer a basis for cultural development, religious beliefs, and way of life, (4) to grant the foundation for ownership of land and resources, and (5) to justify claims and grievances of the group.

The movement from colonialism and totalitarianism to political pluralism is connected to the construction of a state and the reshaping of national identities. Most of the postcolonial, postsocialist, and post-Soviet national identities are now political and are defined by the state. In many cases, when a country declares itself a "national state," it leads to an ethnic conception of nationality. As Brubaker (1996) stresses, ethnic identity politics and minority grievances lead to tensions; the formation of a nation in a newly independent state evokes the activities of national minorities and their proclivity to initiate conflicts.

Since the most usual characteristic of nations is their residence in common territory, many people in newly nationalized states become members of new nations only because they reside within the same borders. However, acquisition of national identity also depends on: (1) the adoption of the specific elements of the national identity, including shared beliefs, history, values, assumptions, and expectations; (2) the development of an orientation to the nation itself (Herman 1977); and (3) self-definition as members of the nation (Kelman 1997a). As Kelman (1997a) points out, the establishment of new states engenders incentives for ethnic homogeneity, and thus, systematic efforts to marginalize or destroy ethnic "others." Conflict can develop when the identity chosen by an individual is incompatible with the identity imposed by others or the social context in which identity is constantly being recreated (Kelman 1982; Stein 1998; Stern 1995).

The establishment of new states, however, embodies the potential for economic independence, human dignity, and higher self-esteem of ethnic groups within the state (Kelman 1997a). In addition to being a contribution to the escalation and self-perpetuation of identity-based conflicts, building a national identity in postcolonial and postcommunist societies is also a process that may create a superordinate peaceful identity and opportunities for the resolution of the conflict. It can be argued that in the formation of national identities, nationalism and patriotism can be connected to the development of attitudes and stereotypes and can produce either conflict or tolerant behavior.

The development of a national identity of minorities is connected to levels within the development of stereotypical systems, a strong feeling of group affinity, and opposition to other groups. The formation of national identity embodies a system that combines the positive stereotypes of one's own nation (patriotism) and negative stereotypes and attitudes toward the other nations (nationalism).

There are two approaches to the study of differences between patriotism and nationalism in social psychology. The first approach suggests that nationalism and patriotism are two different styles of behavior and perception. The research of Feshbach (1987) and his colleagues identified two independent factors: (1) feelings about one's own country and (2) feelings of national superiority along with a need for national power and dominance. Patriotism is connected with a strong attachment and loyalty to one's nation without the corresponding hostility toward other nations, while nationalism is seen as a positive feeling toward one's nation with negative feelings toward others. Adorno's study of the authoritarian personality (1950) also showed a difference between a healthy patriotic love of one's own country, not associated with prejudice against outgroups, and an ethnocentric patriotism which is associated with prejudice.

The second approach suggests that nationalism is merely a more complex form of patriotism. Patriotism is viewed as the simpler relationship between the individual and the nation, and nationalism as a more elaborate complex embedding one's own nation into a set of nations and differentiating one's nation from them. The reference group theory argues that nationalism does not necessarily imply negative feelings toward another nation. Intense loyalty to one nation does not necessarily lead to hostility toward another. If the reference group provides the self-esteem for individuals in the same way or to a greater extent than current membership groups, negative feelings are reduced. Druckman (1994) shows how loyalties to the European community can be transferred from its member nations. It should be possible to have pride, self-esteem, patriotism, and willingness to cooperate with, and perhaps even include, other nations in one's ingroup.

Many subsequent studies have reported significant associations between identification with national, ethnic, and other groups and negative attitudes toward minority groups (Brown 2000; Huddy and Virtanen 1995; Jackson et al. 1996; Tajfel and Turner 1979; Taylor et al. 1987; Wright, Taylor, and Moghaddam 1990). Research also shows that salient identity can foster positive ingroup stereotypes to compensate for a low status (Lalonde 1992; Otten, Mummendey, and Blanz 1996; Van Knippenberg 1978; Van Knippenberg and Van Oers 1984).

Sterns (2006) provides differences between liberal nationalism and intolerant nationalism. The liberal nationalism of Mazzini, Woodrow Wilson, and Gandhi combines strong support for one's own nation with openness and tolerance for the other. Intolerant nationalism is connected with negative attitudes and biases toward other nations and ethnic minorities within that nation. "The encouragement nationalism provided for almost every conceivable people and territory to think in terms of exclusive identity contributed greatly to a mentality of clash and conflict, even in regions that had traditionally experienced normally peaceful coexistence. This flavor of exclusive nationalism progressively informed non-nationalist movements as well, as in regional loyalties that defied larger national unities but with the same language of us-and-them, and in renewed efforts to use wider religious banners to form identities that might transcend nationalism—as, most notably, in the use of Islamic fundamentalism to capture a larger geography, but with a nationalist-like intolerance for others that countered more traditional Islamic practice" (Sterns 2006: 131).

I suggest that a salient national identity is characterized by advanced systems of political attitudes, opposition to other groups, positive autostereotypes, and negative heterostereotypes. It is very likely that new, developing, and vestigial identities, in comparison with salient and core identities, have connections with a small number of attitudes. In particular, a new national identity can embody a different level of the development of positive stereotypes of one's own nation (patriotism) and negative stereotypes and attitudes toward the other nations (nationalism).

8.2. NATIONAL IDENTITY STRUCTURE

Theory suggests that acquiring a national identity depends on three factors: (1) the adoption of the specific elements of national identity, that is, of the beliefs, values, assumptions, and expectations that make up national identity as a collective product; (2) the development of an orientation to the nation itself (Herman 1977); and (3) self-definition as members of the nation (Kelman 1997). Brubaker and Cooper (2000) argue for a tripartite structure of identity that includes (1) identifications and categorizations, (2) self-understanding and social location, and (3) communality, connectedness, and groupness. Identification develops as self-identification and identification of oneself by others (external identification). Identification is connected with categorizations, locations, situations, and places in life. Authors define self-understanding as "one's sense of who one is, of one's social location, and of how (given the first two) one is prepared to act" (Brubaker and Cooper 2000: 17). Self-understanding provides conception of possible variability and/or stability over time and space. "'Communality' denotes the sharing of some common attribute, 'connectedness' the relational ties that link people" (Brubaker and Cooper 2000: 20). Groupness is seen as "the sense of belonging to a distinctive, bounded, solidarity group" (Brubaker and Cooper 2000: 20). For large-scale collectivities, connectedness plays a minor role "when a diffuse self-understanding as a member of a particular nation crystallizes into a strongly bounded sense of groupness, this is likely to depend not on relational connectedness, but rather on a powerfully imagined and strongly felt communality" (Brubaker and Cooper 2000: 20).

Based on my previous research, I suggest the following structure of national identity: (1) salience of national identity, (2) satisfaction by fulfillment of its functions, and (3) adoption of national culture.

Salience of National Identity

Salient national identity can be understood to be the importance of a national identity for an individual, including strong feelings of belonging to one's nation and shared positive attitudes toward the ingroup and negative attitudes toward other countries. This identity has a strong influence on behavior, and for some people can become a central identity.

Satisfaction by Fulfillment of Its Functions

As I already showed, social identity serves five psychological functions for group members: (1) providing self-esteem, (2) bestowing social status, (3) personal safety, (4) group support and protection, and (5) recognition by ingroup. If the new national identity begins to fulfill these necessary functions, it can lead to the quick disappearance of other social identities, such as ethnic or regional identities (Korostelina 2003).

Adoption of National Culture

Each culture has a set of traditions, values, customs, meanings, ethics, holidays, clothes, and foods. The acquirement of a new national identity requires the adoption of specific elements of culture that represent cultural identity. For example, it is important to study to what degree representatives of ethnic minorities in Ukraine accept Ukrainian tradition and values, for example, do they participate in holidays, use traditional clothes in every day life, read books and see movies in the Ukrainian language, because cultural distance is one of the factors that will determine the adoption of national culture by ethnic minorities.

These three components are interconnected, but can have different levels of development. Some groups can be very satisfied with national identity, but do not adopt normative culture and traditions. Other groups can have a very salient national identity, but have little satisfaction with it.

8.3. CONCEPTS OF NATIONAL IDENTITY

The meaning of a new national identity can have a significant impact on the readiness for conflict. Research stresses the importance of meaning in both shaping identities and determining conflictive or tolerant behavior (Deaux 1993; Huddy 2001; Gurin, Hurtado, and Peng 1994; Simon and Hamilton

1994). Breakwell (2004) shows that different meanings of European identity shape reactions to policies that were designed to create the European Union. The meaning of the African American identity influences the willingness to support programs designed to improve the situations of other minority groups: African Americans who emphasize their African identity as a minority are less inclined to support affirmative actions for other minorities than African Americans who accentuate their national American identity (Sellers et al. 1998). Research also shows that the meaning of national identity can influence attitudes toward other groups and political situations, thus individuals with a nativist sense of American identity (such as being Christian) regard immigrants negatively, and see the adoption of American customs as obligatory for them (Citrin, Wong, and Duff 2000).

One of the central problems of forming a national identity is the interrelation between different groups, such as, majority and minority, dominant and small minorities, and natives and immigrants. The core issue of the concept of national identity is the position of ethnic minorities within the nation: whether minorities are oppressed by the majority or have opportunities for maintaining their ethnic culture. Based on this issue, people can have three different concepts or meanings of national identity: *ethnic, multicultural, and civic*. Similar political concepts were developed by Brown (2006), who introduced three types of national identities (civic, ethnocultural, and multiculturalist) that hold nation-states together.

The Ethnic Concept

Some people perceive that their nation is built around a core ethnic community into which ethnic minorities should assimilate. They see their nation as monoethnic and monolingual. For them, people who have inherited or assimilated the values and attributes of the ethnic core should have higher status within a nation.

The Multicultural Concept

Other people view their nation as multicultural, with equal rights for all ethnic groups and elements of autonomy and self-governance. They see their state as a society within which ethnic minorities should be guaranteed resources to maintain their ethnic culture and communities. Different ethnic groups should have an opportunity to receive education in their language, and their cultural heritage should be part of the national heritage.

The Civic Concept

Other people see their citizenship as a contract between the people and the state concerning both rights and obligations. They view the constitution, rule of law, and civic responsibilities as the main features of the nation, and see ethnicity as insignificant. They perceive their nation as having been built on a distinctive nonethnic civic culture into which all citizens should be integrated. In old nations, such as France and Germany, citizens developed a common understanding of their nation and national identity over centuries. In newly developed nations, however, people often differ in their understanding of national identity and this influences their estimations of situations, expectations, and behavior (Korostelina 2003).

The meaning of national identity influences attitudes and behavior toward different ethnic groups within one's own nation and in the approach to other nations. Research shows that in Europe concepts of the nation are associated with specific methods of integrating immigrants into society and also have influence on the process of integrating the nation into the broader European community (Munch 2001). Thus, an ethnic concept of national identity in Germany leads to the rejection of immigrants and a belief that they are granted too many rights. A multicultural concept of national identity, such as in the United States, produces an appreciation of different cultures and an acceptance of differences among citizens and other permanent and temporary residents. A civic concept of national identity, such as in Great Britain, allows the integration of immigrants into society by providing them a place in the community of citizens. Thus, the concept of national identity can influence the readiness of both a majority and minority to fight with other groups and can increase or decrease the influence of other conflict indicators.

Study I. National Identity Structure and the Readiness for Conflict

The analysis of national and ethnic identity resulted in the general research hypothesis: the effect of conflict indicators (salient ethnic identity, economic deprivation, and minority position) on readiness for conflict or for compromise will be mitigated by three features of national identity formation: (1) salience of national identity, (2) satisfaction with fulfillment of national identity functions, and (3) adoption of a national (Ukrainian) culture.

Predictors: salient ethnic identity, ethnocentrism, economic deprivation, and minority position.
Moderators: salience of national identity, satisfaction with fulfillment of national identity functions, and adoption of a national (Ukrainian) culture.
Dependent variable: readiness to fight.

This general hypothesis generated the following nine propositions:

Salience of Ethnic Identity

1. Salient national identity will reduce the effect of salience of ethnic identity on readiness for conflict. This effect will be stronger for respondents with weak ethnic identity.
2. Satisfaction with national identity functions will reduce the effect of salience of ethnic identity on readiness for conflict, which would hold

when controlled for other variables. This effect will be stronger for respondents with a nonsalient ethnic identity.
3. Adoption of national culture will reduce the effect of salience of ethnic identity on readiness for conflict.

Economic Deprivation

4. Salient national identity will reduce the effect of economic deprivation on readiness for conflict.
5. Satisfaction with national identity functions will reduce the effect of economic deprivation on readiness for conflict.
6. Adoption of national culture will reduce the effect of economic deprivation on readiness for conflict.

Majority/Minority Position

7. Salient national identity will reduce readiness for conflict if respondents consider their group a minority. It will have no effects if respondents perceive their group as a majority.
8. The satisfaction with national identity functions will reduce the effect of minority position on readiness for conflict. That effect will be weaker for the majority position.
9. Adoption of national culture will reduce the influence of majority/minority position on readiness for conflict.

Sampling

To test these propositions, an opinion survey was conducted from January to May 2003 in several towns and villages in Crimea. The sample was stratified by location, number of resettlements, and rural-urban status. Participants were Russians and Crimean Tatars, distributed across these locations in equal proportions. Of the participants, 42 percent are male and 58 percent are female; 39 percent are between 20 and 30 years old, 31 percent between 30 and 45, 20 percent between 45 and 60, and 10 percent above 60; 55 percent are residents of towns, and 45 percent are residents of villages. Participation was voluntary. Respondents were provided with a questionnaire and selected answers from a list.

Results

Crimean Tatars identify more strongly with the ethnic Tatar ingroup ($M = 9.94$ on a scale from 3 to 12) than Russians identify with the ethnic Russian ingroup ($M = 7.70$; $F(823) = 50.52$; $p < .001$). Crimean Tatars identify strongly with the nation ($M = 7.29$ on a scale from 3 to 12) than Russians identify with the nation ($M = 6.64$), but the difference is not significant ($F(828) = 0.50$; n.s.). Crimean Tatars show higher satisfaction with national identity ($M = 8.17$ on a scale from 5 to 20) than Russians ($M = 7.4$; $F(824) = 10.92$; $p < .005$), but the level of adaptation of Ukrainian culture does not differ significantly between groups ($F(822) = 0.966$;

n.s.). Russians show more readiness for group conflict behavior ($M = 4.72$ on a scale from 2 to 6) than Crimean Tatars ($M = 4.58$; $F(821) = 11.48$; $p < .001$).

Analysis shows that correlations between moderating variables are significant, but variables are independent (correlation between salience of national identity and satisfaction with national identity is $r = 0.39$, $p < .01$; correlation between salience of national identity and adoption of culture is $r = 0.20$, $p < .01$; and correlation between satisfaction with national identity and adoption of culture is $r = 0.13$, $p < .05$).

The Impact of Ethnic Identity as Moderated by National Identity. The proposition that the high level of acquisition of a new national identity will reduce effect of salience of ethnic identity on readiness for conflict was tested in 2 (Salience of ethnic identification: high versus low) × 2 (Salience of national identification: high versus low) analysis of variance (ANOVA), in 2 (Salience of ethnic identification: high versus low) × 2 (Level of satisfaction with national identity: high versus low) ANOVA, and in 2 (Salience of ethnic identification: high versus low) × 2 (Level of adoption of culture: high versus low) ANOVA for groups of Crimean Tatar respondents and Russian respondents. For Russians, the results show the main effects of ethnic identity, salience of national identity, satisfaction with national identity, adoption of Ukrainian culture, the interaction effect of ethnic identity by level of satisfaction with national identity and by level of adoption of Ukrainian culture on the readiness for conflict behavior (see Table 8.1). The main effects show that that a salient ethnic identity and satisfaction with national identity strengthen the readiness conflict behavior. The interaction effect

Table 8.1 Ethnic Identity Effect on Russians' and Crimean Tatars' Readiness to Fight Moderated by the Structure of National Identity

Variables	Russians		Crimean Tatars	
	High Salience ($N = 251$)	Low Salience ($N = 157$)	High Salience ($N = 364$)	Low Salience ($N = 57$)
Ethnic identity	4.73	4.54	4.59	4.03
Low salience of national identity (RN = 219; CTN = 161)	4.79	4.66	4.65	4.10
High salience of national identity (RN = 189; CTN = 260)	4.57	4.28	4.49	3.95
Low level of satisfaction with national identity (RN = 339; CTN = 275)	4.38	4.43	4.65	4.13
High level of satisfaction with national identity (RN = 69; CTN = 146)	4.77	4.63	4.49	3.82
Low level of adoption of national culture (RN = 165; CTN = 250)	4.83	4.58	4.66	4.15
High level of adoption of national culture (RN = 243; CTN = 171)	4.33	4.48	4.48	3.92

shows that satisfaction with national identity and adopted Ukrainian culture moderate the influence of ethnic identity on the readiness to fight among Russians. When there is a low level of adoption of national culture, ethnic identity has significant influence on readiness to fight, but when level of adoption of national culture is high, salient ethnic identity produces lesser readiness to fight. On the contrary, when there is a low satisfaction with national identity, ethnic identity has no significant influence on the readiness to fight, but when satisfaction with national identity is high, salient ethnic identity generates a higher readiness to fight. Results support Proposition 3 that adoption of Ukrainian culture would reduce impact of ethnic identity on the readiness to fight, but they are differing from what was expected from Russians in the Proposition 2, namely, the weakening effect of satisfaction with national identity.

For Crimean Tatars the results show an interaction effect of ethnic identity by level of satisfaction with national identity (see Table 8.1). When there is a low satisfaction with national identity, ethnic identity produces significant influence on the readiness to fight, but when level of satisfaction with national identity is high, salient ethnic identity has virtually no impact on personal readiness to fight. Thus, satisfaction with national identity weakens the influence of ethnic identity on the readiness of group to fight with other ethnic groups. This is what was expected in the hypothesis (Proposition 2).

The Impact of Economic Deprivation as Moderated by National Identity. The proposition that the high level of acquisition of new national identity will reduce the effect of economic deprivation on readiness for conflict was tested in 2 (Level of economic deprivation: high versus low) × 2 (Salience of national identification: high versus low) ANOVA, in 2 (Level of economic deprivation: high versus low) × 2 (Level of satisfaction with national identity: high versus low) ANOVA, and in 2 (Level of economic deprivation: high versus low) × 2 (Level of adoption of Ukrainian culture: high versus low) ANOVA for groups of Crimean Tatars respondents and Russians respondents (see Table 8.2).

For Russians, economic deprivation impacts the readiness for conflict in interaction with satisfaction with national identity functions. Thus, satisfaction with national identity increases the influence of economic deprivation on the individual and group readiness to fight. This differs from what was expected from Russians in Proposition 5, namely, a weakening of the impact of economic deprivation on conflict behavior. For Crimean Tatars, economic deprivation influences the readiness for conflict behavior in interaction with the salience of national identity and the level of satisfaction with national identity. When there is a low salience of national identity, economic deprivation produces practically no effect on the readiness to fight, but when national identity is salient, economic deprivation has significant impact on the readiness to fight. Thus, salient national identity strengthens the impact of economic deprivation on the readiness to fight. Satisfaction with national

Table 8.2 Economic Deprivation Effect on Russians' and Crimean Tatars' Readiness to Fight Moderated by the Structure of National Identity

Variables	Russians		Crimean Tatars	
	High Level ($N=177$)	Low Level ($N=231$)	High Level ($N=100$)	Low Level ($N=321$)
Economic deprivation	4.54	4.48	4.38	4.56
Low salience of national identity (RN = 219; CTN = 161)	4.47	4.58	4.00	4.60
High salience of national identity (RN = 189; CTN = 260)	4.65	4.56	4.70	4.54
Low level of satisfaction with national identity (RN = 339; CTN = 275)	4.49	4.42	4.42	4.57
High level of satisfaction with national identity (RN = 69; CTN = 146)	4.95	4.72	4.26	4.56
Low level of adoption of national culture (RN = 165; CTN = 250)	4.54	4.61	4.47	4.63
High level of adoption of national culture (RN = 243; CTN = 171)	4.55	4.40	4.40	4.43

identity weakens the effect of economic deprivation on the readiness to fight. The moderation effect of satisfaction with national identity is stronger than moderation effects of national identity salience.

The Impact of Minority Position as Moderated by National Identity.   The proposition that the high level of acquisition of a new national identity will modify the effect of the minority/majority position on readiness for conflict was tested in 2 (Perceived position: minority versus majority) × 2 (Salience of national identification: high versus low) ANOVA, in 2 (Perceived position: minority versus majority) × 2 (Level of satisfaction with national identity: high versus low) ANOVA, and in 2 (Perceived position: minority versus majority) × 2 (Level of adoption of culture: high versus low) ANOVA for groups of Crimean Tatars respondents and Russians respondents. Data analysis shows that Russians who perceive themselves to be in a majority position in Ukraine have higher readiness to fight with the outgroup than Russians who perceive themselves to be in a minority position. For Russians, ANOVA shows an interaction effect between the majority position and the level of satisfaction with national identity and between the level of adoption of Ukrainian culture and the readiness for conflict behavior. When there is low satisfaction with national identity, the majority position has less influence on readiness to fight, but when the level of satisfaction with national identity is high, the majority position has significant impact on the readiness to fight. A similar effect was found for the adoption of Ukrainian culture. Thus, satisfaction with national identity and the adoption of Ukrainian culture increase the influence of the majority position on the readiness to fight (see Table 8.3).

Table 8.3 Majority/Minority Position Effect on Russians' and Crimean Tatars' Readiness to Fight Moderated by the Structure of National Identity

Variables	Russians		Crimean Tatars	
	Minority Position in Ukraine ($N=130$)	Majority Position in Ukraine ($N=278$)	Minority Position in Crimea ($N=346$)	Majority Position in Crimea ($N=75$)
Perceived position	4.24	4.63	4.56	4.33
Low salience of national identity (RN = 219; CTN = 161)	4.22	4.67	4.47	4.30
High salience of national identity (RN = 189; CTN = 260)	4.26	4.59	4.61	4.37
Low level of satisfaction with national identity (RN = 339; CTN = 275)	4.25	4.55	4.65	4.24
High level of satisfaction with national identity (RN = 69; CTN = 146)	4.21	4.93	4.40	4.54
Low level of adoption of national culture (RN = 165; CTN = 250)	4.48	4.70	4.64	4.35
High level of adoption of national culture (RN = 243; CTN = 171)	4.09	4.59	4.43	4.31

For Crimean Tatars, analysis reveals several interaction effects: an interaction effect of minority position with the level of satisfaction with national identity and an interaction effect of majority position with the level of national identity salience (see Table 8.3). When there is low satisfaction with national identity, a minority position has significant impact on the readiness to fight, but when level of satisfaction with national identity is high, a minority position has a lesser effect on personal readiness to fight. So, for Crimean Tatars, satisfaction with national identity weakens the effect of the minority position on the readiness to fight with other ethnic groups. When there is a low salience of national identity, the majority position has practically no effect on the readiness to fight, but when the level of national identity is salient, the majority position has significant impact on the group readiness to fight. Thus, salient national identity strengthens the impact of the majority position on the group readiness to fight.

Discussion

My research shows that national identity moderates the effect of ethnic identity, economic deprivation, and majority/minority positions on individual and group conflict behavior, and that these effects differ between two ethnic groups—the Russians and Crimean Tatars. For both groups, ethnic identity produced the strongest moderation effect.

Salient national identity strengthens the effect of economic deprivation and perceived majority position on perceived readiness to fight for Crimean Tatars. No interaction effects of national identity with ethnic identity, economic deprivation, and majority/minority position were found for Russians. Interpreting the effect of national identity, if Crimean Tatars have salient national identity, they have higher personal loyalty to Ukraine and all ethnic groups within the state. However, if Crimean Tatars consider their group a majority in Crimea, they feel themselves to be a part of Ukrainian community and perceive Russians as aliens in Crimea without social rights. Further analysis showed that Crimean Tatars with salient national identity and perceived majority position have a less developed concept of Ukraine as a multicultural nation than Crimean Tatars with a low level of salience of national identity and perceived majority position. Accordingly, if Crimean Tatars have a strong feeling of belonging to the nation, they believe the experience of strong economic deprivation will reinforce the social activity of their group and readiness to fight for their rights. Moreover, our data showed that Crimean Tatars with salient national identity and perceived strong economic deprivation have a more developed concept of Ukraine as a civic society than Crimean Tatars with a low level of national identity salience ($M = 7.32$; $F(423) = 4.64$; $p < .05$).

For Russians, satisfaction with national identity increases the impact of ethnic identity and economic deprivation on the readiness to fight. For Crimean Tatars, satisfaction with national identity weakens influence of economic deprivation and minority position on the readiness to fight. Russians who adopt Ukrainian culture and customs feel comfortable with being incorporated into Ukrainian society and have less negative attitudes toward people of other ethnic groups. But, if they judge themselves to be a majority or are very ethnocentric, adoption of Ukrainian culture could lead to more negative intentions toward outgroups. Russian and Ukrainian cultures share many common values and customs. As a result, Russians accept their position of "Ukrainian Russians" and do not expect Crimean Tatars to be deeply integrated into the Ukrainian cultural context. Thus, they will be more ready to defend the stable unity of Ukrainian society. For Crimean Tatars, correspondingly, the adoption of Ukrainian culture strengthens positive attitudes toward other ethnic groups who have similar cultures and decreases ethnocentric views.

It was expected that national identity would reduce the negative impact of conflict indicators. This hypothesis was confirmed for Crimean Tatars except for the moderation effect of salient national identity on impact of economic deprivation and perceived majority position on group readiness for conflict behavior. However, the hypothesis failed for most effects on personal and group conflict behavior of Russians, for whom national identity shapes their readiness to fight. It can be explained by the social position and political goals of the two groups.

Russians that adopted the national identity and are satisfied with the fulfillment of national identity functions have salient ethnic identity and ethnocentrism and perceive themselves a "majority" in Ukraine. They have a new identity: "Ukrainian Russians," which is different from the Russian ethnic identity, but does not presuppose a deep adoption of Ukrainian culture (Korostelina 2003). Consequently, they have a stronger readiness to fight with Crimean Tatars—a Muslim minority in Crimea—who possess different culture, value, and goal-sets. If they adopted the Ukrainian identity and experienced economic deprivation, they did not blame Ukraine but considered Crimean Tatars guilty of causing their economic problems because the latter required additional resources for their resettlement and cultural revival.

If Crimean Tatars adopt Ukrainian identity and culture, and are satisfied with national identity, they show less readiness to fight and are fully incorporated in Ukrainian community. But, if Crimean Tatars have a salient national identity, they believe that experiencing strong economic deprivation and perceived majority position in Crimea would reinforce the social activity of their group and their readiness to defend their rights. They accuse the Russians of negative changes in their economic situation and see fighting with them as a goal for the ingroup.

According to the common identity theory, national identity could unite ethnic minorities within the state and reduce negative attitudes and conflict intentions toward other ethnic groups. We could expect that the adoption of national identity by representatives of ethnic minorities would reduce the influence of conflict indicators and lead to more tolerant behavior toward outgroups. This prediction was confirmed for the group of Crimean Tatars—a political and numerical minority—in the Ukraine. However, the hypothesis failed for the group of Russians, who self-identified as a language majority. Results showed that national identity reinforced the readiness to fight with outgroups that significantly differ in religion and culture from the "national group," groups that have intentions for sovereignty or close relations with other countries, and groups that could became the most powerful minority group.

We conclude our empirical study by positing that, in some cases, the adoption of national identity does not create common meaning and a sense of unity. Rather, some ethnic minorities can use loyalty to the nation to accomplish their own goals and receive more benefits. The readiness for conflict behavior is reinforced if the state provides social and personal security and helps to increase the social status of a given ethnic minority. National identity can reduce readiness to fight only if ethnic minorities do not hold ethnocentric views and are ready to adopt national identity or if they perceive that the state can provide more opportunities and defend the rights of their ethnic groups.

Study II. The Concepts of National Identity and the Readiness for Conflict

The study examines how the position of a minority within the nation can regulate the impact of ethnic and multicultural concepts on readiness to fight with other groups.

Predictors: salient ethnic identity.
Moderators: concepts of national identity.
Dependent variable: readiness to fight.

On the basis of this model, I proposed some prospective interrelations between the independent and dependent variables and the moderator:

1. A salient national identity will decrease readiness to fight with other groups and weaken the effect of ethnic identity salience on conflict readiness.
2. Possession of the ethnic concept of national identity will increase readiness to fight with other groups and strengthen the effect of ethnic identity salience on conflict readiness.
3. Possession of the multicultural concept of national identity will reduce readiness to fight with other groups and weaken the effect of ethnic identity salience on conflict readiness.
4. Possession of the civic concept of national identity will reduce readiness to fight with other groups and weaken the effect of ethnic identity salience on conflict readiness. This effect will be more significant than the effect of the multicultural concept.
5. The meaning of national identity will have a different effect on minority groups than on majority groups.

Method

To test these propositions, I designed an opinion survey that was conducted between January and May 2003 in several towns and villages in Crimea. The sample was stratified by location, number of resettlements, and rural-urban status. The survey strata include the towns of Simferopol and Alushta and the counties of Bahchisarai (including the city of Bahchisarai), Krasnoperekopsk, and Sudak, with 997 respondents distributed across these locations in equal proportion.

Five-point scales were recoded to four-point scales, excluding "No answer." All missing data and the answers "don't know" were deleted from the analysis.

Results

Crimean Tatars identify more strongly with the ethnic Tatar ingroup ($M = 16.74$ on a scale from 3 to 20) than Russians identify with the ethnic Russian ingroup ($M = 12.46$; $F(1,827) = 50.52$; $p < .001$). Crimean Tatars also identify more strongly with the nation of Ukraine ($M = 7.29$ on a scale from 3 to 12) than Russians do ($M = 6.64$), but the difference is not significant ($F(1,828) = 0.50$; n.s.).

The multicultural concept of national identity is stronger among Crimean Tatars ($M = 9.29$ on a scale from 3 to 12) than it is among Russians ($M = 8.81$; $F(1,828) = 8.74$; $p < .005$), while the civic concept of national identity is stronger among Russians ($M = 7.63$ on a scale from 3 to 12) than it is among Crimean Tatars ($M = 7.51$; $F(1,826) = 5.35$; $p < .05$). The ethnic concept of national identity does not differ significantly between the groups ($F(1,827) = 2.35$; n.s.). Crimean Tatars and Russians have very similar levels of conflict readiness ($M = 4.52$ and $M = 4.51$; n.s. on a scale from 1 to 8).

A partially saturated general linear model was used to simultaneously test the effects of all the above-mentioned predictors on conflict readiness.

Table 8.4 Main Effects of the Concepts of National Identity on Conflict Readiness

Concepts of National Identity	Russians			Crimean Tatars		
	Beta	Mean Readiness to Fight		Beta	Mean Readiness to Fight	
		With Concept	Without Concept		With Concept	Without Concept
Ethnic	2.05*	4.67	4.14	3.44**	4.07	4.81
Multicultural	1.90*	4.33	4.51	3.92**	4.20	4.68
Civic	2.27**	4.28	4.56	3.04**	4.16	4.71

Note: $*p < .05$; $**p < .01$. Standardized beta coefficients from a partially saturated general linear model of data from the 2003 Crimean survey.

Table 8.5 Moderating Effects of Salience and Concepts of National Identity on the Readiness for Conflict

Effects of Ethnic Identity	Russians	Crimean Tatars
Without salient national identity	2.56*	3.726**
With salient national identity	3.01**	2.198*
Without ethnic concept	1.95*	2.47*
With ethnic concept	2.54*	2.02*
Without multicultural concept	4.01**	2.23*
With multicultural concept	3.25**	3.03**
Without civic concept	4.02**	2.27*
With civic concept	3.12**	1.93*

Note: $*p < .05$; $**p < .01$. Standardized beta coefficients from a partially saturated general linear model of data from the 2003 Crimean survey.

For both ethnic groups, a salient ethnic identity strengthens conflict readiness, and a salient national identity reduces conflict readiness. The results also show that a salient ethnic concept of national identity among Russians contributes to conflict readiness, while among Crimean Tatars it substantially reduces conflict readiness (Table 8.4).

Among Russians, the multicultural concept of national identity reduces conflict readiness, while among Crimean Tatars it makes a significant contribution to conflict readiness. The civic concept of national identity significantly reduces conflict readiness among both Russians and Crimean Tatars; this impact is more significant for Crimean Tatars.

The moderating roles of identity salience and of the different concepts of national identity were determined by comparing the direct effect of ethnic identity on conflict readiness relative to the model above, in which salience and each concept of national identity operated as a moderator. Identity salience and possession of the different concepts of national identity do have moderating effects on the impact of ethnic identity for Russians and Crimean Tatars (Table 8.5).

Possession of a salient national identity and of the ethnic concept of national identity strengthens the influence of salient ethnic identity on conflict readiness among Russians and weakens it among Crimean Tatars. Possession of the multicultural concept weakens the influence of salient ethnic identity on conflict readiness among Russians and strengthens it among Crimean Tatars. Possession of the civic concept weakens the influence of salient ethnic identity on conflict readiness among representatives of both ethnic groups.

Discussion
The results of my survey demonstrate that the possession of salient national identity increases the influence of ethnic identity on the personal and group conflict readiness of Russians. When Russians adopt a salient national identity and believe that they are the main and more powerful minority group in Ukraine, their readiness to fight with other ethnic minorities is strengthened. When Russians accept Ukrainian identity without adopting a salient ethnic identity and ethnocentric views, however, they perceive the Ukrainian identity as common to all ethnic groups in Ukraine. For Crimean Tatars, conversely, the possession of salient national identity weakens the effect of ethnic identity on conflict readiness: in Crimean Tatars with low national identity salience, ethnic identity leads to readiness to fight with other ethnic minorities who can compete with them, but if national identity is salient, it decreases the influence of ethnic identity on conflict readiness.

I expected to find that possession of an ethnic concept of national identity would increase conflict readiness and strengthen the negative impact of ethnic identity. This hypothesis was confirmed for Russians, but it failed for Crimean Tatars, for whom possession of the ethnic concept of national identity decreases conflict readiness and weakens the impact of ethnic identity. I also assumed that possession of the multicultural concept of national identity would reduce conflict readiness and weaken the impact of conflict indicators. This hypothesis, too, was confirmed for Russians but failed for Crimean Tatars, among whom the multicultural concept of national identity contributes to conflict readiness and strengthens the impact of ethnic identity. My hypothesis that possession of the civic concept of national identity would reduce the influence of conflict indicators was completely confirmed. Therefore, my research shows that different conceptions of national identity *do* affect the readiness for conflict with outgroups among ethnic minorities. They also moderate the impact of salient ethnic identity on conflict readiness.

However, these effects depend on the position of an ethnic minority in Ukrainian society. Thus, Russians and Crimean Tatars have different ethnic concepts of national identity: the Russians have a concept of Russian-Ukrainian national identity, while the Crimean Tatars have a concept of simple Ukrainian national identity. For Russians, a numerous and powerful minority, particularly in Crimea, possession of an ethnic concept of national identity increases the impact of the salience of ethnic identity on the readiness to fight with other ethnic groups. When Russians have an ethnic concept of national identity, they perceive the nation as a single ethnic entity in which Ukrainian Russians must have the highest status among other groups (Korostelina 2003, 2006a). They believe that national identity in Ukraine has to be built around the Russian community. Therefore, as the dominant minority (and even the numerous majority in Crimea), Russians are ready to fight other ethnic groups for their privileged position. When Crimean Tatars, a small minority in Ukraine, have an ethnic concept of national identity, on the other hand, they accept the leading role of the Ukrainian ethnic group in the nation. They feel themselves to be secure within the nation and are ready to accept Ukrainian culture and language if Ukraine will help the Crimean Tatars deter the pro-Russian movement in Crimea (Korostelina 2003a). Thus, the possession of an ethnic concept of national identity weakens the impact of ethnic identity on the readiness of Crimean Tatars to fight with other groups.

Possession of a multicultural concept of national identity decreases the impact of ethnic identity on conflict readiness among Russians and increases its impact among Crimean Tatars. When Russians have a multicultural concept of national identity, they see Ukraine as a society within which ethnic minorities should be guaranteed resources to maintain their ethnic cultures and communities. As a numerous and powerful minority, Russians expect that they will receive major benefits from the state, and they want to preserve their position without having to struggle against other ethnic groups. Such beliefs reduce the influence of salient ethnic identity among Russians in Crimea. When Crimean Tatars, as a small minority, see the nation as multicultural, however, they are more ready to fight against other ethnic groups for their rights and some privileges. They think they can get more resources than other ethnic groups because of their history of deportation and their unique position as an indigenous people. In this case, the multicultural concept strengthens the impact of salient ethnic identity on readiness to fight for resources to maintain the ethnic culture and community of Crimean Tatars.

Possession of a civic concept of national identity reduces the impact of salient ethnic identity for both groups. When people perceive their nation as built on a distinctive, nonethnic civic culture into which all citizens should integrate, their ethnic identity does not have an important influence on their conflict readiness. If representatives of both large and small minorities see civic responsibility as the main feature of the nation, their ethnicity is less significant. Thus, the civic concept of national identity mitigates readiness to fight among ethnic minorities and moderates the impact of ethnic identity.

The hypotheses, which were derived from conventional theory, suggested that possession of the ethnic concept of national identity would increase readiness to fight with other groups and strengthen the effects of ethnic identity salience on conflict readiness. They also predicted that possession of the multicultural concept of national identity would reduce readiness to fight with other groups and weaken the effects of ethnic identity salience, ethnocentrism, and economic deprivation on conflict readiness. My results show that such propositions are accurate for some groups and incorrect for others. The critical moderating variable, I would suggest, is the position of a minority within the state as a major or minor minority. For numerous and powerful minorities, possession of the ethnic concept of national identity strengthens their willingness to fight for a privileged position within society; the multicultural concept, on the other hand, reduces their readiness to fight, because they expect to obtain the major benefits in a multicultural nation. For small minorities, possession of the ethnic concept encourages assimilation and reduces willingness to fight, while possession of the multicultural concept evokes competition with other ethnic groups for rights and social and economic position within the society. Generalizing from my findings, I would propose that the position of a minority within a nation regulates the impact of the ethnic and multicultural concepts of national identity on members of that minority's readiness to fight with members of other groups. The only proposition that appears to have been correct for both groups is my hypothesis about the moderation effect of the civic concept. My results show that possession of the civic concept of national identity significantly reduces conflict readiness among ethnic minorities.

The findings provide ample empirical support for my hypothesis that a salient social identity can influence the impact of other identities on conflict intentions. I have shown that possession of a salient national identity can mitigate the impact of ethnic identity on readiness for conflict with other ethnic groups. I have also demonstrated that the meaning of other social identity can be a powerful moderator of the influence of a particular identity on behavioral intention: the three different concepts of national identity, I argue, weaken or strengthen the impact of ethnic identity on the readiness for conflict among ethnic groups. Thus, my study confirms that analysis of the impact of social identity on attitudes or behavior requires assessment of the interconnections between different identities. To understand the effects of a single social identity, it is necessary to analyze the influence, salience, and meaning of other social identities.

CHAPTER 9

IDENTITY AND CONFLICT: IMPLICATIONS
FOR IDENTITY CONFLICT MANAGEMENT

9.1. THEORETICAL APPROACHES FOR THE RESOLUTION OF IDENTITY-BASED CONFLICTS

According to contact theory in social psychology (Allport 1954; Pettigrew 1998; Pettigrew and Tropp 2000), the more contacts with representatives of an outgroup a person has, the more positive his or her attitudes toward the outgroup will be. Additionally, the theory stresses that simple contact among groups is not sufficient to improve intergroup relations. Several conditions are essential for reducing prejudice and bias: equal status among groups; cooperative intergroup interaction; opportunities for personal acquaintances among group members, especially with those whose personal characteristics do not support stereotypic expectations; and supportive norms by authorities within and outside the contact situation (Cook 1985; Pettigrew 1998). The effectiveness of these required conditions for improving intergroup relations has been confirmed in laboratory and field research (Pettigrew and Tropp 2000).

Some studies provide an explanation of the process of reducing prejudice and bias: changing the nature of interdependence from competition to cooperation and creating opportunities for equal status reduce negative stereotypes toward members of other groups. Conflict intentions can also be reduced when people experience cognitive dissonance between current positive interaction and previous negative attitudes and stereotypes; their stereotypes become more positive (Miller and Brewer 1984).

If all conditions are not present, the intergroup contact can actually increase prejudice. A study by the National Conference for Community and Justice shows the tendency for an increase in interaction and contact between racial and ethnic groups during the 1993–2000 period. However, this study also demonstrates the escalation of racial, religious, and ethnic tensions in schools, in neighborhoods, and at work.

The realistic conflict theory clearly demonstrates that contact alone is not sufficient for reducing intergroup conflicts. As I stressed above, this theory not only describes the sources for conflict among groups but also stresses the role of cooperative interdependence and superordinate goals as means of conflict resolution. It also shows the influence of superordinate identity on the process of conflict mitigation. Cooperative interdependence requires compatible goals; the activity of one party in achieving its goals is useful for another party in achieving its goals. There are several types of cooperative interdependence. In some cases, it can lie in the basis of social structures and does not require coordination for performing activities. In other cases, a common activity is important for achieving goals. The realistic conflict theory suggests that superordinate goals and positive interdependence are the bases for the development of a common, shared identity. Brewer (2000) stresses that, on the contrary, a common identity is the foundation for the development of superordinate goals and positive interdependence. In spite of this contradiction, both approaches agree that conflict resolution is possible only in the presence of two conditions: intergroup cooperative activity and common shared identities.

The common identity model developed by Gaertner et al. (1999, 2000a, 2000b) suggests that cognitive representations of the intergroup context depend on different types of intergroup interaction as well as cognitive, emotional, and social factors. Changes in these factors can lead to the perception of several groups as one common group, as groups with several subgroups, or as an association of separate individuals. The perception of groups as an association of separate individuals is called decategorization. It can be achieved, for example, by stressing the variation of opinions among ingroup members and some similarities between different opinions of ingroup and outgroup members or by creating more personalized interactions on the basis of personal information.

The perception of several groups as one common group is called supercategorization. It is based on the revaluation of former outgroup members as members of a new common ingroup. Supercategorization does not eliminate ingroup favoritism; it readdresses favoritism and leads to the acceptance of former outgroup members. The new common identity changes people's conceptions of the membership from different groups to a much more inclusive group and makes individual attitudes toward former outgroup members more positive, even if they had a long history of offences. According to Gaertner et al. (1999, 2000a, 2000b), this result can be achieved by increasing the importance of common superordinate goals or by introducing new factors such as common tasks or destinies, which will be shared by both groups.

The aim of supercategorization is the creation of a new, broader identity that unites groups. New identities can be formed by creating one group with several subgroups. In this case, members of the new group have a dual identity, one of which is connected with the new common group and the other reflects membership in a subgroup. On the basis of a positive balance of differences and similarities, all members of the new group have positive attitudes and stereotypes toward others.

As Gaertner et al. (1999, 2000a, 2000b) show in their studies, an increase in group differentiation, the creation of conditions for cooperative interactions, and the context of interdependence with positive emotional experience are the factors that influence the formation of a common identity and subsequently a decrease in intergroup prejudice. It is important that members of the new common group have equal status and position within the group. But even if subgroups have different statuses, the dual identity can develop a feeling of commonality and decrease negative attitudes toward members of other subgroups. If people continue to perceive themselves as members of different groups but also feel themselves to be members of a common large group, intergroup relations become more positive in comparison with the context of a single ingroup and single outgroup (Dovidio and Gaertner 2004).

Another interesting approach to identity-based conflict was developed by Rothman (1997). He stresses that participants have to gain insight into the nature of conflict and only then develop new ways for effectively engaging it. This intensive diagnostic and intervention process—ARIA—has four stages. First, participants have to develop their understanding of the type and level of a given conflict and produce diagnosis. This analysis includes stage one, Surfacing Antagonism (What caused the conflict between the parties in the first place? What are the main symptoms of the problem?), and stage two, Fostering Resonance (What does each side care about most, and why? Where is an overlap of underlying concerns?) (Rothman 1997). Once the conflict has been assessed, participants can select an appropriate intervention strategy. Then they go through stage three, Generating Inventions (What solutions can the parties apply to convert the negative dynamics of conflict to an opportunity for addressing underlying—and often shared—concerns?), and stage four, Planning Action (How can the parties design a specific action plan for clarifying who will do what, why, when, and how?). Rothman stresses that the ARIA framework can help transform the "dissonance of conflict" into the "resonance of creativity and cooperation" through an active learning process.

9.2. THE MODEL OF DEALING WITH IDENTITY CONFLICTS

The clear role of social identity in the conflict dynamic stresses the importance of analyzing the complex relationship between social identity and conflict. The following scheme shows this interrelation as well as some political and research implications (see Figure 9.1).

The analysis of the impact of conflict among and within groups on social identity becomes an important element in the field of *conflict analysis*. Having knowledge about the influence of conflict structure and dynamics

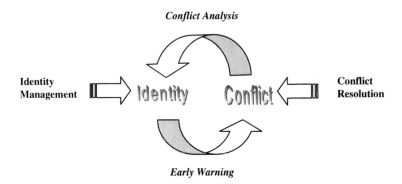

Figure 9.1   The model of analysis and resolution of identity-based conflicts.

on ethnic, religious, national, and other identities and the processes of identity formation expands the understanding of conflict processes and the complexity of conflict situations. The study of the effects of identity on conflict escalation creates the opportunity for *early warning* models, which are based on the salience, forms, types, and levels of identity, the meaning of group membership, interrelations between identities, and the specificity of the identity system. A description of the early warning system based on identity will be presented in Section 9.3. Together with the established techniques of *conflict resolution* that deal directly with the structures, components, and dynamics of conflict, this scheme shows another path to conflict prevention and resolution: *identity management,* which uses different interventions to change or redefine identity in order to mitigate conflicts. Several methods of identity management will be presented in Section 9.4.

The interrelations between instrumental interests and identity in emergent conflicts can be used as a framework for developing a system of conflict mitigation and peacebuilding. The methods of dealing with identity issues must be combined with conflict resolution methods such as demilitarization, constitutional reforms, power sharing, and economic development. It is important to stress that the conflict resolution methods that involve the acknowledgment of ingroup violent actions and recognition of human rights of an outgroup pose a threat to the ingroup identity that rests on the idea of "positive We–negative They." The acknowledgement of negative ingroup actions requires the reviewing and reconceptualization of the ingroup identity that always invokes strong resistance. Thus, for example, the main problem in the relationship between Armenia and Turkey is the 1915–1923 period, during which more than 1.5 million Armenians were killed by the Turkish people. The Armenians insist that the deaths of their people be defined as genocide. The Turkish government denies the act of genocide, declaring that the Armenians died during a civic war that began during World War II and continued after its end. Scholars, planning to organize a conference in Istanbul in the summer of 2005 to analyze different conceptions of the events of

1915–1923, discovered firsthand how the very idea of such a conference provokes strong negative reactions among political leaders. As it happened, the Turkish minister of justice stressed in his speech at Parliament that the conference was a stab in the back of Turkey. It is important to facilitate the transformation of identity with the prevailing narratives of the "We-They" opposition to identity characterized by different meanings and sources of pride and self-esteem.

9.3. EARLY WARNING MODEL FOR IDENTITY CONFLICTS

The importance of early warning models and systems based on the systematic collection and analysis of information was stressed in numerous publications. Based on the collection and analysis of specific indicators, such systems help to anticipate the escalation of violent conflict, produce best- and worst-case scenarios, and develop a basis for the decision making and conflict prevention. The predictors in early warning systems reflect the stages of conflict or different spheres of a conflict situation. Thus, FAST International (Krummenacher 2006) describes four types of causes: root, proximate, positive intervening, and negative intervening. Root causes expose background factors that are necessary but not sufficient sources for conflict. They are usually static and embedded in historical context, such as ethnic diversity, colonial history, and economic situation. In other models they are presented as systemic factors and reflect social, political, and economic structures. Proximate factors change over time and can provoke conflict and violence. Any changes in economic or political situations, such as an increase in poverty and unemployment, drought, migration, human rights violation, change of regime, can lead to an open conflict. Positive intervening factors can help prevent conflict and include humanitarian aid, investments, seasonal factors, and so forth. Negative intervening factors increase the likelihood of violent conflict (e.g., arms trade, criminal groups).

Other early warning systems are based on the description of different sectors and segments of society and point to political, economic, judicial, legal, social, and cultural issues as well as military and security issues on different levels: subregional, regional, and geopolitical. Many systems stress the importance of such factors as fragility of state, type of government, mass migration, and so on.

In spite of the advanced level and complexity of these models, social identity is barely presented among indicators. The previous chapters showed the impact of social identity on the dynamic of conflict and emphasized the importance of the development of an early warning model based on the characteristics of social identity. Such a model does not dismiss other systems but, in contrast, complements, enhances, and strengthens them by introducing the issue of identity. This chapter shows the factors of the early warning model that is based on the results of the research presented in this book. Figure 9.2 shows the five main groups of factors.

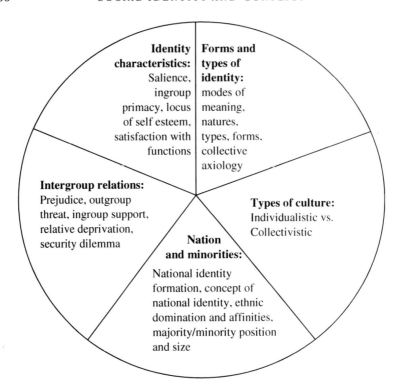

Figure 9.2 The model of the identity-based early warning system.

Identity characteristics

1. Salience of identity (see Korostelina 2006b, Section 4.1; Studies I, II, and III in Chapter 4; and Studies I, II, and III in Chapter 7). As it was shown in numerous studies and this book, a salient identity provokes active actions against other groups and leads to conflict. The monitoring of the salience of identity, especially rapid changes in the importance of group membership, can help predict ingroup members' involvement in conflict.

2. Ingroup primacy (see Section 4.1 and Study I in Chapter 7), or the feeling of supremacy of ingroup goals and values over individual goals and values. The higher the level of ingroup primacy for ingroup members, the stronger their willingness to disregard their own goals and values and to follow the ways of behavior required by the ingroup. Ingroup primacy can increase or decrease the influence of identity salience on the conflict behavior of ingroup members. People with a low level of social identity salience show the readiness for conflict behavior only if they have high ingroup primacy and believe that the existence of an enemy unites ingroup against outgroup. For people with a salient ethnic identity, the readiness for conflict is a result of identity salience; ingroup supremacy is derived from identity salience and does not have a direct impact on the

readiness for conflict behavior. Thus, it is important to consider the level of ingroup primacy if social identity is not salient.

3. Locus of self-esteem (see Section 4.7). In cases of *internal locus for self-esteem,* ingroup members are satisfied with their position, proud to be ingroup members, and have a high sense of confidence even if they do not make a favorable comparison between their groups and outgroups. They show few conflict intentions and do not consider fighting with other groups. If group members need to use favorable comparisons with outgroups to increase their self-esteem, or if they do not have the opportunity to promote, develop, or revive their culture, an *external locus of self-esteem* usually creates a solid basis for conflict intentions and a readiness to fight with outgroups.

4. Satisfaction with identity functions (see Sections 3.3 and 8.3 and Studies I in Chapters 3 and 8). A study of the functions of social identities can help understand the basic needs of a particular group and develop an early warning of triggering events and situations. Thus, if social status is the most important function for ethnic identity, any threat to the status of an ethnic group or its members can provoke negative reactions and conflict activities. If self-esteem is the most significant function for national identity, any threat to the self-respect as a member of a particular nation can inflame the readiness for conflict behavior (see Study I in Chapter 3). The fulfillment of the most important functions can increase the salience of identity and strengthen the readiness for conflict. If ingroup members attach important factors to a new identity, it develops into a salient identity and can replace other identities that previously provided corresponding functions. However, if a common (national, regional, etc.) identity fulfills the main functions, including increasing self-esteem and social status and providing personal safety, group support, and protection and recognition to an ingroup, it significantly reduces the readiness to fight between subgroups (see Study I in Chapters 8).

Forms and types of identity

5. Mode of the meaning of identity (see Section 4.2). The depictive mode of the meaning of identity has a very small implication for conflict, while other modes can provoke violence on the basis of different motives: the ideological mode on the basis of ideological differences; the historical mode on the basis of chosen traumas and history of intergroup violence; and the relative mode on the basis of intergroup prejudice and biases. If multiple identities with multimodal meaning transform to a single identity with prevailing threat narratives—a *dominant* identity—conflict and violence among groups can increase significantly. The most important components of its meaning are interrelations with outgroups and negative outgroup images; thus a dominant identity leads to the perception of the world in terms of "positive we–negative they." The fighting with the outgroup becomes the main goal and condition of individual and ingroup survival.

6. Forms of identity (see Section 4.5). The cultural form (based on characteristics of the everyday life of a group) and the reflected form (which includes a reflective or advanced understanding of the group's past, present, and future) of identity have a less impact on conflict behavior than mobilized form. The main content and meaning of this identity are contradiction and competition among groups. The core aim is to increase the status or power of the ingroup, which leads to conflict intentions and a readiness to fight against outgroups.

7. Type of identity (see Section 4.4.). The types of social identity moderate the influence of identity on a person's behavior and attitudes. Dual and collective identities have a very significant effect on a person's values, beliefs, and positions. Descriptive and collective identities influence the perceptions and evaluations of the world in terms of group categories and intergroup relations. Therefore, the collective type of identity has the highest potential for conflict.

8. Type of collective axiology (see Rothbart and Korostelina 2006 and Section 4.6). The protracted conflict usually rests on a collective axiology with *low* axiological balance and *high* collective generality. While generating degrading stories, a group becomes incapable of understanding and perceiving the Other, as the ingroup loses its ability to see the virtues of the Other, to understand their complexities, and to evaluate their decisions. This kind of identity is often associated with extreme forms of nationalism, fascism, racism, and sectarianism. Another type of collective axiology that can also lead to conflict is the collective axiology characterized by a *low* axiological balance and a low collective generality. Such an ingroup views itself as morally pure, sacred, and glorified, while an outgroup is characterized as exhibiting mixed values and virtues. Two types of collective axiology with a high degree of axiological balance (and a high/low degree of collective generality) are less prone to conflict. In such cases, both the ingroup and the outgroup identities portray a balanced axiology of virtues and vices.

9. Nature of identity (ascribed vs. acquired) (see Section 4.3). Acquired social identities have a greater impact on a person's behavior than ascribed ones. In many cases, people who adopt new religious, ethnic, or national identities show stronger devotion to ingroup beliefs, values, and norms than people with ascribed identities.

Type of culture

10. Individualistic/collectivistic cultures (see Chapter 2). For representatives of collectivistic cultures, a strong sense of belonging to an ingroup determines the readiness for conflict behavior, whereas for representatives of individualistic cultures, individual estimation of a situation carries the strongest impact on the readiness for conflict behavior. Thus, for representatives of collectivistic cultures, a salient social identity plays a determinant role in the formation of conflict behavior. It influences attitudes and perceptions of situations: group values and perceptions

dominate individual opinions and attitudes. People are ready to defend and fight for ethnic identity to ensure personal security and social stability. For representatives of individualistic cultures, personal development and achievements are more important than involvement and connections with an ingroup. The personal perception and estimation of a situation (attitudes) precedes and determines the readiness for conflict behavior. A salient social identity also influences the readiness for conflict behavior; nevertheless, attitudes can increase or decrease this influence.

State of intergroup relations

11. Intergroup prejudice (see Section 6.1). Positive evaluations of ingroups and negative evaluations of outgroups increase the potential of conflict. The majority of studies of social identity provide evidence of a relationship between the salience of identity and attitudes toward outgroups.
12. Outgroup threat (see Section 6.6 and Study III in Chapter 7). Studies show that outgroup threats increase intergroup prejudice and lead to more hostility toward outgroups, which helps justify the conflict and the unfavorable treatment of outgroup members. The situations of competition, proximity, and contact increase intergroup hostility rather than decreasing it. Among the factors contributing to the perception of outgroup threat are the following: unequal economical, cultural, or political positions of ethnic groups; different citizenship of ethnic groups; memories of the former domination of an outgroup and attribution of the desire for revival; the perception that groups have weaker or worse positions in comparison with outgroups; limitation of the socioeconomic opportunities of the ingroup by outgroups' political extremism, violence, and nationalism. Changes in intergroup positions have an even stronger impact on the perception of outgroup threat. Among the triggering factors are the following: (a) changes in the demography of groups (including asymmetrical birth rate, the politics of natalism, or baby boom); (b) economic competition; (c) new territorial claims of outgroups; (d) new barriers to upward mobility, economic competition, and the rise of the educational level and mobility of outgroups; and (e) intentions to change the existing intergroup positions.
13. Ingroup support (see Section 6.8 and Study III in Chapter 7). Ingroup support reflects the expectation that all outgroup members maintain the same goals and aspirations, a common perception of the outgroup, and similar intentions to change the current social situation. It increases the level of participation in decision-making processes and collective actions of ingroups. If more ingroup members are willing to fight with outgroups, the readiness for conflict will increase.
14. Relative deprivation (see Section 6.3 and Chapter 7). The perceptions of deprivation or disadvantage that are based on comparisons among groups provoke social activity if people recognize that a higher standard of living exists and that they will have the opportunity and ability to achieve it. Thus, relative deprivation can lead to violence.

15. Security dilemma (see Section 6.7). In situations of competition among groups, such factors as information failure, credible commitments, and the security dilemma can reshape social identities and provoke identity conflict. A perceived external threat produces feelings of insecurity among ingroup members who perceive the ingroup as a target of this threat, and leads to the ingroup taking actions against all outgroups. These actions are, in turn, perceived by outgroups as threatening, and their counteractions develop a new turn in the spiral of conflict and violence.

Nation building and minorities' positions

16. National identity formation (see Chapter 8). The establishment of new states engenders incentives for ethnic homogeneity and thus systematic efforts to marginalize or destroy ethnic "others." Conflict develops when the identity chosen by a minority group is incompatible with that imposed by others.

17. Concepts of national identity (see Chapter 8). These concepts influences people's attitudes and behaviors toward different ethnic groups within their own nation and their approach to other nations. The ethnic concept (the perception that the nation is built around a core ethnic community into which the ethnic minorities should assimilate) leads to the increasing resistance of ethnic minorities and intergroup conflict. In some cases (see Study II in Chapter 8), it can decrease the readiness to fight. The multicultural concept (the view of the nation as multicultural, with equal rights for all ethnic groups and autonomy) usually decreases the potential of conflict between the majority and minorities but can lead to conflicts among minorities. The civic concept (the perception of citizenship as a contract between the people and the state concerning both rights and obligations) decreases prospective tensions and violence.

18. Majority/minority position and size (see Section 6.4). Minority groups appear to be more prone to bias and show the largest amount of discriminatory behavior. Minority group members are more socially mobile and ready for transformations. Political goals of minorities are connected with the changes in social and political situations, and numerous minorities show a higher readiness for conflict.

19. Experience of domination (see Chapters 6 and 7). Ethnic, religious, and national groups that experienced domination in the past can try to reclaim their power and supremacy. Previously subordinate groups have a strong potential for conflict based on motives of revenge and revival as well as fear of restoration of outgroup domination.

20. Transnational affinities (see Chapters 6 and 7). Ingroup members not only perceive outgroups in terms of stereotypes, but also attribute goals to them. If a minority group has a strong nation-state of the same ethnicity near the border, it can be perceived as a "fifth column" that aims for cultural autonomy or changes of borders. This goal attribution

results in the perception of such groups as a threat to the well-being and position of the nation.

The logistic of the identity-based early warning system is presented in Figure 9.3.

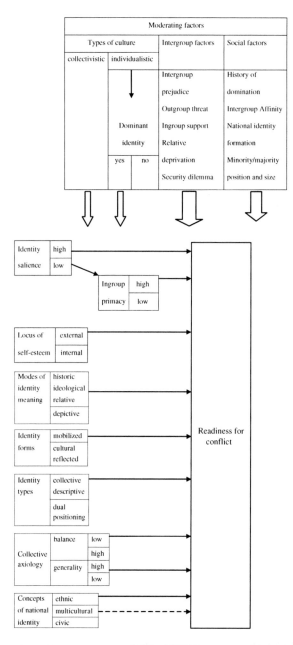

Figure 9.3 The logistic of the identity-based early warning system.

All factors listed on the left represent different aspects of identity that contribute to the readiness for conflict. The arrows show the specificity of each factor's influence. To develop a complete diagnosis of the conflict, it is important to collect information about every identity feature and summarize its impact. Factors on the top have a moderating effect: they can increase or decrease the influence of identity functions on the readiness for conflict. Thus, collectivistic cultures are more prone to identity conflicts; however, the presence of a dominant identity in an individualistic culture can strongly contribute to the readiness to fight with other groups. Intergroup factors, including prejudice ingroup support, outgroup threat, relative deprivation, and security dilemma, are interconnected with identity aspects (e.g., salience of identity and ingroup support are interrelated, and external locus of self-esteem contributes to the feeling of relative deprivation). Social factors, including history of domination of one of the groups, transnational or national affinities, minority/majority position and size, and formation of national identity, are relatively independent and increase the effect of identity on the readiness for conflict.

9.4. METHODS AND TECHNIQUES OF IDENTITY MANAGEMENT

Six main trends of identity management can be defined on the basis of different types of identity:

1. An increase in identity awareness, including knowledge about the role of identity as a source of conflict or tolerance;
2. An increase in group esteem and positive ingroup image through the revival of ingroup identity;
3. Actualization of the cultural form of identity through the support of cultural identity;
4. Reduction of the salience of categorization and transformation of dominant identity;
5. Formation of a common identity;
6. Negotiation of identity.

Several methods can be used to successfully manage and transform identity. Among them are identity-based training (Korostelina 2001, 2002a), identity reconstruction workshops (Korostelina 2002b, 2003), problem-solving workshops (Kelman 1982, 1997, 2002, 2004), consultations with the elite (Byman 1997; Mezran 2001), formal negotiations (Rosoux 2001), and management of multicultural communities (Korostelina 2000b, 2000c).

Identity-Based Training

Identity awareness is the first basic stage in the process of mitigation of identity-based conflicts. It helps people understand the role of identity in the increasing conflict or in developing tolerance (Korostelina 2001, 2002a).

The identity-based training that I developed aims (1) to show the existence of multiple system of identities; (2) to demonstrate the influence of a salient identity on stereotypes and attitudes; (3) to develop the tolerant multi-identity approach for situations, groups, and people; (4) to show the patterns of formation of identities and to introduce the intergroup dynamics as roots of conflict; (5) to build skills of analysis and recognition of identity-based conflicts; (6) to demonstrate methods for tolerance building such as decategorization, recategorization, and mutual differentiation; and (7) to develop skills of conflict resolution using knowledge about group dynamics.

The training contains three segments: (1) multiplicity of identity; (2) identity as a source for conflict; (3) ways for tolerance. The first part is devoted to identity as a source of behavior— specifically, to the multiplicity of identity, identity salience, and the influence of identity on our behavior. The aim of the second part is to show the patterns of formation of identities and such phenomena as negative comparison, ingroup favoritism, biases, the ultimate attribution error, metacontrast, the outgroup homogeneity effect, and images of the enemy. By introducing the intergroup dynamics as roots of conflict, we show how identity leads to conflict. The third part is devoted to the ways of tolerance through identity change such as decategorization, recategorization, and mutual differentiation.

The training includes a set exercises followed by debriefing and discussion. These exercises are described below, accordingly, for each part.

Part I. Multiplicity and Salience of Identity

I have created some exercises in order to introduce the multiplicity of identities and decreases in the salience of ethnicity. During the exercise "Circle of Identities," the trainees could see the differences between the different types of identities and the possibilities of using these types in their lives. They understood that not only they were members of ethnic groups or families but also had multiple identities that helped to make their salient identities "softer" and more "flexible."

At the beginning of the exercise, the participants were asked to answer the question Who am I? in a nested system of five circles. The main answer had to be written in the center circle, while considerably less important answers were to be enclosed in various other circles. The least important identity must be written in the last or fifth circle. They then fastened their written circles to their clothes and walked around the room, viewing the circles of other participants. They found that the others' circles were similar to their own and were able to discuss these similarities with the others. At the end of this stage, all participants arranged group discussions of their impressions. After returning to their places, they were asked to write three to four personal features that characterized each identity in their circles. Then one of them introduced all five of his or her identities and one set of features. The others tried to guess the connection between the identities and the features.

Another exercise, "Changing the Identities," showed the influence of identities on behavior in certain situations. It was conducted in the form of a role-play game. Four participants played two role games about family conflicts. In the first, the father played the role of a lawyer who used his professional principles in his everyday life. In the second, he played the role of a family father who valued his family's honor.

Others participants also changed their identities, and after finishing the role game, they discussed how their behavior changed depending on their adopted identities.

Part II. *Identity as a Basis for Conflict*

In the second part, I created win-or-lose situations for teams by using a simple exercise. We divided the participants into two teams and put together two lines of chairs. Each participant was asked to stand on the chair and one chair was free in each line. Then I asked participants to pass the free chair to the end of the line, put it down, and step over the chairs in order to have a free chair at the beginning of the line. The two teams had to reach the finish line advancing in this way. In this competition, only one team could win (in some trainings, participants played with a ball in two teams). Then I introduced discriminative rules for the losing team. The participants of this team could not sit down, could not have breaks during their work, had to raise their hands to ask questions, and could not begin conversations with representatives of the winning team. The participants from the winning team could sit, stand, or walk and could take breaks and ask any questions they wished (in one training, which we conducted together with our colleagues from the ICAR, George Mason University in Crimea, during the summer of 2002, the members of the winning team could even swim in the pool). The aim of such discrimination was to show the different mechanisms of intergroup relations. All participants had to use these rules throughout the next exercises and discussions: the members of both teams had to prepare a list of value triads. Two values in this triad had to be controversial, and the third value had to serve as a frame for the conciliation of the two conflict values (e.g., a contradiction between a housewife's responsibilities and her career; peace and love in the family as the basis for conflict resolution). Each team had to prepare as many value triads as they could.

Then I asked people to send a greeting to another participant, either a member of the outgroup or their ingroup. This exercise demonstrated the phenomenon of ingroup favoritism. In debriefings, we discussed all the emotions, feelings, and thoughts that arose during the exercises, such as anger, feelings of being a "second-rate person," indignation, and such phenomena as negative comparison, stereotypes, and biases.

Such situations were used in the famous "Blue Eyes–Brown Eyes" experiment (Brewer 2003), where the advantages for people with blue eyes were sufficient to produce a preference for fellow group members and to elicit discrimination against outsiders. Instead of using the color of people's eyes as a reason for discrimination, our training created a situation of competition and winning where people were discriminated against on the basis of their losing status. We think that the reality of the situations were very important for our purposes. After this exercise, we were able to demonstrate the movie about the "Blue Eyes–Brown Eyes" experiment and discussed the role of identity in intergroup relations.

As the training showed, after only an a hour of work, the participants from the losing team became angry, wanted to stop the training, did not like people from the winning team, and attributed to these people the feelings of superiority, hard-heartedness, and arrogance. They acted aggressively toward the leader of the training (and even expressed hatred toward me) and felt very uncomfortable, declaring themselves "people of a second sort." To increase their self-esteem, the members of the losing team attributed to themselves such peculiarities as magnanimity and creativity and denied the presence of these peculiarities among the winning team members. Their lists of value triads were shorter than those of the winning team and reflected their position: most of the values were connected with values of self-esteem, competition, and equality. The exercise's condition did not influence the values of the winning team.

When I asked people to send a greeting to another participant, members of the losing team demonstrated ingroup favoritism: they sent greetings only to the members of their team. The members of the winning team did not prefer members of their group: they sent greetings to members of both teams.

Part III. Ways for Tolerance
To show the influence of decategorization, I divided the participants into two teams and asked them to discuss the roots of identity. One team had to defend the thesis that identity is situational and can be constructed. The other team had to defend the thesis that people receive identity from birth and it cannot be changed. I asked the participants to begin all their phrases in the discussion with the words "My team suggests . . ." or "My team considers . . ." After half an hour, we offered to continue the discussion in pairs (two participants from each team). The discussion of the exercise showed that working in two teams led to negative emotions and attitudes toward the other group, and that working in pairs helped to reduce such negative feelings.

To show the effect of mutual differentiation, I used a version of the prisoners' dilemma. In the game "By the Lake," five different plants and enterprises worked by using the water from the lake for their manufacturing. Their actions included the dropping of polluted water; therefore, a fine was imposed and the lake had to be cleaned, thus linking the five plants. Only one strategy, real cooperation, could help them to get the biggest profits.

To show the effect of recategorization, we proposed the game "The Common Holiday and Common Heroes." The participants had to discuss values, goals, and histories that could be estimated as common for different people.

Results and Effectiveness of Training
To evaluate the effectiveness of training, my team conducted four trainings during 2000–2001. The first training was conducted for 24 members of civil society, including NGO members, teachers, and leaders of the ethnic

Crimean Tatar community, during August 14–16, 2000, in the Kamenka village of Simferopol district. The second training was conducted for 14 leaders of youth organizations of the town of Simferopol in January 2001. Both the third and fourth trainings were conducted in Simferopol during September 2001, with 48 members of NGOs and leaders of ethnic communities participating.

After the first two trainings, we organized debriefings. According to the results of the debriefing discussions, all of the exercises and information were useful and valuable for the participants. Many of them said that they would use the knowledge and skills in their work and share their new understanding of the roots of conflict with their friends and contacts. This discussion showed that people realized the ways of tolerance; they had a real desire to use the new skills and experience to resolve conflicts in their communities. The participants told us after the training, "Now I know why we have such problems, and I know—it is more important—what to do with conflict." One woman said, "It is very useful to show all people in Crimea all these exercises, to teach them how people discriminate [against] each other and why they do it. I will use these ways for tolerance in my work in community."

The role of evaluation is to determine what works and what does not in terms of the goals of the training. As Ross (1998, 2001) stressed, the success of training should be understood in terms of multiple (often continuous) dimensions. As many practitioners point out, the main purpose and success of training is connected with improving the relationships between opposing communities and building capacity for disputing parties to manage future problems. It is difficult to find adequate methods of training evaluation because of the existence of numerous independent variables, changing contexts of the trainings, problems of instrumentation, and so on. As Ross claims, a "good enough" evaluation requires using the best possible measurement under difficult circumstances. To evaluate our training, we decided to apply pre- and posttest measures.

Our purpose was to study how training influenced the estimation of ethnic relations in Crimea and the opportunities of conflict resolution. To study the effectiveness of our training, we used comparative methods, confronting the traditional and identity-based trainings. The traditional training design contains such skills as conflict analysis, problem solving, cross-cultural communication, negotiation, mediation, and facilitation. During traditional training, we introduced strategies for conflict resolution; the Blake and Mouton diagram; the "standard" mediation model and the role of culture; the standard approaches to negotiation, prisoner's dilemma, and "principled negotiation"; the basic roles a third party can play in an integrative process; respectful listening; and the general model for an integrative third-party process.

To study the effectiveness of our trainings, we used a method of semantic differential. This method was chosen because of the following reasons:

1. It gave an opportunity to estimate two opposite view for each situation;
2. It provided a seven-point scale, which was more differentiated than dichotomous answers for questions;

3. In comparison with questionnaires, it could reduce the effect of the situation, because the participants did not tell the trainer what they thought he or she wanted to hear.

Eight pairs of the phrases about conflict in Crimea were proposed for each participant before and after training; 59 trainees taking part in the traditional training and 63 in the identity-based training participated in the experiment. For the semantic differential method, it is recommended that there be a minimum $N = 100$ in order to have statistically reliable results. Regardless of the fact that we have a lesser sample, we consider that the levels of difference were sufficiently significant.

We organized three series of research, each of which included one traditional and one identity-based training. The first series was conducted for members of civil society, including NGO members, teachers, and leaders of the ethnic Crimean Tatar community in two resettlements in the Simferopol district. The conditions of their lives, the time of the village's founding, and the compositions of the trainees (by gender, age, and level of education) in both trainings were equal. Twenty-one trainees took part in the traditional training, and 24 in the identity-based training. The training "Methods of Conflict resolution" was conducted during August 10–12, 2000, in Marino village, and "Identity-Based Peace Building" was conducted during August 14–16 in Kamenca village, with the participation of Tamra Pearson d'Estree, then associate professor at the Institute of Conflict Analysis and Resolution at George Mason University. The second series was conducted for leaders of youth organizations in the town of Simferopol. Fifteen trainees took part in the traditional training, and 14 in the identity-based training. Both were conducted in Simferopol during January 2001. The third series was conducted for members of ethnic NGOs and leaders of ethnic communities of Crimea during September 2001 in Simferopol. Twenty-three trainees took part in the traditional training, and 25 in the identity-based training. Again, the compositions of trainees (by gender, age, and level of education) in all trainings were equal.

The similarity of the groups selected for traditional and identity-based trainings is supported by the results of the semantic differential before trainings: the paired samples t-test analysis did not indicate any significant differences (Tables 9.1 and 9.2).

The results of three traditional trainings are presented in the Table 9.1. The paired samples t-test analysis indicated that the most significant changes were connected with the following:

1. Estimation of third-party intervention, $t(59) = 5.07$, $p < .000$, with the mean level before the trainings at -2.00 ($SD = -1.2$, $n = 59$) and after the trainings at 0.5 ($SD = 0.1$, $n = 59$);
2. The possibility to avoid conflict on the basis of the knowledge of its causes $t(59) = 4.31$, $p < . 000$, with the mean level before the trainings at -2.80 ($SD = -2.0$, $n = 59$) and after the trainings at -1.11 ($SD = -0.6$, $n = 59$).

Table 9.1 Semantic Differential Results in Traditional Trainings

Left statement	3	2	1	0	1	2	3	Right statement
Ethnic relations in Crimea are conflict			*1.5* / **1.64**					Ethnic relations in Crimea are not conflict
Ethnic conflict in Crimea is hardly resolvable			*1.4* / **1.20**					Ethnic conflict in Crimea can be resolved
Ethnic conflict in Crimea is based profoundly		*2.2*	**1.43**					Ethnic conflict in Crimea is situational
Ethnic conflict in Crimea is easily controlled		**1.9**	*1.5*					Ethnic conflict in Crimea is spontaneous and uncontrollable
The intervention of third party is useful		**2**		*0.5*				The intervention of third party is dangerous
Ethnic conflict in Crimea is inveterate				*0.25* / **0**				Ethnic conflict in Crimea is changeable
There is a possibility to construct the common "We"				*0.8* / **0.6**				Differences between peoples in Crimea are too big
The conflicts between ethnic groups are inevitable	*2.8*		**1.11**					The conflicts can be avoided through the knowledge of their causes

*Note: Italic type, values before training; **bold type,** values after training.*

After the trainings, the trainees considered that third-party intervention would be useful for conflict resolution in Crimea and that the knowledge of the roots of conflict could help to prevent conflict. The paired samples t-test analysis of the results of identity-based training (Table 9.2) indicated that the most significant changes were connected with the following:

1. The possibility to resolve and control conflict, $t(63) = 6.11$, $p < .000$, with the mean level before the trainings at -1.60 ($SD = -1.0$, $n = 63$) and after the trainings at 1.45 ($SD = 0.9$, $n = 63$);
2. The construction of common "We," $t(63) = 7.12$, $p < .000$, with the mean level before the trainings at -1.00 ($SD = -0.3$, $n = 63$) and after the trainings at 2.5 ($SD = 1.9$, $n = 63$);
3. The prevention of conflict on the basis of knowledge, $t(63) = 7.67$, $p < .000$, with the mean level before the trainings at -2.40 ($SD = -1.7$, $n = 63$) and after the trainings at 1.09 ($SD = 0.8$, $n = 63$).

After the trainings, they asserted that conflict could be prevented and resolved and pointed out that the development of a common identity is one of the most important ways to create tolerance. The revaluation of the importance of knowledge for conflict prevention was more significant for the participants of the identity-based training.

Table 9.2 Semantic Differential Results in Identity-Based Trainings

Left pole	3	2	1	0	1	2	3	Right pole
Ethnic relations in Crimea are conflict			*1.4* **1.1**					Ethnic relations in Crimea are not in conflict
Ethnic conflict in Crimea is hardly resolvable			*1.6*		**1.45**			Ethnic conflict in Crimea can be resolved
Ethnic conflict in Crimea is based profoundly			*1.9* **1.3**					Ethnic conflict in Crimea is situational
Ethnic conflict in Crimea is easily controlled		**2.48**	*1.25*					Ethnic conflict in Crimea is spontaneous and uncontrollable
The intervention of third party is useful			**0.9**	*0*				The intervention of third party is dangerous
Ethnic conflict in Crimea is inveterate				*0*	**1.6**			Ethnic conflict in Crimea is changeable
There is a possibility to construct the common "We"		**2.5**			*1*			Differences between peoples in Crimea are too big
The conflicts between ethnic groups are inevitable		*2.4*			**1.09**			The conflicts can be avoided through the knowledge of their causes

Note: Italic type, values before training; **bold type,** values after training.

A comparative analysis of the results from two groups (NGO leaders and young leaders) showed no significant differences between these groups, except that young leaders showed larger changes in both trainings.

The results demonstrated that the traditional training dealt mostly with third-party skills and did not significantly change the attitudes toward the possibility of conflict prevention and resolution in societies with community conflicts. The identity-based training gave less attention to third-party intervention, but influenced the transformation of conflict evaluation toward more changeable and resolvable ends. It provided more knowledge and understanding of the roots of conflict and skills to create tolerance among parties and improve the relation between opposing communities. We suggest that identity-based methods must be used with traditional methods as a basis for third-party methods of conflict resolution. Understanding intergroup and interethnic dynamics, stereotypes, biases, and discrimination will help adopt third-party methods and appreciate their role in conflict resolution.

Management of Multicultural Communities

It has been repeatedly stressed in this book that a salient identity provokes negative intergroup comparison, negative attitudes, and conflict behavior toward members of other groups. A cultural revival that provides sources for ingroup respect and positive self-image can reduce negative perceptions of outgroups by reducing favorable comparison and developing internal sources for self-esteem. Stressing the cultural components of the meaning of identity can help transform a mobilized form of identity with a "We-They" perception into a cultural form. In addition, cultural events and dialogues develop cross-cultural understanding, an appreciation of differences, and a search for common values and decrease the salience of a particular identity by penetrating borders and increasing positive attitudes.

This chapter describes activities on the management of multicultural communities in Crimea, where more than 100 relatively small ethnic groups share the small peninsula. One of the central problems at the end of 1990s was the preservation or revival of different cultures together with the formation of tolerance.

The Crimean Republican Culture Fund (CRCF) was established in September 1987 to support the further development of ethnic cultures. Their first actions include the exhibition of Crimean painters' pictures (December 1987), the auction of Crimean artists' works (November 1988), the charity concert of Crimean artists (December 1988), and the auction-entertainment "Southern Night" in Kherson (an old Crimean town). All financial resources gained during these events were allocated to the development of ethnic minorities associations and cultural centers. With the assistance of the CRFC, the ethnic cultural centers and associations started to be established. In the period between April 1989 and December 1990, the Armenian Culture Society, the Crimean Karaims Society, the Jewish national-cultural association "Zibn Likht," the Azerbaijani society "Odjag," the Crimean Greek Culture Society, the Coordinated Center of Renaissance of Crimean Tatar Culture, the Georgian Crimean Community, and the Crimean Enlightenment German Society were established. In total, during that period, nine ethnic-cultural centers were founded with the assistance of the CRFC. Thus, the necessity rose to coordinate these associations, plan common actions, and share experiences.

Therefore, in December 1990, the roundtable was organized. The meeting discussed the main activities of newly established ethnic-cultural associations. Finally, an appeal to the people of the republic was announced. It stressed the notion that the society could not progress without the combined efforts of all ethnic groups. Soon, three new associations were established (Russian, Belorussian, and Bulgarian).

The main task of the CRCF was to emphasize the idea that Crimea is the "common house." Certain awards were established for distinguished people in the sphere of culture and sciences—for instance, the Evsey Peisakh, Stepan Rudansky, and Peter Palas awards. However, in our opinion, the awards for contributing to the development of multiethnic Crimean culture, and for assisting minorities associations, are more significant.

The next step was the establishment of the Crimean Publishing House. *Unknown Crimea: A History in Faces* (issued in January 1992) was the first book it published. The book demonstrated that the existence of multiple ethnic groups was not an obstacle to friendship and the mutual understanding among different ethnic groups. Moreover, it stimulated the development of regional culture.

At the same time, activities directed to organize and conduct cultural events with the active participation of all ethnic communities were continuing—for example, June 1991, the auction-performance "Southern Night" in the Bakhchisarai Palace; July 1992, holiday of the Sudak Genuezian Castle; summer 1993, the days of Slavonic literature and holidays of Greek culture in Yalta; and July 1994, the festival of German culture in Yalta. The number of cultural associations was increasing; Italian, Czech, Jewish, Ukrainian, Korean, Polish, Osethian, and Estonian societies were being established. Societies were conducting activities for the development and popularization of ethnic cultures; however, a more significant feature of such actions was the joint activities of different ethnic groups.

The teamwork of ethnic cultural centers required an in-depth comprehension, planning, and summarizing of their activities. The most meaningful events were the an international conference of CRCF representatives in 1993, press conferences, a "roundtable" dedicated to establishing interethnic cooperation (1995), and a seminar on the activities of nongovernmental organizations. These meetings and conferences have shown the importance of activities and further development of cooperation among ethnic cultural groups. Moreover, the main activities have to be conducted not only in the framework of certain ethnic organizations (at the local level), but also throughout the region. In that sense, the collaboration-oriented actions are very important. Thus, the necessity of a new organization, which was to supervise and assist the joint activities of ethnic cultural associations, had arisen.

The Association of Ethnic Societies and Communities of Crimea (AESCC) was established in August 1995. The AESCC has been distributing its newspaper *Krymsky Dom* (The Crimean Home) since September 20, 1996. In the first issue, the newspaper's main aim was pointed out: "elimination of existing inequality in promotion of cultural heritage among all ethnic groups of Crimea, assistance of stability in inter-ethnic relations."

One of the first significant actions was the organizing of the international conference "Dialogue of Cultures: The Ethnic Realities and the Future of Crimea" (Yalta, November 1996). The International Fund "Renaissance" conducted the preparation for the conference. Among the most interesting performances for children was a New Eve celebration.

Another significant action of the AESCC was the organization of the First International Folklore Festival "Crimean Rainbow," which took place in Yalta during September 1997. It included the following programs:

- Concerts of different folklore groups representatives;
- The international research conference "Ethnic-Cultural Integration as the Basis for Interethnic Stability in Crimea";
- A national mass media holiday (during which national newspapers exhibited reports about their activities);

- Exhibitions of regional artists and applied handicrafts artists;
- An award ceremony in the sphere of national cultures;
- The opening ceremony of "Friendship Alley" in Yalta city square;
- An ethnic tales carnival in Yalta.

The main activities of the association required the establishment of a more powerful center, functioning not only as a coordination core but also as a leadership link between ethnic cultural centers and the republic's government and Supreme Council. Moreover, it was essential to support the initiative of the ethnic associations and communities of Crimea and to attract these organizations to the discussion and decision-making processes on ethnic questions and their achievement at the level of the Crimean Cabinet of Ministers.

On August 25, 1998, the decision about the establishment of the Inter-Ethnic Council (IEC) under the Cabinet of Ministers of the Autonomic Republic of Crimea (ARC) was ratified. The council is a consultative, expert-analytical body and was established in order to consider issues connected to the realization of judicial acts of the ARC as well as to supervise the fulfillment of the national rights and interests of ethnic associations and communities of Crimea.

Every registered Crimean association and community is represented in the IEC. Recently, organized republican ethnic organizations could send their delegates to the IEC. Also, scientists, researchers, specialists, and representatives of local governments can join the council.

Among the central objectives and responsibilities of the IEC were the following:

- Participating in the organization of regional programs in the sphere of national culture, projects, and decisions concerning the rights and interests of ARC folks considering themselves as determined ethnic groups;
- Consulting the Supreme Council and the government on the central problems of Crimean folks;
- Assisting in establishing cooperative activities among ethnic associations and communities;
- Organizing and conducting international seminars and schools.

The first session of the IEC took place in Partenit in October 1998. The discussions were conducted with the active support of the Adenauer Foundation. Later, in November, a session of the Presidium on the issue of cult memorials in Feodosia and interethnic relations in the region took place.

More than 25 ethnic-cultural organizations have been established since 1998. Their main objective is to encourage cultural activities toward the preservation and development of ethnic cultures. The AESCC aims to continue the friendship and cooperation among ethnic organizations of Crimea through concerted action and participation of ethnic group representatives in the ethnic-cultural activities of other ethnic groups.

The IEC has moved the established and productive cooperation of ethnic groups to the political level. The establishment of and provisions for ethnic policies of the Crimea have progressed into a common matter for all ethnic group representatives. Although the decisions of the IEC have a recommending character, they influence the economic, political, social, and cultural policies in Crimea. According to UN and OSCE representatives' evaluation, this is a significant message for the formation of ethnic tolerance and friendship among ethnic groups of Crimea. The main results of these activities are as follows:

1. The establishment of ethnic-cultural associations of Crimea not only stimulated activities on the preservation, development, and popularization of ethnic cultures and identities, but also assisted ethnic groups to gain a deeper understanding of their cultural and ethnic identity.
2. The establishment of organizations that provide the coordination for ethnic-cultural associations' activities in the sphere of culture and sport (AESCC and CRCF) led to the further development of cultural identities and formation of tolerance through collaboration and active participation in the activities of other ethnic groups. The revival of Crimea's culture turned into a common task for all ethnic associations.
3. The establishment of the IEC allowed increased cooperation of ethnic groups on a higher political level. The cooperation is directed to forming the ethnic policy in Crimea and creating a new type of tolerance, so that the region is considered a common house.

Formation of a Common National Identity

Analysis has shown that in Ukraine in 1999 there was a need to decrease ethnic tension through the creation of common values and a common view of the future of society. The creation of a common national identity and common regional—or Crimean—identity was perceived as the basis for resolving ethnic conflict and became the main goal of the project. The National Taurida University (Crimea, Ukraine) in cooperation with the Institute for Conflict Analysis and Resolution (Virginia, United States) became the center of public education in national and regional identity formation and peacebuilding on the peninsula. The activities of the project "Institute for Conflict Analysis and Resolution at George Mason University/National Tavrida University Partnership for Conflict Resolution Development in Ukraine," supported by the Bureau of Educational and Cultural Affairs, U.S. Department of State, and the NIS College and University Partnerships Program (NISCUPP), were planed to develop local capabilities for building a common identity to counteract the divisive factors that contribute to the instability in the region, to increase cooperation and stability on the Crimean peninsula in order to prevent violence, and to create the momentum necessary for economic and social recovery.

Together with the development of a new emphasis on peacebuilding and conflict resolution across National Taurida Vernadsky University's curriculum, this project included a variety of activities in ethnic communities of Crimea. Two new institutions, the Crimean Institute of Peace (CIP) and the student-led University Dispute Resolution Center, were established during the first year of the project. The CIP aimed to provide outreach in the form of consulting and training for government executives, NGOs and business leaders, educators, and community leaders; to conduct collaborative research on interethnic conflict and peacebuilding; and to facilitate the resolution of conflicts of regional or national significance. In addition, the University Dispute Resolution Center provided consultations and training to the Crimean community.

Activities in the Political Sphere
The members of the CIP and the IEC had organized discussions with representatives of multicultural ethnic associations. During several meetings, the active members of the CIP discussed multicultural politics at the regional level with Pedro Pablo Vilianueva, the councilor of the UN Development Program in Ukraine and coordinator of the UN system; Max van der Stool, the supreme commissioner of OSCE on ethnic minorities affairs; Michael Gordon Vaigant, the head of OSCE mission in Ukraine; and Sadako Ogata, the supreme commissioner of UN on refugees. Together with the participation in the organization of regional programs in the sphere of national culture, projects, and decisions concerning the rights and interests of Crimean peoples, members of the CIP provided consultations to the Supreme Council and the Crimean government on the problems of peacebuilding, national identity formation, and multiculturalism; submitted proposals and recommendations on the ethnic policy in Crimea; and assisted in the organization and conduction of international seminars and schools in the region.

Activities in Educational Sector
To achieve the goal of developing an emphasis on peacebuilding and conflict resolution across Crimean institutes of higher education, three workshops for the professors of the departments of history, psychology, sociology, linguistics, and political science from National Tavrida University, Crimean Engineering and Pedagogical Institute, Tavrida Ecological Institute and Crimean Medical Institute were conducted. The workshops included informational sessions on peace education, cross-cultural education, and the formation of national identity as well as the discussions on how to introduce these topics into the system of higher education of Crimea and into particular syllabi.

The program of the first workshop, "Cross-Cultural Adaptation," included such topics as the interrelation between culture and ethnos, cultural differences, the processes of stereotypization, biases and attitudes, analyses of ways of ethnic coexistence in Crimea, and recommendations on the formation of interethnic tolerance in university (during lectures, seminars, and practices). The program of the second workshop, "Methods of Conflict Resolution," integrated such topics as types of conflicts, negotiation processes, conversation and styles, and methods of third-party facilitation, mediation, and arbitration. The program of the third workshop, "Identity-Based Peace Building," included such topics as identity as a bases of conflict, processes of categorization, ways for tolerance, decategorization, mutual differentation, and recategorization.

The discussion with faculty who took part in the workshops showed that there was a need to confer how academics could contribute creating the culture of peace in Crimea. The follow-up workshop was conducted on the issues of peace education and peacebuilding in Crimea.

Three special educational curricula and programs on peace education, cross-cultural communication, and identity management were prepared. A training handbook on peaceful conflict management was produced and published. About 90 faculties were trained and prepared to continue teaching and training work in higher educational institutions and local communities.

The faculty of the Institute for Conflict Analysis and Resolution at George Mason University and Crimean Peace Institute at National Tavrida University conducted the Summer Training Institute for students—members of the Student Dispute Resolution Center—during the summer of 2001. This program integrated such topics as spheres of conflict, influences on conflict, processes to address conflict, negotiation/integrative solutions, conflict resolution processes and their interrelationships, intercultural interaction, culture and conflict, identity issues in conflict, mediation, facilitation, dialogue, problem-solving workshops, consensus building, and energizing community change. For six days, 20 students were involved in the interactive process of education, including lectures, discussions, games, role –plays, and other training activities.

The second round of the training institute was held at the Institute for Conflict Analysis and Resolution in October 2002. Ten students of National Tavrida University traveled to the United States for a two-week training session. The faculty of the institute conducted nine lectures and five seminars. The students also visited such organizations as the Unitcs States Institute of Peace (USIP), the Institute for Multi-Track Diplomacy, and Search for Common Ground and participated in numerous student activities at the GMU. As a follow-up activity, each of the students conducted a workshop on one topic of the training institute for students of National Tavrida University.

The conference "Intercultural Communication: Reality and Perspectives" was organized in Alushta, Crimea, Ukraine, during May 27–31, 2002. It aimed to present the research that was conducted by faculties, students, and Ph.D. students in the framework of the project. The participants discussed the problems of roots of conflict and tolerant behavior, stereotypes, attitudes among representatives of different ethnic groups, the formation of the understanding of war and peace, political activity, and civic participation. The conference included six sections: (1) national-cultural specifics of inter-language communication; (2) intercultural interaction: psychological aspects; (3) ethnic group and family: cultural roots of identity and conflict behavior; (4) social and political activeness: on the ways to tolerance building; (5) social dimensions and conflict; and (6) social identity and intergroup conflict.

More than 90 faculties, students, and Ph.D. students from Ukraine, Russia, Belarusia, Kazakhstan, and the United States participated in the conference's discussions and roundtables, as well as in the cultural program.

Activities in Communities
Leaders of ethnic communities in Crimea, who were the main target of the activities of the CIP, had considerable input into the CIP programs that would be affecting them. Leaders of Crimean Tatar, Greek, Armenian, and German communities made important recommendations in the villages Kamenca and Marino (Simferopol district) during the winter–spring training sessions in 2001. In addition, the members of the CIP regularly arranged meetings with the leaders from ethnic communities to discuss with them issues that were crucial for them but difficult to raise in their own communities. The issues that were raised served for the institute members as one of the main determinants for the activities of the CIP and the Student Center. During these meetings, the CIP members also asked participants to mark which skills from the "Skills and Abilities Checklist" they would like the members of the CIP and the Student Center to address and advance through the institute's and center's programs of training, role plays, and innovative workshops.

During the project, six trainings were conducted for ethnic leaders of different Crimean communities. The first two, "Cross-Cultural Understanding" and "Communities Management," were conducted in Simferopol in 2000.

The goals of the trainings included the following:

1. To develop the awareness about culture, traditions, values, and myths and their influence on cross-cultural communication;
2. To show the nature of such negative phenomena as stereotypes, biases, and intolerance;
3. To develop the skills of multicultural relations, dealing with differences, and understanding of others cultures;
4. The facilitate change in the community.

The next two trainings were devoted to the processes of negotiation, facilitation, and mediation in communities.

The program for these trainings included the following:

1. The development of the awareness of the range of third-party roles and their relative benefits;
2. The development of skills as third parties (listening, reframing, conflict analysis, reconciliation);
3. An increase in the awareness of cultural assumptions in conflict resolution processes and responses to intercultural conflict settings;
4. The development of knowledge about conflict resolution and peacebuilding in a local context.

The last two trainings were devoted to the analysis and resolution of identity-based conflicts. They aimed to show the role of identity in increasing conflict and the ways for tolerance. These trainings consisted of three parts:

1. Identity as a source of behavior—that is, issues of identity, system of identity, and influence of identity on our behavior;
2. Negative effects of identity on intergroup relations;
3. Ways for tolerance.

Twenty participants took part in each training session—community leaders, trainers, project coordinators, and other community catalysts from four regions of Crimea. At the end of each session, they were asked to present ideas for projects in communities. After each presentation, a discussion of the projects developed by participants was facilitated. They were encouraged to discuss how such projects can be realized in their communities. At the end of the day, they were asked to evaluate projects and define the five best projects.

Four workshops were conducted with the community and NGO leaders on negotiating the meaning of national identity (see below) and on sources for the formation of a new common identity.

A very significant feature of these workshops was a joint activity of different ethnic groups. For example, the Azerbaijani society organized several performances where poems were read in Russian, Crimean Tatar, and Azerbaijani. Representatives from different cultural societies participated in those performances.

The Crimean Armenian Society organized the open backgammon championship of Crimea where different ethnic groups were represented. The Belorussian society prepared the photo exhibition "Belarus," which was visited by two thousand people. These pictures showed various architectural memorials, unique sites of nature, and national traditions (Ivan Kupala's holiday, wedding ceremonies, christening parties, and other ceremonies). Also, an exhibition of the well-known philologist A. I. Germanovich was opened.

The Greek Society established a Greek library, which held a rich collection of literature, task-books, and tutorials. Several Greek culture performances were organized with the active assistance of the library staff. Other ethnic groups' representatives were invited to participate. Other activities included the holidays of "Holy Trinity" and "Holy Konstantin and Elena."

Under the supervision of the Jewish Society, a Sunday school and a charity fund were established. Independent of ethnic status, anyone can apply to the Open University of Israel and to mathematics courses (distance learning) at the Veitsman Institute. Distinguished students are awarded with a one-week trip to Israel.

The Italian Culture Society arranged several TV programs on traditions, different ceremonies, and Italian national cuisine.

The Karaim Society prepared several books on the following ethnic topics: "Crimean Karaims," "Karaims in Chufut-Kale," "Ceremonies and customs of Crimean Karaims," "Russian-Karaim Phrase Book," and "Karaim's Cuisine." Under the supervision of the Crimean Karaims' Association, the Scientific and Research Council, headed by Professor Yu. A. Polkanovbegan, was established.

The Czech Association organized Czech culture days in Crimea, where local and invited folk orchestras participated. Russian, Ukrainian, and Belorussian societies organized yearly festivals of Slavonic culture.

Another example of the cooperative activity of the Institute and Center members and leaders of ethnic communities is the facilitation of the dialogue among students of Taurida National Verandsky University (Simferopol, Ukraine). In May 2001, after several instances of social exclusion and violence among students with different ethnic backgrounds, the members of the Student Center were asked to facilitate dialogue in National Taurida University. In June, a training of peer mediators was conducted for Ph.D. students, which had a positive impact on interethnic relations and reduced tension among students with different ethnic backgrounds. During this training, students were not only taught to reject violence but were involved in "educating" others who provided alternatives to violent behavior. They were shown innovative forms of democratic participation and active citizenship.

Increase in Skills and Knowledge
The participants reported that the trainings were effective in increasing knowledge about cultural roots of conflict and gave them an opportunity to discuss particular projects, which could be realized in their communities. For example, the participants proposed to organize a cross-cultural holiday of spring greetings using different cultural traditions; to prepare at schools decorative pictures devoted to different cultures, with special lessons; and to organize *kermis* with dishes and articles of different cultures. The trainings also provided the basic knowledge about mediation, facilitation, and negotiation. All participants showed great interest in such methods and proposed real situations for their communities from the mediation sessions. In addition, the trainings gave the participants an insight into the role of identity in conflicts. The results of the discussions showed that all exercises and information were useful and valuable for participants.

The participants of the trainings also became active leaders of their communities and applied the new skills and knowledge in developing new projects. According to Dr. Oleg Smirnov, director of the Crimean branch of Soros Foundation, the number of project applications in communities increased three times after project activities in the areas. Moreover, the proposed projects were more advanced and received increasing support from several foundations.

The faculty at four leading Crimean institutions of higher education—National Tavrida University, Crimean Engineering and Pedagogical Institute, Tavrida Ecological Institute, and Crimean Medical Institute—incorporated new knowledge and skills on conflict resolution and cross-cultural understanding in their syllabi. More than 10 courses on political science, psychology, sociology, and history were revised to include lectures and seminars on peacebuilding and conflict management. Five new courses were developed and taught at the National Tavrida University, including "Ethnic Conflict Resolution and Peace Building," "Conflict Management," and "The Problem of Nationalism and Minorities in the Former Soviet Union."

The students who had participated in the two training institutes developed and conducted trainings and dialogues in communities and created their own programs of intervention, such as conflict resolution and self-efficacy, "Dialogue on Cultural Dimensions and Conflict" and "Training for Adolescents on Identity Formation."

The students defended two Ph.D. dissertations and more then 20 theses on the topics of social identity, conflict resolution, and peacebuilding. Among them were the following: N. Mishchenko, "The Process of Inculturation among 5- to 7-Year-Old Children in Different Ethnic Groups"; I. Kalisezhka, "Cultural Peculiarities of Self-Effectiveness"; D. Ostanina, "Ethnic Peculiarities of Personal Social Activity"; L. Kuzmyshcheva, "Cognitive Models of Ethnic Situation in the Crimea: Psychological Analysis"; O. Dzhuzha, "Perspectives of Study of Personal Ethnic Identity in Psychoanalytical Perceptions"; and T. Kalinina, "The Influence of Identity of the Effectiveness of Negotiation Process."

New Actions and Projects
The project began to initiate and involve new activities in the first stages of its implementation. Thus, the president of Division 48, "Peace Psychology," of the American Psychological Association, Dr. Leila Dane, traveled to Crimea to participate in the conference titled "Intercultural Communication" and conduct a workshop in the framework of the project. The international seminar "The Role of NGOs in Local Communities' Development" was conducted on the basis of experience in Crimean communities. Representatives from seven Eastern European countries took part in it and discussed different approaches to peacebuilding and coexistence in multiethnic communities. I received a grant from the International Research and Exchanges Broad (IREX) for developing a peace education curriculum in Ukraine.

Many activities that began during the ICAR project continued after it ended. The spring conference "Intercultural Communication" organized in Alushta, Crimea, became annual and was conducted each May from 2003 to 2005. The conferences provided opportunities to present the research conducted by faculties, students, and Ph.D. students on the topics of interethnic and intercultural relations and identity formation. Representatives from Ukraine, Russia, Belarusia, Kazakhstan, and other countries took part in these conferences.

New projects and activities were developed as a result of the project. The USIP supported the project, which included the production of training courses for workshops on conflict resolution, cross-cultural communication, negotiation, and mediation by using new technologies, with special attention to case study, conduction of scientific research, and book publishing. The book *The Ethnic Conflicts in Crimea: Finding a New Framework for Understanding Tensions in the Search for Peace* was published.

Another project, the roundtables on the ethnic problems in Crimea, was supported by the United Nations. It consisted of series of roundtables with representatives from Crimea and Ukraine (scientists, policy makers, and practitioners). The aim of this project was define the elements the conception of ethnic policy in Crimea.

The series of seminars for leaders of ethnic communities was conducted with the support of OUN. The main goal was to develop the active citizenship, values of civic duty, and values of peace and democracy. Seminars were conducted in 10 regions of Crimea. The project contributed to the establishment of a sustainable cooperation among organizations and led to the networking with other conflict prevention organizations. It also prepared trainers for work on a community level and forced the development of a healthy civil society in the region.

The CIP also participated in the research project of the Council of Europe, "Universities as a Site of Citizenship." The study of the formation of civic responsibility, the university's role in community development, and establishing the values of democracy in society was conducted.

Changes in National and Regional Identity
During –1999–2002 I conducted several studies of social identities and attitudes among representatives of ethnic minorities in Crimea. This research was supported by MacArtur Foundation, Soros Foundation, and INTAS. Four opinion surveys were conducted during the winter and spring of each year in several towns and villages in Crimea. The samples were stratified by location, number of resettlements, and rural-urban status. The survey's strata included the regions' trainings, seminars, and dialogues, and the project took place in the towns of Simferopol and Alushta and the counties of Bahchisarai (including the city of Bahchisarai), Dzhankoy, and Sudak. Every study involved nearly 500 Russians and 500 Crimean Tatars distributed across these locations in equal proportions. In 1999, 42 percent of the participants were male and 58 percent female; 39 percent were between 20 and 30 years old, 31 percent between 30 and 45, 20 percent between 45 and 60, and 10 percent above 60; and 55 percent were residents of towns and 45 percent those of villages. In 2000, 44 percent of the participants were male and 56 percent female; 36 percent were between 20 and 30 years old, 32 percent between 30 and 45, 22 percent between 45 and 60, and 10 percent above 60; and 51 percent were residents of towns and 49 percent those of villages. In 2001, 43 percent of the participants were male and 57 percent female; 41 percent were between 20 and 30 years old, 30 percent between 30 and 45, 18 percent between 45 and 60, and 11 percent above 60; and 60 percent were residents of towns and 40 percent those of villages. In 2002, 48 percent of the participants were male and 52 percent female; 40 percent were

between 20 and 30 years old, 31 percent between 30 and 45, 20 percent between 45 and 60, and 9 percent above 60; and 53 percent were residents of towns and 47 percent those of villages. Participation was voluntary. The respondents were run individually. They were given a questionnaire and were asked to select answers from a list, and they filled out the questionnaire in about 20 to 30 minutes.

Every survey included statements to measure the salience of national ethnic and regional identity: national identity by three questions such as "It is important for me to be a citizen of Ukraine," to be assessed on a five-point scale from "disagree" to "agree"; and ethnic identity by three questions such as "It is important for me to be a representative of my ethnic group," to be answered on a five-point scale from "disagree" to "agree."

The analysis of the dynamic of social identity among Russians and Crimean Tatars shows that the salience of national identity increased during the four years of the project. Thus, in 1999, only 3 percent of Russians considered this identity important, and in 2002, more than one-third of them stressed the significance of belonging to the Ukrainian nation. In 1999, 20 percent of Crimean Tatars had a salient national identity, and in 2002, more than half of them considered this identity very important. The salience of regional identity among Russians and Crimean Tatars also increased during 1999–2002. The percentage of Russians with salient regional identity increased from 49 in 1999 to 85 in 2002.

In 1999, nearly 10 percent of Russians denied the importance of their belonging to Crimean people; in 2002, less than 1 percent of them shared such an attitude. For Crimean Tatars, the dynamic of regional identity is weaker: the percentage of Crimean Tatars with a salient regional identity increased from 67 in 1999 to 77 in 2002.

The project "Institute for Conflict Analysis and Resolution at George Mason University/National Tavrida University Partnership for Conflict Resolution Development in Ukraine" concentrated on a very important dimension of the peacebuilding process: developing local capabilities for building a common identity and increasing cooperation and stability on the Crimean peninsula. This stage of the process was built on the assessment of previous activities, the existing capacity to deal with ethnic conflicts, and theoretical and practical approaches to identity formation. Through the development of new knowledge and skills, transformation of attitudes and stereotypes, and formation of common national and regional identities, the project counteracted the divisive factors that were contributing to the instability in Crimea. The establishment of new institutions and development of new actions and projects promoted the sustainability of the project.

The CIP remains active after the project has officially ended; it aims to further facilitate the friendship and cooperation among ethnic communities in Crimea. Although the institute can provide only recommendations to the government, they influence the economic, political, social, and cultural policy in Crimea. According to the UN and OSCE representatives' evaluation, its activity had a significant message for the formation of ethnic tolerance and friendship among ethnic groups of Crimea. Undoubtedly, the absence of serious ethnic conflicts in Crimea is a merit of the project and the CIP.

Negotiation of National Identity

The negotiation of national identity aims at bringing together previously incompatible identities into a common group concept that would be mutually acceptable and would connect all groups and parties. As Kelman (1997b, 2001) stresses, the possibility to negotiate and change identity rests on two reasons: (1) identities are not zero-sum concepts like territory and resources; and (2) as social constructs, they can be reconstructed and redefined. "In fact, the reconstruction of identity is a regular, ongoing process in the life of any national group. Identities are commonly reconstructed, sometimes gradually and sometimes radically, as historical circumstances change, crises emerge, opportunities present themselves, or new elites come to fore" (Kelman 1997b:338).

Undoubtedly, national identities contain some core elements that could not be negotiated: sense of peoplehood, attachment to the land, confidence in history, and commitment to culture and religion (Kelman 2001). Nevertheless, only a few central elements can be reconsidered and redefined in order to protect the essential components of identity. To reduce intergroup tensions and develop a common understanding, these elements can be negotiated and discussed during specially organized workshops.

One of the basic assumptions of the theory of protracted identity-based conflict is that basic needs are not negotiable and that people need universal justice. In reality, basic needs and conceptions of justice are also identity-based categories, and their meaning depends on the meaning and structure of ingroup identity. Security, freedom, and community have different senses and are perceived in various ways among people with different social identities. Even for the same person, a basic human need can have a different meaning depending on what social identity would be most salient at the moment.

The concepts of justice also differ among groups. For some, justice means revenge and prosecution of perpetrators; for others, it suggests reimbursement in terms of money, contributions, or labor. Some people can be satisfied with truth and reconciliation committees where people who have committed violence would confess and admit their crimes, and some communities are ready to forgive the perpetrators if they show their commitment to peace. The study conducted in Uganda (Pham et al. 2005) showed that four groups within the country (the Gulu, Kitgum, Lira, and Soroti regions) have different perceptions of justice. Nearly half of the respondents perceived "reconciliation" as "forgiveness" (52%). Thirty-one percent defined justice as trials; however, the respondents in Soroti showed only 15 percent agreement with this statement. For one-third (35%) of them in Soroti, justice meant reconciliation, while only 12 percent and 3 percent of Gulu and Kitgum, respectively, stated that justice was reconciliation. Eleven percent of all respondents associated justice with "truth and fairness," while 22 percent of the respondents in Kitgum considered justice as truth and fairness.

Out of all respondents, 24 percent considered that reconciliation required confession, while 23 percent said that reconciliation was connected with "togetherness, unity, and peace." Only 9 percent associated reconciliation with a traditional ceremony. The understanding of human rights also varied among the respondents: 29 percent said that human rights meant a "life with peace and security and without fear"; more than one-third of them mentioned freedom of speech, 21 percent mentioned dignity, 18 percent noted socioeconomic rights, 16 percent cited justice, and 12 percent mentioned freedom of movement.

The understanding of differences in conceptions of justice and reconciliation and basic human needs can help to reconcile different identities, even conflictual ones. Identity negotiation workshop includes forming a dialogue around differences in the meaning of these basic conceptions and developing ways for their accommodation. Because of variations in perceptions of basic human needs and justice among different groups, it is possible to negotiate these concepts among groups in order to develop a new common identity or reconcile existing identities.

The informal identity negotiation process in a workshop setting has been described by Kelman (1982, 1997b, 2001, 2004) as an informal, unofficial process of give-and-take among groups whose ideas about their respective national identities conflict with one another. In this chapter I describe negotiation processes that are designed to create a new common identity or reconcile conflictual identities. Such a practice can be organized into different forms, ranging from mediation between ethnic groups in the process of self-determination of a new nation to the redefinition of identity through reworking history, and from negotiations among political leaders to discussion workshops in communities.

Kelman (2001) describes negotiation of national identity in the –Israeli-Palestinian conflict. He stresses that each group perceives relationship to land and history, the defining element of identity, as its exclusive right and considers claims of another group as illegitimate. The parties have to "accept the possibility that certain elements of identity may be *shared* with the other, acknowledging that the other also has a profound attachment to the land, anchored in authentic historical ties to it" (Kelman 2001:193). Sharing the land requires developing the common elements of identity and understanding that land can belong to two groups. As Kelman shows, the Israelis and Palestinians began to accept a shared concept of land but failed to perceive Jerusalem as a mutual element of their identities.

The example of Morocco shows that national identity can be negotiated in two ways: through an exchange within the new nationalist elites and by stressing characteristics and traditions common for all groups. A vision of the national identity of the Moroccans was developed during the negotiation led by the king as a compromise among various visions of the elite (for a more in-depth analysis, see Mezran 2001).

One of the most important problems for the new independent Morocco was the confrontation between the mainly urban Arab Istiqlal and the Berber

tribes of the interior. During its period of dominance, the Istiqlal government forced the assimilation of the Berbers into a larger Moroccan identity.
It was argued that a Berber was a man who had never been to school and
that the Istiqlal goal was to change the Berbers' identity, language, and way
of life to fit its Arab nationalist model. During 1956–1958, the Istiqlal Party
developed policies to impose a dominant Arab identity on the Berber parts
of Morocco. All the local leadership posts were held by the Arabs; the Berber
college, established by the French, was transferred into an ordinary school;
Berber-language broadcasts were prohibited. These Istiqlal policies led to
the Berber uprisings against the Arab-dominated government and policies.

King Mohammed realized the importance of the common concept of
Morocco's national identity and decided to act as a mediator who facilitated agreement around the various identity concepts. The meaning of
national identity varied among several parties, including the Arabist party,
the Islamicist conservative part of the Istiqlal, the Democratic Party, the
Berberist socialism of the Popular Movement, and the secular republican
Marxism. Instead of acting as a party in conflict over identity, Mohammed V
announced himself a national leader and symbol of national unity. He aimed
to develop a shared national identity and unite fragmented elites under a
monarchy. To force the negotiation process, the king posited himself as a
mediator among various competing visions and interests.

A series of meetings with the leaders of all groups were organized to
discuss the vision of national identity and find the ground for the final
agreement. The basic concept of national identity included three main
identity-forming beliefs: Islam, Arabism, and Moroccanism. Moroccan
Islam became the central component of the uniting national identity.
Mohammed V stressed the strong connection between Islamic and democratic principles, the "innovative" role of Islam in society, and its function as
a basis for national identity.

To mediate differences between the Arabist Istiqlal and the Berberist
Popular Movement, the king developed the idea of Moroccan Arabism,
stressing that the Moroccans for their vast majority are not pure Arabs but
Berbers Arabized. As a basis for territorial nationalism that would unite
different elites, Mohammed V developed the conception of Moroccanism
(Marocaineté). This national territorial idea became the main content of
Moroccan national identity that overarched, but never denied, local Arab or
Berber, tribal or urban identities.

Using these three conceptions, King Mohammed was developing agreement between all the rival groups. He conducted his negotiations on the
basis of an "issue" approach, approaching the development of a common
identity by discussing single issues. As Mezran (2001) describes,

> For example, in dealing with the democratization issue, he [the King] acted in
> such a way as to appease each party within this framework while asking con-
> cessions of others. Thus, in exchange for their consent to the formation of a
> National Consultative Assembly, the King offered to the left wing of the Istiqlal

a wide agrarian reform. To the Berbers, after secret negotiations the monarch offered recognition of their political party, the Popular Movement. On another table, in exchange for their acquiescence on the Berber issue, the King offered to the Istiqlal the implementation of a wide campaign of Arabization through the school development program to be held in Arabic and to the Berbers wider representation in the army and in the bureaucracy.

(156)

Compromises were not negotiated with oppositions and served as a tool for reaching the agreement.

Thus, while negotiating a new national identity, the king of Morocco invented the concept of "Arabized Berbers" and satisfied the most important concerns of Arabs (such as teaching Arabic in all schools) and Berbers (recognition of political party) within the framework of a unified nation (Byman 1997; Mezran 2001).

The negotiation of identities is also an important part of the process developing peaceful coexistence between former adversaries. Conflictual identities have to be redefined to accept a new type of intergroup relations and to accept multiple meanings of the events. The cooperation of both parties and the step-by-step process of re-creating identity characterized the negotiations between France and Germany. These negotiations focused on overcoming the conflictual past and accentuating their commonalities through a process of mutual reidentification: "brothers who have engaged in a long fratricidal war" (for a more in-depth analysis, see Rosoux 2001).

For centuries, French and German people had negative stereotypes and perceived each other as unfriendly and aggressive. As Rosoux (2001) stresses, in the last century, the French associated the German and Prussian identities with "barbarism" that symbolized Protestantism in the eyes of Catholics and militarism for Republicans. The French considered the Germans physically and intellectually inferior as well as morally uncivilized. The Germans accused the French of lacking fundamental public and private ethical norms and religious beliefs. The Germans perceived their nation as dynamic and prosperous, while describing France as weak and decadent. The mutual hatred and opposition were developed through numerous wars and conflicts. These negative perceptions were a significant part of each nation's identity and stressed opposition and differences between the two nations.

In 1958, Charles de Gaulle and Konrad Adenauer decided to redefine the relationship between France and Germany. This required a reconsideration of perceptions and memories and reconstruction of their common past, as well as the development of the basis for a common interpretation of future events and collaboration. This process included the acceptance of complexity and all contradictions of the past and the understanding of the other party's meaning of events and actions.

In 1958–1962, de Gaulle and Adenauer had several meetings aimed to overcome negative perceptions rooted in past events and to archive reconciliation. They stressed that former enemies are determined to become friends.

One of the most important steps was understanding and officially recognizing the sufferings of the other nation. The new changes in the German national identity included confrontation of the past and acceptance of responsibility for the most difficult episodes of national history. De Gaulle also recognized the negative actions of France and described Germany as a "great nation." Both nations decided not to emphasize the conflictual past, but highlight the solidarity that also characterized relations between them. Past wars and conflicts between the French and Germans were redefined as a common past of collective sufferings, and both nations became brothers that mutually endured a common tragedy.

In Ukraine, I conducted workshops with community and NGO leaders on negotiating the meaning of national identity and sources for the formation of a new common identity. The participants discussed the values, needs, and traditions of each ethnic group and the possibilities for the creation of a common identity concept that would satisfy and respect the values and needs of all groups. By using the appreciative inquiry method, I encouraged the participants to think about the possible actions for national identity formation. A catalogue of such actions was created and several activities were developed in communities. Among them were celebrations of holidays of other ethnic groups, the Common Culture festival, and the Day of Crimea. One of the most amazing initiatives was the creation of a collage of Common Culture elements that represented different cultures of Crimea—for example, scarves, plates, toys—in several schools. Students drew different objects that characterized their culture and then created a wall collage that included all the ethnic groups of Ukraine.

Identity Reconstruction Workshops

Another approach for reducing the salience of identity and destabilizing "positive We–negative They" perceptions and behavior is through identity restructuring workshops. These workshops aim to transform dominant identities into multiple identities with polymodal meanings. The structure of narratives, based on the perception of "They as an enemy" and reflecting negative attitudes, feeling, and stereotypes, can be replaced by a nonoppositional structure rooted in a nonviolent self-image.

The first step for identity reconstruction includes increasing the awareness about the role of identity in conflicts, We-They perception, and collective axiology, which lead to violence. The stories of different conflicts and violent actions, analyzed through the prism of identity, provide insights about salience and dominance of identity, changes and destruction of perception, misbalances and projective axiologies, and accepted or expected ferocious behaviors. It is important that conflicts and vicious situations discussed at this stage of the workshop be dissimilar to the conflict that participants involved in. Similar events and situations will provoke comparison, develop analogies, and strengthen negative attitudes and emotions. The more distinctive the stories, the lower the resistance to understand wrong perceptions and actions. Thus, in Crimea, where conflict developed between Muslim Crimean Tatars and Orthodox Russians, the discussion of conflict in Bosnia exacerbates strong negative feelings and aggravates aggressive attitudes toward other ethnic groups (e.g., see Chapter 7). The discussion of conflicts perceived as very distinctive from the Crimean situation, such as discriminative practices in the Dominican Republic and violence in Sudan and Rwanda, increases the understanding of roots of vicious actions and alleviates changes in perceptions, leading to the recognition of ferocious behaviors of ingroups.

The recognition of ingroup violent actions and human rights of outgroups poses a threat to ingroup identity, which rests on the idea of positive We–negative They. The acknowledgment of negative ingroup actions requires reviewing and reconceptualization of ingroup identity that always invokes strong resistance. Ingroup members have a strong aspiration to defend the positive self-image and defy accepting negative information that can destroy it. Stressing other important components of the meaning of identity, such as cultural heritage, deep traditions, history of peaceful coexistence with other groups, and so on, can help preserve a high level of self-esteem and ingroup pride.

Such narrative intervention has to emphasize the positive features in the self-description of an ingroup, such as "peaceful people," "value of tolerance," "open-mindedness and understanding," and "pleasure of forgiveness." These images always exist in the self-portrayal of all people and serve as powerful sources for self-esteem and pride. By stressing peaceful images of the ingroup, an intervener can provoke supporting narratives that describe the ingroup's peaceful history and glory and positive situations in interethnic relations. Such storytelling by different people will reinforce them through complementary ideas and constructive character. The positive emotions produced during the workshops will strengthen the formation of peaceful self-concepts, with an emphasis on tolerance, reconciliation, and goodwill.

To turn such models into positive attitudes and actions, the intervener has to take the next step: form a common, overarching identity that can lead to the de-escalation of conflict. The common or shared identities can reduce intergroup hostility by minimizing the attention to ethnic/racial/religious differences and thinking of themselves as "one unit." The sources for the basis of an overarching identity can be found in the common territorial position, national ideas, community problems, and so forth. By asking questions about the present and future positive developments and the possibilities of collaboration with others, the intervener can reinforce the formation of a common identity. The intervener's task is to facilitate the production of the narratives of productive partnership, which are based on peaceful concepts of the ingroup and which emphasize possible positive images of others.

The formation of a new common identity is possible only if ingroup members do not perceive any danger or threat to their primary identity (ethnic/racial/religious) from a new overarching identity. If values, core ideas, or new identity needs contradict the possible (perceived) values and ideas of the existing identity, a new circle of violence can begin. The intervener has to construct the perception and concept of the new common identity very carefully, using narratives of existing collaboration and situations of successful teamwork. By asking such questions as What can we do together to make our future better? and What can we do for our children? practitioners will change the emphasis of narratives from opposition in the past to mutual under-standing and responsibilities, and mutual defending of human rights among former enemies. In this case, the concepts of a peaceful ingroup and of a new "We-ness" will be developed simultaneously and strengthen each other.

CONCLUSION

Thus, the formation of a peaceful national identity requires a set of actions that includes increasing identity awareness, reconceptualizing salient identi-ties, negotiating a common identity concept, and forming a civic and multi-cultural meaning of national identity. The construction and understanding of national identity would be created by the facilitation and mediation of *ongoing dialogue* between representatives of ethnic and religious groups. A new common identity would include elements of the particular ethnic and religious identities and common goals, values, and aims. It would be based on the reconciliation of past grievances, with an emphasis on the future mutual development and peaceful coexistence within the state. Dialogue about the meaning and content of a common national identity includes the planning and discussion of specific actions for specific regions that must be accomplished for a successful formation of this identity. The formation of a national identity with an emphasis on multicultural and civic meanings will help to construct society with (1) equal rights for all ethnic groups and resources to maintain their ethnic culture and (2) a distinctive nonethnic civic culture with peaceful coexistence and civic responsibility among all citizens.

BIBLIOGRAPHY

Abbott, A. 1995. Things of Boundaries. *Social Research* 62: 857–882.

Abrams, D. 1999. Social Identity, Social Cognition, and the Self: The Flexibility and Stability of Self-Categorization. In *Social Identity and Social Cognition*, ed. D. Abrams and M. Hogg, 197–229. Oxford: Blackwell.

Ackerman, N., ed. 1970. Family Therapy in Transition. *International Psychiatry Clinics* 7 (14).

Adler, H. G. 1994. "Mischling" Attempts to Fight for His Rights. In *Displacements: Cultural Identities in Question*, ed. A. Bammer, 205–215. Bloomington, IN: Indiana University Press.

Adorno, T. W. 1950. The Authoritarian Personality. New York: Harper.

Ageev V. S. 1990. *Mezhgrupovie Bzaimodeistvie* [Intergroup interaction]. Moskow: Academic Press.

Ageev, V. S., and Tolmasova, A. K. 2000. *Teoria Social'noi Identichnosti* [Theory of social identity]. Samara: Bahrad M.

Aharpour, S. 1997. Functions of Identification: Group Differences and Their Implications for Intergroup Attitudes. *Applied Psychology* 48: 185–206.

Allen, V. L., and Wilder, D. A. 1975. Categorization, Belief Similarity, and Group Discrimination. *Journal of Personality and Social Psychology* 32: 971–977.

Allport, G. W. 1954. *The Nature of Prejudice.* Cambridge, MA: Addison-Wesley.

Alwin, D. F., Cohen, R. L., and Newcomb, T. M. 1992. *Political Attitudes over the Life Span: The Bennington Women after Fifty Years.* Madison, WI: University of Wisconsin Press.

Anderson, B. 1991. *Imagined Communities: Reflections on the Origin and Spread of Nationalism.* Rev. ed. London and New York: Verso.

Arcuri, L. 1982. Three Patterns of Social Categorization in Attribution Memory. *European Journal of Social Psychology* 12: 271–282.

Augoustinos, M., Ahrens, C., and Innes, J. M. 1994. Stereotypes and Prejudice: The Australian Experience. *British Journal of Social Psychology* 33: 125–141.

Azar, E. E. 1990. *The Management of Protracted Social Conflict.* Hampshire, UK: Dartmouth.

———. 1991. The Analysis and Management of Protracted Social Conflict. In *The Psychodynamics of International Relationships*, vol. 2, ed. J. Volkan, J. Montville, and D. Julius, 93–120. Lexington, MA: D. C. Heath.

Barth, F., ed. 1969. *Ethnic Groups and Boundaries: The Social Organization of Culture Difference.* Boston: Little, Brown.

Barth, F. 1981. *Process and Form in Social Life.* London: Routledge and Kegan Paul.

Bar-Tal, D. 1990. *Group Beliefs: A Conception for Analyzing Group Structure, Processes, and Behavior.* New York: Springer Verlag.

———. 1998. Group Beliefs as an Expression of Social Identity. In *Social Identity*, ed. S. Worchel, J. F. Morales, D. Paez, and J. C. Deschamps, 93–113. London: Sage.

Bauman, Z. 1999. *In Search of Politics*. Cambridge: Polity Press.
_____. 2002. *The Individualized Society*. Oxford: Blackwell.
Berry, J., Kim, U., Power, S., Young, M., and Bujaki, M. 1989. Acculturation Attitudes in Plural Societies. *Applied Psychology* 38: 185–206.
Bilinsky Y. 1999. *Endgame in NATO's Enlargement: The Baltic States and Ukraine*. Westport, CT: Praeger.
Billig, M., and Tajfel, H. 1973. Social Categorization and Similarity in Intergroup Behavior. *European Journal of Social Psychology* 3: 27–52.
Blumer, H. 1958. Race Prejudice as a Sense of Group Position. *Pacific Sociological Review* 1: 3–7.
Bobo, L. 1999. Prejudice as Group Position: Micro-foundations of a Sociological Approach to Racism and Race Relations. *Journal of Social Issues* 55: 445–472.
Bobo, L., and Hutchings, V. 1996. Perceptions of Racial Group Competition: Extending Blumer's Theory of Group Position to a Multiracial Social Context. *American Sociological Review* 61: 951–972.
Booth, K. 1979. *Strategy and Ethnocentrism*. New York: Holmes and Meier.
Branscombe, N., and Wann, D. 1994. Collective Self-Esteem Consequences of Outgroup Derogation When a Valued Social Identity Is on Trial. *European Journal of Social psychology* 2: 641–657.
Breakwell, G. M. 2004. Identity Change in the Context of the Growing Influence of European Union Institutions. In *Transnational Identities: Becoming European in the EU*, ed. R. K. Herrmann, T. Risse, and M. B. Brewer. Lanham, MD: Rowman and Littlefield.
Brewer, M. B. 1991. The Social Self: Being Same and Different at the Same Time. *Personality and Social Psychology Bulletin* 17: 475–482.
_____. 1996. When Contact Is Not Enough: Social Identity and Intergroup Cooperation. *International Journal of Intercultural Relations* 2: 291–303.
_____. 2000. Superordinate Goals versus Superordinate Identity as Bases of Intergroup Cooperation. In *Social Identity Processes*, ed. D. Capozza and R. Brown. London: Sage.
_____. 2001. The Many Faces of Social Identity: Implications for Political Psychology. *Political Psychology* 22: 115–126.
_____. 2003. *Intergroup Relations*. 2nd ed. Berkshire, UK: Open University Press.
Brewer, M. B., and Weber, J. G. 1994. Self-Evaluation Effects of Interpersonal versus Intergroup Social Comparison. *Journal of Personality and Social Psychology* 66: 268–275.
Brewer, M. B., and Gardner, W. 1996. Who Is This We? Levels of Collective Identity and Self Representations. *Journal of Personality and Social Psychology* 71 (1): 83–93.
Brewer, M. B., and Miller, N. 1984. Beyond the Contact Hypothesis: Theoretical Perspectives on Desegregation. In *Groups in Contact: The Psychology of Desegregation*, ed. N. Miler and M. Brewer, 281–302. Orlando, FL: Academic Press.
Brewer, M. B., and Silver, M. 1978. In-group Bias as a Function of Task Characteristics. *European Journal of Social Psychology* 8: 393–400.
Brigham, J. C. 1971. Ethnic Stereotypes. *Psychological Bulletin*, 76: 15–33.
Brown, D. 2007. Ethnic Conflict and Civic Nationalism: A Model. In *Identity Matter*, ed. J. L. Peacock, P. Thornton, and P. Inman. Oxford: Berghahn.
Brown, R. 2000. Social Identity Theory: Past Achievements, Current Problems and Future Challenges. *European Journal of Social Psychology* 30: 746–778.

Brown, R., and Capozza, D. 2000. Social Identity Theory in Retrospect and Prospect. In *Social Identity Processes,* ed. D. Capozza and R. Brown. London: Sage.

Brown, R., Hinkle, S., Ely, P. G., Maras, P., and Taylor, L. A. 1992. Recognizing Group Diversity: Individualist-Collectivist and Autonomous-Relational Social Orientations and Their Implications for Intergroup Process. *British Journal of Social Psychology* 31: 327–342.

Brubaker, R. 1996. *Nationalism Reframed: Nationhood and the National Question in the New Europe.* Cambridge: Cambridge University Press.

Brubaker, R., and Cooper, F. 2000. Beyond "Identity." *Theory and Society* 29: 1–47.

Buadaeng, K. 2007. Ethnic Identities of the Karen Peoples in Burma and Thailand. In *Identity matters,* ed. J. L. Peacock, P. Thornton, and P. Inman Oxford: Berghahn.

Burton, J. W. 1987. *Resolving Deep-Rooted Conflict: A Handbook.* Lanham, MD: University Press of America.

––––––––––––. 1990. *Conflict: Resolution and Prevention.* New York: St. Martin's Press.

Butler, J. 1990. *Gender Trouble.* New York: Routledge.

Byman, D. 1997. Explaining Ethnic Peace in Morocco. *Harvard Middle Eastern and Islamic Review* 4: 1–29.

Canidu, M., and Reggiori, C. 2002. Discrimination of Low-Status Outgroup: The Role of Ingroup Threat. *European Journal of Social Psychology* 32: 501–515.

Carrigan, A. 1995. Chiapas: The First Post-modern Revolution. *Fletcher Forum* 19: 1–87.

Cheldelin, S. 2006. Gender and Violence: Redefining the Moral Ground. In *Identity, Morality and Threat,* ed. D. Rothbart and K. V. Korostelina, 279–300. Lexington, MA: Lexington Books.

Citrin, J., Reingold, B., and Green, D. P. 1990. American Identity and the Politics of Ethnic Change. *Journal of Politics* 5: 1124–1154.

Citrin, J., Wong, C., and Duff, B. 2000. The Meaning of American Identity: Patterns of Ethnic Conflict and Consensus. In *Social Identity, Intergroup Conflict and Conflict Resolution,* ed. R. Ashmore et al. New York: Oxford University Press.

Clark, K. G., and Clark, M. L. 1939. The Development of Consciousness of Self and the Emergence of Racial Identification in Negro Preschool Children. *Journal of Social Psychology* 1: 591–599.

Clary, E. G., Snyder, M., Ridge, R. D., Copeland, J., and Stukas, A. A. 1998. Understanding and Assessing the Motivations of Volunteers: A Functional Approach. *Journal of Personality and Social Psychology* 74: 1516–1530.

Cohen, A. P. 1985. *The Symbolic Construction of Community.* London, Tavistock.

––––––––––––. 1986. Belonging: The Experience of Culture. In *Symbolising Boundaries: Identity and Diversity in British Cultures,* ed. A. P. Cohen, 1–17. Manchester: Manchester University Press.

Collins, A. 1997. *The Security Dilemma and the End of the Cold War.* Edinburgh: Keele University Press.

––––––––––––. 1998. The Ethnic Security Dilemma: Evidence from Malaysia. Contemporary Southeast Asia. *A Journal of International and Strategic Affairs* 20 (3): 261–278.

Conover, P. J. 1988. The Role of Social Groups in Political Thinking. *British Journal of Political Science* 18: 51–76.

Cook, S. W. 1985. Experimenting on Social Issues: The Case of School Desegration. *American Psychologist* 40: 452–460.

Corneille, O., Huart, J., Becquart, E., and Brédart, S. 2004. When Memory Shifts Towards More Typical Category Exemplars: Accentuation Effects in the Recollection of Ethnically Ambiguous Faces. *Journal of Personality and Social Psychology* 86: 236–250.

Crano, W. D. 1983. Assumed Consensus of Attitudes: The Effect of Vested Interest. *Personality and Social Psychology Bulletin* 9: 597–608.

Crenshaw, K. 1998. Demarginalizing the Intersection of Race and Sex: A Black Feminist Critique of Antidiscrimination Doctrine, Feminist Theory, and Antiracist Politics. In *Feminism and Politics*, ed. A. Phillips, 9–36. New York: Oxford University Press.

Crighton, E., and MacIver, M. 1991. The Evolution of Protracted Ethnic Conflict: Group Dominance and Political Underdevelopment in Northern Ireland and Lebanon. *Comparative Politics* 2: 127–142.

Crisp, R. J., and Hewstone, M. 2000. Multiple Categorization and Social Identity. In *Social Identity Processes*, ed. D. Capozza and R. Brown London: Sage.

Crocker, J., and Luhtanen, R. 1990. Collective Self-Esteem and Ingroup Bias. *Journal of Personality and Social Psychology* 58: 323–338.

Crosby, F. 1984. The Denial of Personal Discrimination. *American Behavioral Scientist* 27: 371–386.

Cross, W. E. 1991. *Shades of Black: Diversity in African-American Identity.* Philadelphia: Temple University Press.

Davis, J. A. 1959. A Formal Interpretation of the Theory of Relative Deprivation. *Sociometry* 22: 280–296.

Deaux, K. 1993. Reconstructing Social Identity. *Personality and Social Psychology Bulletin* 19: 4–12.

_____. 1996. Social Identification. In *Social Psychology: Handbook of Basic Principles*, ed. E. T. Higgins and A. Kruglanski. 777–798. New York: Guilford.

_____. 2000. Models, Meaning and Motivations. In *Social Identity Processes*, ed. D. Capozza and R. Brown London: Sage.

Deaux, K., Reid, A., Mizrahi, K., and Cotting, D. 1999. Connecting the Person to the Social: The Functions of Identification. In *The Psychology of the Social Self*, ed. T. Tyler, R. Kramer and O. John, 91–113 Mahwah: Lawrence Erlbaum Associates.

Deaux, K., Reid, A., Mizrahi, K., and Ethier, K. A. 1995. Parameters of Social Identity. *Journal of Personality and Social Psychology* 68: 280–291.

Deschamps, J. C., and Devos, T. 1998. Regarding the Relationship Between Social Identity and Personal Identity. In *Identity: Social International Perspective*, ed. S. Worchel , J. F. Morales, D. Paez, J. Deschamps, 1–12. London: Sage.

Deschamps, J. C., and Doise, W. 1978. Crossed Category Memberships in Intergroup Relations. In *Differentiations between Social Groups: Studies in the Social Psychology of Intergroup Relations*, ed. H. Tajfel, 141–158. London: Academic Press.

Devine, P. G. 1989. Stereotypes and Prejudice: Their Automatic and Controlled Components. *Journal of Personality and Social Psychology* 56: 5–18.

Doise, W., and Sinclair, A. 1973. The Categorization Process in Intergroup Relations. *European Journal of Social Psychology* 3: 145–157.

Dovidio, J. F., and Gaertner, S. L. 2004. Aversive Racism. In *Advances in Experimental Social Psychology* 36, ed. M. P. Zanna, 1–51. San Diego: Academic Press.

Dovidio, J. F., Brigham, J. C., Johnson, B. T., and Gaertner, S. L. 1996. Stereotyping, Prejudice and Discrimination: Another Look. In *Stereotypes and Stereotyping*, ed. C. N. Macrae, C. Stangor, and M. Hewstone, 276–319. New York: Guilford.

Druckman, D. 1994. Nationalism, Patriotism and Group Loyalty: A Social Psychological Perspective. *Mershon International Studies Review* 38: 43–68.

Druckman, D., and Korostelina, K. V. 2001. Negotiating Ethnic Conflicts: Some Results of the Role-Play Simulation. Unpublished Paper, National Taurida University.

Duckitt, J. H. 1989. Authoritarianism and Group Identification: A New View of an Old Construct. *Political Psychology* 10: 63–84.

Duckitt, J. H., and Mphuthing, T. 1998. Group Identification and Intergroup Attitudes: A Longitudinal Analysis in South Africa. *Journal of Personality and Social Psychology* 74: 80–85.

Durkheim, E. 1969. *The Elementary Forms of the Religious Life.* New York: Free Press. (Originally published in 1915.)

Eagly, A. H., and Chaiken, S. 1993. *The Psychology of Attitudes.* San Diego: Harcourt Brace.

Ellemers, N., Kortekaas, P., and Ouwerkerk, J. W. 1999. Perceived Intragroup Variability as a Function of Group Status and Identification. *Journal of Experimental Social Psychology* 31: 410–436.

Ellemers, N., Spears, R., and Doosje, B. 1997. Sticking Together or Falling Apart: Ingroup Identification as a Psychological Determinant of Group Commitment versus Individual Mobility. *Journal of Personality and Social Psychology* 72: 617–626.

Ellemers, N., Wilke, H., and Van Knippenberg, A. 1993. Effects of the Legitimacy of Low Group or Individual Status on Individual and Collective Identity and Enhancement Strategies. *Journal of Personality and Social Psychology* 64: 766–758.

Ellemers, N., Doosje, B. J., van Knippenberg, A., and Wilke, H. 1992. Status Protection in High Status Minority Groups. *European Journal of Social Psychology* 22: 123–140.

Eriksen, T. H. 2001. Ethnic Identity, National Identity and Intergroup Conflict: The Significance of Personal Experiences. In *Social Identity, Intergroup Conflict, and Conflict Reduction,* ed. Ashmore, Jussim, Wilder. New York: Oxford University Press.

Erikson, E. H. 1974. *Identity: Youth and Crisis.* London: Faber and Faber.

Espinoza, J. A., and Garza, R. T. 1985. Social Group Salience and Interethnic Cooperation. *Journal of Experimental Social Psychology* 21: 380–392.

Esses, V. M., Haddock, G., and Zanna, M. P. 1993. Values, Stereotypes, and Emotions as Determinants of Intergroup Attitudes. In *Affect, Cognition, and Stereotyping: Interactive Processes in Group Perception,* ed. D. M. Mackie and D. L. Hamilton, 137–166. New York: Academic Press.

Ethier, K. A., and Deaux, K. 1994. Negotiating Social Identity When Contexts Change: Maintaining Identification and Responding to Threat. *Journal of Personality and Social Psychology* 67: 243–251.

Fenton, S. 2004. Beyond Ethnicity: The Global Comparative Analysis of Ethnic Conflict. *International Journal of Comparative Sociology* 3–4: 179–194.

Feshbach, S. 1987. Individual Aggression, National Attachment, and the Search for Peace. *Aggressive Behavior* 5: 315–326.

Ferdman, B. M. 1995. Cultural Identity and Diversity in Organizations. In *Diversity in Organizations: New Perspectives for Changing Workplace,* ed. M. Cheremers, S. Oskamp, and M. Costanzo, 37–61. London: Sage.

Festinger, L. 1957. *A Theory of Cognitive Dissonance,* Stanford University, Stanford, CA.

Fisher, R. 1997. *Interactive Conflict Resolution.* Syracuse, NY: Syracuse University Press.

Fiske, S. T., and Taylor, S. E. 1991. *Social Cognition.* 2nd ed. New York: McGraw-Hill.

Freud, S. 1959. *Group Psychology and Analysis of Ego.* London: Institute of Psycho-Analysis.

Friedman, J. 1999. The Hybridization of Roots and the Abhorrence of the Bush. In *Spaces of Culture,* ed. M. Featherstone, and S. Lash. London: Sage.

Gaertner, S. L., Dovidio, J. F., Nier, J. A., Ward, C. M., and Banker, B. S. 2000. The Common Ingroup Identity Model for Reducing Intergroup Bias: Progress and Challenges. In *Social Identity Processes,* ed. D. Capozza, and R. Brown. London: Sage.

Gaertner, S. L., Dovidio, J. F., Houlette, M., Johnson, K. M., and McGlynn, E. A. 2000. Reducing Intergroup Conflict: From Superordinate Goals to Decategorization, Recategorization, and Mutual Differentiation. *Group Dynamics: Theory, Research, and Practice* 4: 98–114.

Gaertner, S. L., Dovidio, J. F., Nier, J. A., Ward, C. M., and Banker, B. S. 1999. Across Cultural Divides: The Value of a Superordinate Identity. In *Cultural Divides: Understanding and Overcoming Group Conflict,* ed. D. Prentice and D. Miller, 173–212. New York: Sage.

Gamson, W. A. 1992. *Talking Politics.* Cambridge: Cambridge University Press.

Gellner, E. 1994. Nationalism and Modernization. In *Nationalism,* ed. J. Hutchinson. and A. Smith. Oxford: Oxford University Press.

Gerard, H., and Hoyt, M. F. 1974. Distinctiveness of Social Categorization and Attitude toward Ingroup Members. *Journal of Personality and Social Psychology* 29: 836–842.

Gerson, J. M. 2001. In between States: National Identity Practices among German Jewish Immigrants. *Political Psychology* 1: 179–198.

Gibson, J. L., and Gouwa, A. 1998. *Social Identity Theory and Political Intolerance in South Africa.* Unpublished Manuscript, University of Houston.

Giddens, A. 1991. *Modernity and Self Identity: Self and Society in the Late Modern Age.* Cambridge: Polity.

Granberg, D. 1987. Candidate Preference, Membership Group, and Estimates of Voting Behavior. *Social Cognition* 5: 323–335.

Grant, P., and Brown, P. 1995. From Ethnocentrism to Collective Protest: Responses to Relative Deprivation and Threats to Social Identity. *Social Psychology Quarterly* 58: 195–211.

Gurin, P., Hurtado, A., and Peng, T. 1994. Group Contacts and Ethnicity in the Social Identities of Mexicanos and Chicanos. *Personality and Social Psychology Bulletin* 20: 521–532.

Gurin, P., and Townsend, A. 1986. Properties of Gender Identity and Their Implications for Gender Consciousness. *British Journal of Social Psychology* 25: 139–148.

Gurr, T. R. 1970. *Why Men Rebel.* Princeton, NJ: Princeton University Press.

————. 1993. *Minorities at Risk: A Global View of Ethnopolitical Conflict.* Washington, DC: United States Institute of Peace.

Gurr, T., and Harff, B. 1994. *Ethnic Conflict in World Politics.* 2nd ed. Boulder, CO: Westview Press.

Habermas, J. 1990. *Moral Consciousness and Communicative Action.* Cambridge: MIT Press.

Hagendoorn, L., Csepeli, G., Dekker, H., and Farnen, R. 2000. European Nations and Nationalism: Theoretical and Historical Perspectives. Aldershot: Ashgate.

Hagendoorn, L., Linssen, H., Rotman, D., and Tumanov, S. 1996. Russians as Minorities in Belarus, Ukraine, Moldova, Georgia and Kazakhstan. Paper presented to the International Political Science Association Conference. Boon, NC.

Hagendoorn, L., Linssen, H., and Tumanov, S. 2001. *Inter-group Relations in States of the Former Soviet Union: The Perception of Russians.* Hove: Psychology Press.

Hardin, R. 1995. *One for All, the Logic of Group Conflict.* Princeton: Princeton University Press.

Harre, R. 2006. The Texture of Threat. In *Identity, Morality, and Threat,* ed. D. Rothbart. and K. Korostelina. 19–28. Lexington, MA: Lexington Books.

Hampden-Turner, C., and Trompenaars, F. 2000. Building Cross-Cultural Competence: How to Create Wealth from Conflicting Values. Chichester: Wiley.

Heider, Fritz. 1958. *The Psychology of Interpersonal Relations.* New York: John Wiley and Sons.

Helton, A. 1996. *Crimean Tatars: Repatriation and Conflict Prevention.* New York: Open Society Institute.

Herman, S. 1977. *Jewish Identity: A Social Psychological Perspective.* Beverly Hills, CA: Sage.

Herz, John. 1950. Idealist Internationalism and the Security Dilemma. *World Politics* 2 (2): 157–180.

Hewstone, M. 1989. *Causal Attribution: From Cognitive Processes to Cognitive Beliefs.* Oxford: Blackwell.

Hinkle, S., and Brown, R. 1990. Intergroup Comparisons and Social Identity: Some Links and Lacunae. In *Social Identity Theory: Constructive and Critical Advances,* ed. D. Abrams. and M. A. Hogg. New York: Harvester Wheatsheaf.

Hirt, E. R., Zillmann, D., Erickson, G., and Kennedy, C. 1992. Costs and Benefits of Allegiance: Changes in Fans' Self-Ascribed Competencies after Team Victory versus Defeat. *Journal of Personality and Social Psychology* 63: 724–738.

Hobsbawm, E. 1994. *The Age of Extremes.* London: Michael Joseph.

Hofstede, G. 1980. *Culture's Consequences: International Differences in Work-Related Values.* Beverly Hills, CA: Sage.

_____2001. *Culture's Consequences, Comparing Values, Behaviors, Institutions, and Organizations Across Nations.* Thousand Oaks CA: Sage.

Hogg, M. A. 1992. *The Social Psychology of Group Cohesiveness.* New York: Hemel Hempstead/Harvester Wheatsheaf.

_____. 1996. Intragroup Processes, Group Structure and Social Identity. In *Social Groups and Identities: Developing the Legacy of Henri Tajfel,* ed. W. P. Robinson. 65–93. Oxford: Butterworth-Heinemann.

Hogg, M. A., and Abrams, D. 1993. *Group Motivation.* London: Harvester Wheatsheaf.

Holland, D., W. Lachicotte, D. Skinner and C. Cain. 1998. *Identity and Agency in Cultural Worlds.* Cambridge: Harvard University Press.

Holland, D., and Lave J. 2001. *History in Person: Enduring Struggles, Contentious Practice, Intimate Identities.* Santa Fe, NM: School of American Research Press.

Holtz, R., and Miller, N. 1985. Assumed Similarity and Opinion Certainty. *Journal of Personality and Social Psychology* 48: 890–898.

Homans, G. 1950. *The Human Group.* New York: Harcourt Brace.

Horowitz, D. L. 1985. *Ethnic Groups in Conflict*. Berkeley: University of California Press.

Horowitz, D. L. 1975. Ethnic Identity. In *Ethnicity, Theory and Experience*, ed. N. Glazer and D. Moynihan. Cambridge: Harvard University Press.

Huddy, L. 2001. From Social to Political Identity: A Critical Examination of Social Identity Theory. *Political Psychology* 1: 127–156.

Huddy, L. and Virtanen, S. 1995. Subgroup Differentiation and Subgroup Bias among Latinos as a Function of Familiarity and Positive Distinctiveness. *Journal of Personality and Social Psychology* 68: 97–108.

Hutnik N. 1986. Patterns of Ethnic Minority Identification and Modes of Social Adaptation. Ethnic and Racial Studies 9: 150–167. Inkeles.

_____. 1991. *Ethnic Minority Identity*. Oxford: Clarendon Press.

Hyers, L. L., and Swim, J. K. 1998. A Comparison of the Experiences of Dominant and Minority Group Members during an Intergroup Encounter. *Group Processes and Intergroup Relations* 1 (2): 143–163.

Jackson, J. 1993. Realistic Group Conflict Theory: A Review and Evaluation of the Theoretical and Empirical Literature. *Psychological Record* 43: 395–414.

_____. 2002. The Relationship between Group Identity and Intergroup Prejudice Is Moderated by Socio-structural Variation. *Journal of Applied Social Psychology* 32: 908–933.

Jackson, L. A., Sullivan, L. A., Harnish, R., and Hodge, C. N. 1996. Achieving Positive Social Identity: Social Mobility, Social Creativity, and Permeability of Group Boundaries. *Journal of Personality and Social Psychology* 70: 241–252.

James, W. 1890. *The Principles of Psychology*. 2 vols. Mineola, NY: Dover.

Jaromowic, M. 1998. Self-We-Others Schemata and Social Identification. In *Social Identity: International Perspective*, ed. S. Worchel, J. F. Morales, D. Paez, and J. Deschamps, 44–52. Thousand Oaks, CA: Sage.

Jenkins, R. 1996. *Social Identity*. London: Routledge.

Jervis, R. 1976. *Perception and Misperception in World Politics*. Princeton: Princeton University Press.

_____. 1978. Cooperation Under the Security Dilemma. *World Politics* 40 (1): 167–214.

Jones, E. E., and Harris, V. A. 1967. The Attribution of Attitudes. *Journal of Experimental Social Psychology* 3: 1–24.

Jung, C. 2003. The Politics of Indigenous Identity: Neoliberalism, Cultural Rights, and the Mexican Zapatistas. *Social Research* 70 (2): 433–462.

Karasawa, M. 1991. Toward an Assessment of Social Identity: The Structure of Group Identification and Its Effects on In-group Evaluations. *British Journal of Social Psychology* 30: 293–307.

Katz, D., and Braly, D. 1933. Racial Stereotypes of One Hundred College Students. *Journal of Abnormal and Social Psychology* 28: 280–290.

Kawakami, K., and Dion, K. L. 1993. The Impact of Salient Self-Identities on Relative Deprivation and Action Intentions. *European Journal of Social Psychology* 23: 525–540.

Kellner, D. 1992. *The Persian Gulf TV War*. Boulder, CO: Westview Press.

Kelman, H. C. 1982. Creating the Conditions for Israeli-Palestinian Negotiations. *Journal of Conflict Resolution* 1: 39–76.

_____. 1997a. Nationalism, Patriotism, and National Identity: Social-Psychological Dimensions. In *Patriotism in the Lives of Individuals and Nations*, ed. D. Bar-Tal and E. Staub, 165–189. Chicago: Nelson-Hall.

_____. 1997b. Negotiating National Identity and Self-Determination in Ethnic Conflicts: The Choice between Pluralism and Ethnic Cleansing. *Negotiation Journal* 13: 327–340.

_____. 2001. The Role of National Identity in Conflict Resolution. In *Social Identity, Intergroup Conflict, and Conflict Reduction*, ed. R. D. Ashmore, L. Jussim, and D. Wilder, 187–212. Oxford: Oxford University Press.

_____. 2002. Interactive Problem Solving: Informal Mediation by the Scholar-Practitioner. In *Studies in International Mediation: Essays in Honor of Jeffrey Z. Rubin*, ed. J. Bercovitch, 167–193. New York: Palgrave Macmillan.

_____. 2004. Reconciliation as Identity Change: A Social-Psychological Perspective. In *From Conflict Resolution to Reconciliation*, ed. Y. Bar-Siman-Tov, 111–124. Oxford: Oxford University Press.

Kelly,G. 1955. *Principles of Personal Construct Psychology*. New York: Norton.

Kempny, M. J., and Jawłowska, A. 2002. Identity in Transformation: Postmodernism, Postcommunism, Globalization. Westport, CT: Praeger.

King, D. 1988. Multiple Jeopardy, Multiple Consciousness: The Context of Black Feminist Ideology. *Signs* 14: 42–72.

Kinket, B., and Verkuyten, M. 1997. Levels of Ethnic Self-Identification and Social Context. *Social Psychology Quarterly* 60: 338–354.

Klandermans, B. 1997. *The Social Psychology of Protest*. Oxford: Blackwell.

Klink, A., Mumendey, A., Mielke, R., and Blanz, M. 1997. A Multicomponennt Approach to Group Identification: Results from Field Study in East Germany. *Social Psychology Quarterly* 60: 135–151.

Kofta, M., Weary G., and Sędek, G., eds. 1985. *Personality Functioning and Social Cognition: An Action Control View*. New York: Plenum.

Korostelina, K. V. 2000a. The Social-Psychological Roots of the Ethnic Problems in Crimea. *Democratizatsiya* 8: 219–231.

_____. 2000b. Peace Building in Multiethnic Crimea. *Give and Take: A Journal on Civil Society in Eurasia* 3(1): 26–27.

_____. 2000c. Crimean Psychologists Investigate Multi-ethnic Conflict and Social Change. *Psychology International: Journal of American Psychological Association Office of International Affairs* 11: 1–3.

_____. 2001. Identity-Based Training. *Nauka i Osvita* [Science and education] 6: 59–64. Odessa.

_____. 2002a. *Identity Based Training: Toward Peacebuilding in Multicultural Societies*. Report No. NCRTL-RR-143. East Lansing, MI: National Center for Research on Teaching Learning. ERIC Document Reproduction Service No. ED 462 636.

_____. 2002b. Formuvanya Nacional'noyi Identichnosti Yak Zavdanya Gumanizatsii Osvity [Formation of national identity as task of humanization of education]. *Aktual'ni Problemu Psyhologii* [Topical problems of psychology] 7: 106 – 111. Kiev.

_____. 2003. The Multiethnic State-Building Dilemma: National and Ethnic Minorities' Identities in the Crimea. *National Identities* 5 (2): 141–159.

_____. 2006a. National Identity Formation and Conflict Intensions of Ethnic Minorities. In *The Psychology of Resolving Global Conflicts: From War to Peace* (Contemporary Psychology), ed. Mari Fitzduff and Chris E. Stout. 3 vols. Westport, CT: Praeger.

_____. 2006b. Identity Salience as a Determinant of the Perceptions of Others. In *Identity, Morality, and Threat*, ed. Rothbart, Daniel, and Karina Korostelina. Lexington, MA: Lexington Books.

Kriesberg, L. 2003. *Constructive Conflicts: From Escalation to Resolution.* 2nd ed. Lanham, MD: Rowman and Littlefield.

Krummenacher, Heinz. 2006. Computer Assisted Early Warning: The Fast Example. In *Programming for Peace: Computer Aided Methods for International Conflict Resolution and Prevention,* ed. R. Trapple. Dordrecht: Springer.

Lalonde, R. N. 1992. The Dynamics of Group Differentiation in the Face of Defeat. *Personality and Social Psychology Bulletin* 18: 336–342.

Lake, D., and Rothchild, D. 1998. *The International Spread of Ethnic Conflict: Fear, Diffusion, and Escalation.* Princeton: Princeton University Press.

Lamont, M. 2000. *The Dignity of Working Men: Morality and the Boundaries of Race, Class, and Immigration.* Cambridge, MA: Harvard University Press.

Lamont, M. A., and Molnar V. 2002. The Study of Boundaries in the Social Sciences. *Annual Review of Sociology* 28:167–195.

Lasch, C. 1979. *Culture of Narcissism.* London: Pan Books.

Leont'ev, A. N. 1978. *Activity, Consciousness, and Personality.* Englewood Cliffs, NJ: Prentice-Hall.

_____. 1982. *Problems of the Development of Mind.* Moscow: Progress Publishers.

Levin, S. and Sidanius, J. 1999. Social Dominance and Social Identity in the United States and Israel:Ingroup Favoritism or Outgroup Derogation? *Political Psychology* 20: 99–126.

Levine, R. A., and D. T. Campbell. 1972. *Ethnocentrism: Theories of Conflict, Ethnic Attitudes, and Group Behavior.* New York: John Wiley and Sons.

Luhtanen, R., and Crocker, J. 1992. A Collective Self-Esteem Scale: Self Evaluation of One's Social Identity. *Personality and Social Psychology Bulletin* 18: 302–318.

Mackie, Diane M., and Hamilton, David L. 1993a. Cognitive and Affective Processes in Intergroup Perception: The Developing Interface. In *Affect, Cognition, and Stereotyping: Interactive Processes in Group Perception,* ed. D. M. Mackie and D. L. Hamilton, 1–11. San Diego, CA: Academic Press.

_____. 1993b. Affect, Cognition, and Stereotyping: Concluding Remarks. In *Affect, Cognition, and Stereotyping: Interactive Processes in Group Perception,* ed. D. M. Mackie and D. L. Hamilton, 371–383. San Diego, CA: Academic Press.

McAdam, D., Tarrow, S., and Tilly, C. 2001. *Dynamics of Contention.* New York: Cambridge University Press.

Manz, B. F., ed. 1994. *Central Asia in Historical Perspective.* Boulder, CO: Westview Press.

Marcia, J. E. 1980. Identity in Adolescence. In *Handbook of Adolescent Psychology,* ed. J. Adelson, 159–187. New York: Wiley.

Markus, H., and Kitayama, S. 1991. Culture and the Self: Implications for Cognition, Emotion, and Motivation. *Psychological Review* 98: 224–253.

McGarty, C., Turner, J. C., Hogg, M. A., David, B., and Wetherell, M. S. 1992. Group Polarization as Conformity to the Prototypical Group Member. *British Journal of Social Psychology* 31: 1–20.

McConahay, J. B. 1986. Modern Racism, Ambivalence, and the Modern Racism Scale. In *Prejudice, Discrimination, and Racism,* ed. J. F. Dovidio and S. L. Gaetner, 91–125. Orlando, FL: Academia Press.

McGuire, W. J., McGuire, C. V., Child, P., and Fujioka, T. 1978. Salience of Ethnicity in the Spontaneous Self-Concept as a Function of One's Ethnic Distinctiveness in the Social Environment. *Journal of Personality and Social Psychology* 36: 511–520.

McGuire, W. J., and Padawer-Singer, A. 1976. Trait Salience in the Spontaneous Self-Concept. *Journal of Personality and Social Psychology* 33: 343–754.

Mead, G. H. 1934. *Mind, Self and Society.* Chicago: University of Chicago Press.

Melosik, Z., Szkudlarek, T. 1998. *Culture and Education.* Krakow: Impuls.

Mezran, K. 2001. Negotiating National Identity in North Africa. *International Negotiation* 2: 141–173.

Miller, A. H., Gurin, P., Gurin, G., and Malanchuk, O. 1981. Group Consciousness and Political Participation. *American Journal of Political Science* 25: 495–511.

Miller, N., and M. Brewer, eds. 1984. *Groups in Contact: The Psychology of Desegregation.* Orlando, FL: Academic Press.

Morales, J. F., López-Sáez, M., and Vega, L., 1998. Discrimination and Beliefs on Discrimination in Individualists and Collectivists. In *Social Identity: International Perspectives,* ed. S. Worchel, J. F. Morales, D. Páez, and J. C. Deschamps, 199–210. Thousand Oaks, CA: Sage.

Moscovici, S. 1988. Notes toward a Description of Social Representations. *European Journal of Social Psychology* 18: 211–250.

Moscovici, S., and Paicheler, G. 1978. Social Comparison and Social Recognition: Two Complementary Processes of Identification. In *Differentiation Between Social Groups: Studies in the Social Psychology of Intergroup Relations,* ed. H. Tajfel, 251–266. London: Academic Press.

Motyl, A. 1992. *Thinking Theoretically about Soviet Nationalities.* New York: Columbia University Press.

Mullen, B. 1983. Egocentric Bias in Estimates of Consensus. *Journal of Social Psychology* 121: 31–38.

Mullen, B., Brown, R., and Smith, E. 1992. Ingroup Bias as Function of Salience, Relevance, and Status: An Integration. *European Journal of Social Psychology* 22: 103–122.

Munch, R. 2001. Nation and Citizenship in the Global Age. Houndmills, Basingstoke, Hampshire: Palgrave.

Mummendey, A., and Otten, S. 1998. Positive-Negative Asymmetry in Social Discrimination. In *European Review of Social Psychology,* vol. 9, ed. W. Stroebe and M. Hewstone, 107–143. New York: Wiley.

Mummendey, A., and Schreiber, H. J. 1984. "Different" Just Means "Better": Some Obvious and Some Hidden Pathways to In-group Favouritism. *British Journal of Social Psychology* 23: 363–368.

Nagel, J. 1995. American Indian Ethnic Renewal: Politics and the Resurgence of Identity. *American Sociological Review* 60: 947–965.

Noricks, J. S., Agler, L. H., Bartholomew, M., Howarth-Smith, S., Martin, D., Pyles, S., and Shapiro, W. 1987. Age, Abstract Thinking, and the American Concept of Person. *American Anthropologist* 89: 667–675.

Novotny, K. M. 1998. Taylor-Made? Feminist Theory and the Politics of Identity. *Women and Politics* 19: 1–18.

Oakes, P. 1987. The Salience of Social Categories. In *Rediscovering the Social Group: A Self-Categorization Theory,* ed. M. A. Turner, P. J. Hogg, S. D. Oakes, S. D. Reicher, and M. S. Watherell, 117–134. Oxford: Blackwell.

Oakes, P., Haslam, A., and Turner, J. C. 1998. The Role of Prototypicality In-group Influence and Cohesion. In *Social Identity,* ed. S. Worchel, J. F. Morales, D. Paez, and J. C. Deschamps, 75– 92. London: Sage.

Oberg, K. 1960. Cultural Shock: Adjustment to New Cultural Environments. *Practical Anthropology* 7: 177–182.

Otten, S., Mummendey, A., and Blanz, M. 1996. Intergroup Discrimination in Positive and Negative Outcome Allocations: Impact of Stimulus Valence, Relative Group Status, and Relative Group Size. *Personality and Social Psychology Bulletin* 22: 568–581.

Parsons, T. 1951. *The Social System*. Glencoe, IL: Free Press.

Peacock, J. L. 2007. Cross-Cutting Identities: Singapore's Crabgrass. In *Identity Matter*, ed. J. L. Peacock, P. Thornton, and P. Inman. Oxford: Berghahn.

Peacock, J. L, Thornton, P., and Inman, P., eds. 2007. *Identity Matter*. Oxford: Berghahn.

Perreault, S., and Bourhis, R. Y. 1998. Social Identification, Interdependence, and Discrimination. *Group Processes and Intergroup Relations* 1: 49–66.

Perreault, S., and Bourhis, R. Y. 1999. Ethnocentrism, Social Identification, and Discrimination. *Personality and Social Psychology Bulletin* 25: 92–103.

Pettigrew, T. F. 1979. The Ultimate Attribution Error: Extending Allport's Cognitive Analysis of Prejudice. *Personality and Social Psychology Bulletin* 5: 461–476.

_____. 1998. Intergroup Contact: Theory, Research and New Perspectives. *Annual Review of Psychology* 49: 65–85.

Pettigrew, T. F., and Tropp, L. R. 2000. Does Intergroup Contact Reduce Prejudice? Recent Meta-analytic Findings. In *Reducing Prejudice and Discrimination*, ed. S. Oskamp, 93–114. Hillsdale, NJ: Lawrence Erlbaum.

Pham, P., Vinck. P., Wierda, M., Stover, E., and di Giovanni, A. 2005. *Forgotten Voices: A Population-Based Survey of Attitudes About Peace and Justice in Northern Uganda*. www.ictj.net/downloads/ForgottenVoices.pdf

Phinney, J. S. 1990. Ethnic identity in Adolescence and Adulthood: Review of Research. *Psychological Bulletin* 108: 499–514.

Phinney, J. 1991. Ethnic Identity and Self- Esteem: A Review and Integration. *Hispanic Journal of Behavioral Science* 13: 193–208.

Posen, B. 1993. The Security Dilemma and Ethnic Conflict. *Survival* 35 (1): 27–47.

Prentice, D. A., Miller, D. T., and Lightdale, J. R. 1994. Asymmetries in Attachments to Groups and to Their Members. *Personality and Social Psychology Bulletin* 20: 484–493.

Rabbie, J., Schot, J., and Visser, L. 1989. Social Identity Theory: A Conceptual and Empirical Critique from the Perspective of a Behavioural Interaction Model. *European Journal of Social Psychology* 19: 171–202.

Reel, M. 2005. In Buenos Aires, Researchers Exhume Long-Unclaimed African Roots. *Washington Post Foreign Service*, May 5, A14.

Reid, A., and Deaux, K. 1996. Relationship between Social and Personal Identities: Segregation or Integration? *Journal of Personality and Social Psychology* 71: 1084–1091.

Reykowski, J. 1997. Patriotism and Collective System of Meanings. In *Patriotism in Global Age*, ed. Bar-Tal and E. Staub, 108–128. Chicago: Nelson Hall.

Rogers, C. R. 1961. *On Becoming a Person: A Therapist's View of Psychotherapy*. Boston: Houghton Mifflin.

Rokeach, M. 1973. *The Nature of Human Values*. New York: Free Press.

Ros M., Huici C., and Gomez A. 2000. Comparative Identity, Category Salience and Intergroup Relations. In *Social Identity Processes*, ed. D. Capozza and R. Brown, 81–95. London: Sage.

Ros, M., Huici, C., and Cano, J. I. 1994. Ethnolinguistic Vitality and Social Identity: Their Impact on Ingroup Bias and Social Attribution. *International Journal of the Sociology of Language* 108: 145–166.

Rosenberg, S., and Gara, M. 1985. The Multiplicity of Personal Identity. *Review of Personality and Social Psychology* 6: 87–113.

Rosoux, V. B. 2001. National Identity in France and Germany: From Mutual Exclusion to Negotiation. *International Negotiation* 2: 175–198.

Ross, L. 1977. The Intuitive Psychologist and His Shortcomings: Distortions in the Attribution Process. In *Advances in Experimental Social Psychology*, vol. 10, ed. L. Berkowitz, 173–220. New York: Academic Press.

Ross, L., Greene, D., and House, P. 1977. The "False Consensus Effect": An Egocentric Bias in Social Perception and Attribution Processes. *Journal of Experimental Social Psychology* 13: 279–301.

Ross, M. H. 1998. Cultural Dynamic in Ethnic Conflict. In *Culture in World Politics*, ed. D. Jacquin, A. Oros, and M. Verwij, 156–186. Basingstoke, UK: Macmillan.

_____. 2001. Psychocultural Interpretation and Dramas: Identity Dynamics in Ethnic Conflict. *Political Psychology* 22: 157–178.

Rothbart, D., and Korostelina, K. V. 2006 *Identity, Morality and Threat*. Lexington, MA: Lexington Books.

Rothman, J. 1997. Resolving Identity-Based Conflict in Nations, Organizations, and Communities. San Francisco, CA: Jossey-Bass.

Rothchild, D. 1991. *Ghana: The Political Economy of Structural Adjustment*. Boulder, CO: Lynne Rienner.

Roy, O. 2000. *The New Central Asia: The Creation of Nations*. London: I. B. Tauris.

Runciman, W. G. 1966. *Relative Deprivation and Social Justice: A Study of Attitudes to Social Inequality in Twentieth Century England*. Berkeley: University of California Press.

Sachdev, I., and Bourhis, R. Y. 1984. Minimal Majorities and Minorities. *European Journal of Social Psychology* 14: 35–52.

Sanders, G. S., and Mullen, B. 1983. Accuracy in Perceptions of Consensus: Differential Tendencies of People with Majority and Minority positions. *European Journal of Social Psychology* 13: 57–70.

Sasse, G. 2002. The "New" Ukraine: A State of Regions. In *Ethnicity and Territory in the Former Soviet Union: Regions in Conflict*, ed. J. Hughes and G. Sasse, 69–100. London: Frank Cass.

Schwartz, S. H., and Bilsky, W. 1990. Toward a Theory of the Universal Content and Structure of Values: Extensions and Cross-Cultural Replications. *Journal of Personality and Social Psychology* 58: 878–891.

Sears, D. O., and Henry, P. J. 1999. Ethnic Identity and Group Threat in American Politics. *The Political Psychologist* 4 (2): 12–17.

Sellers, R. M., Smith, M. A., Shelton, J. N., Rowley, S. A., and Chavous, T. M. 1998. Multidimensional Model of Racial Identity: A Reconceptualization of African American Racial Identity. *Personality and Social Psychology Review* 2 (1): 18–39.

Serino, C. 1998. The Personal-Social Interplay: Social-Cognitive Prospects on Identity and Self-Others Comparison. In *Social Identity*, ed. S. Worchel, J. F. Morales, D. Paez, and J. C. Deschamps, 24–43. London: Sage.

Sherif, M., and Sherif C. 1953. *Group in Harmony and Tension*. New York: Harper.

Sherif, M. 1966. Group Conflict and Cooperation: Their Social Psychology. London: Routledge and Kegan Paul.

Shevel, O. 2000. Crimean Tatars in Ukraine: The Politics of Inclusion and Exclusion. *Analysis of Current Events* 12: 9–11.

Sidanius, J., Feshbach, S., Levin, S., and Pratto, F. 1997. The Interface between Ethnic and National Attachment: Ethnic Pluralism or Ethnic Dominance? *Public Opinion Quarterly* 61: 102–133.

Simon, B. 1992. The Perception of Ingroup and Outgroup Homogeneity: Reintroducing the Intergroup Context. In *European Review of Social Psychology,* ed. W. Stroebe and M. Hewstone 3:1–30. Chichester, UK: Wiley.

Simon, B., and Hamilton, D. 1994. Self-Stereotyping and Social Context: The Effects of Relative Ingroup Size and Ingroup Status. *Journal of Personality and Social Psychology* 66: 699–711.

Skevington, S., and Baker, D., eds. 1989. *The Social Identity of Women.* London: Sage.

Smith, Anthony D. 1991. *National Identity.* Reno: University of Nevada Press.

——————. 1994. Gastronomy or Geology? The Role of Nationalism in the Reconstruction of Nations. *Nations and Nationalism* 1 (1): 3–23.

Smith, E. R., and Henry, S. 1996. An In-group Becomes Part of the Self: Response Time Evidence. *Personality and Social psychology Bulletin* 22: 635–642.

Snyder, J., and Jervis, R. 1999. Civil War and the Security Dilemma. In *Civil Wars, Insecurity, and Intervention,* ed. B. F. Walter and J. Snyder, 15–37. New York: Columbia University Press.

Somers, M. R. 1994. Reclaiming the Epistemological "Other": Narrative and the Social Constitution of Identity. In *Social Theory and the Politics of Identity,* ed. C. Calhoun, 37–99. Cambridge, MA: Blackwell.

Spear, J. 1996. Arms Limitations, Confidence-Building Measures, and Internal Conflict. In *The International Dimensions of Internal Conflict,* ed. M. E. Brown, 377–410. Cambridge, MA: MIT Press.

Stein, J. G. 1998. Image, Identity, and Conflict Resolution. In *Managing Global Chaos,* ed. C. A. Crocker and F. O. Hampson. 93–111. Washington, DC: USIP.

Stephan, C. W., and Stephan, W. G. 2004. Intergroup Relations in Multicultural Education Programs. In *Handbook of Research on Multicultural Education,* 2nd ed., ed. J. A. Banks and C. McGee-Banks, 782–798. New York: Jossey-Bass.

Stephan, W. G., Ybarra, O., and Bachman, G. 1999. Prejudice towards Immigrants. *Journal of Applied Social Psychology* 29: 2221–2237.

Stephan, W. G., Ybarra, O., Martinez, C., Schwarzwald, J., and Tur-kaspa, M. 1998. Prejudice toward Immigrants to Spain and Israel: An Integrated Threat Theory Analysis. *Journal of Cross Cultural Psychology* 29: 559–576.

Stern, P. 1995. Why Do People Sacrifice for their Nation. *Political Psychology,* 16 (2): 217–235.

Sterns P. N. Humanitarianism and Intolerance: Two Contemporary Approaches to the Other. In *Identity, Morality and Threat,* ed. D. Rothbart, and K. V. Korostelina, 129–146. 2006, Lexington, MA: Lexington Books.

Stouffer, S. A., Suckman, E A., Devinney, L. C., Star, S. A., Williams, R. M. 1949. *The American Soldier: Adjustment during Army Life,* vol. 1. Princeton: Princeton University Press.

Struch, Naomi, and Shalom H. Schwartz. 1989. Intergroup Aggression: Its Predictors and Distinctness from In-group Bias. *Journal of Personality and Social Psychology* 56: 346–373.

Stryker, S. 1969. Identity Salience and Role Performance: The Relevance of Symbolic Interaction Theory for Family Research. *Journal of Marriage and the Family* 30: 558– 564.

_____. 2000. Identity Competition: Key to Differential Social Movement Participation? In *Self, Identity, and Social Movements*, ed. S. Stryker, T. Owens, and R. White, 21–40. Minneapolis: University of Minnesota Press.

Stryker, S., and Serpe, R. T. 1994. Identity Salience and Psychological Centrality: Equivalent, Overlapping, or Complementary Concepts? *Social Psychology Quarterly* 57: 16–35.

Suls, J., and Wann, C. 1987. In Search of False Uniqueness Phenomenon: Fear and Estimates of Social Consensus. *Journal of Personality and Social Psychology* 52: 211–217.

Swann, S. and Wyer, R. S. 1997. Gender Stereotypes and Social Identity: How Being in the Minority Affects Judgments of Self and Other. *Personality and Social Psychology Bulletin* 23: 1265–1276.

Swidler, A. 2001. *Talk of Love. How Culture Matters*. Chicago: University of Chicago Press.

Sy, H. T. 2007. The Casamance Separatist Conflict: From Identity to the Trap of "Identitism". In *Identity matters*, ed. J. L. Peacock, P. Thornton, and P. Inman Oxford: Berghahn.

Taft, R. 1977. Coping with Unfamiliar Cultures. In *Studies in Cross-Cultural Psychology*, vol. 1, ed. N. Warren, 125–153. London, England: Academic Press.

Tajfel H. 1969. Cognitive Aspects of Prejudice. *Journal of Social Issues* 25: 79–97.

_____1974. Social Identity and Intergroup Behaviour. *Social Science Information* 13: 65–93.

_____1978. *Differentiations between Social Groups: Studies in the Social Psychology of Intergroup Relations*. London: Academic Press.

Tajfel, H., Flament, C., Billig, M., and Bundy, R. 1971. Social Categorisation and Intergroup Behaviour. *European Journal of Social Psychology* 1: 149–178.

Tajfel, H., and Turner, J. C. 1986. The Social Identity Theory of Intergroup Behavior. In *Psychology of Intergroup Relations*, ed. S. Worshel and W. G. Austin, 7–24. Chicago: Nelson Hall.

_____. 1979. An Integrative Theory of Intergroup Conflict. In *The Social Psychology of Intergroup Relations*, eds. W. G. Austin and S. Worchel, 33–48. Monterey, CA: Brooks/Cole.

Tan, L. 2006. From Incorporation to Disengagement: East Timor and Indonesian Identities, 1975–1999. In *Identity, Morality and Threat*, ed. D. Rothbart and K. V. Korostelina, 177–210. 2006, Lexington, MA: Lexington Books.

Taylor, V., and Whittier, N. E. 1992. Collective Identity in Social Movement Communities. In *Frontiers of Social Movement Theory*, ed. A. Morris and C. Mueller, 104–130. New Haven, CT: Yale University Press.

Taylor, S. E., and Brown, J. D. 1988. Illusion and Well-Being: A Social Psychological Perspective on Mental Health. *Psychological Bulletin* 103: 193–210

Taylor, D. M., and Moghaddam, F. M. 1994. *Theories of Intergroup Relations: International Social Psychological Perspectives*. 2nd ed. New York: Praeger.

Taylor, D., Moghaddam, F., Gamble, I. and Zellerer, E. 1987. Disadvantaged Group Responses to Perceived Inequality: From Passive Acceptance to Collective Action. *Journal of Social Psychology* 127: 259–272.

Taylor, D. M., and McKirnan, D. J. 1984. A Five-Stage Model of Intergroup Relations. *British Journal of Social Psychology* 23: 291–300.

Thoits, P. A. and Virshup, L. V. 1997. Me's and We's: Form and Functions of Social Identities. In *Self and Identity: Fundamental Issues*, vol. 1, ed. R. Ashmore and L. Jussim, 106–133. New York: Oxford University Press.

Tilly, C. 1978. *From Mobilization to Revolution*. Reading, MA: Addison-Wesley.
———. 1994. States and Nationalism in Europe, 1492–1992. In *Theory and Society: Renewal and Critique in Social Theory* 23 (1):131–146.
———2005. Identities, Boundaries and Social Ties. Boulder, CO: Paradigm.
Ting-Toomey, S., Yee-Jung, K. K., Shapiro, R., Garcia, W., Wright, T. J., and Oetzel J. G. 2000. Ethnic/Cultural Identity Salience and Conflict Styles in Four US Ethnic Groups. *International Journal of Intercultural Relations* 24: 47–81.
Triandis, H. C. 1995. *Individualism and Collectivism*. San Francisco, CA: Westview Press.
Triandis, H. C., and Gelfand, M. J. 1998. Converging Measurement of Horizontal and Vertical Individualism and Collectivism. *Journal of Personality and Social Psychology* 74 (1): 118–128.
Trompenaars, F., and Hampden-Turner, C. 1997. *Riding the Waves of Culture: Understanding Cultural Diversity in Business*. London: Nicholas Brealey.
Trumbull, E., Rothstein-Fisch, C., and Greenfield, P.M. 2000. *Bridging Cultures in Our Schools: New Approaches That Work* (Knowledge Brief). San Francisco: West Ed.
Turner, J. C., Hogg, M. A., Oakes, P. J., Reicher, S. D., and Watherell, M. S. 1987. *Rediscovering the Social Group: A Self-Categorization Theory*. Oxford: Blackwell.
Turner, J., Hogg, M, Turner, P., and Smith, P. 1984. Failure and Defeat as Determinants of Group Cohesiveness. *British Journal of Social Psychology* 23: 97–111.
Turner, J. C., Oakes, P. J., Haslam, S. A., and McGarty, C. 1994. Self and Collective: Cognition and Social Context. *Personality and Psychology Bulletin* 20: 454–463.
Van Dijk, T. A., ed. 1997. *Discourse Studies*. 2 vols. London: Sage.
Van Evera, S. 1999. *Causes of War: Power and the Roots of Conflict*. Ithaca: Cornell University Press.
Van Knippenberg, A. 1978. *Status Differences, Comparative Relevance and Intergroup Differentiation*. In *Differentiation between Social Groups: Studies in the Social Psychology of Intergroup Relations*, ed. H. Tajfel, 171–199. London: Academic Press.
Van Knippenberg, A., and van Oers, H. 1984. Social Identity and Equity Concerns in Intergroup Perceptions. *British Journal of Social Psychology* 23: 351–361.
Van Oudenhoven, J., and Eisses, A. 1998. Integration and Assimilation of Moroccan Immigrants in Israel and the Netherlands. *International Journal of Intercultural Relations* 22: 293–307.
Verkuyten, M., and Masson, K. 1995. New Racism, Self-Esteem, and Ethnic Relations among Minority and Majority Youth in the Netherlands. *Social Behavior and Personality* 23: 137–154.
Volkan, V. D. 1988. *The Need to Have Enemies and Allies: From Clinical Practice to International Relationship*. New York: Aronson.
———1997. *Bloodlines: From Ethnic Pride to Ethnic Terrorism*. New York: Farrar Straus Giroux.
———2004. *Blind Trust: Large Groups and Their Leaders in Times of Crisis and Terror*. Charlottesville, VA: Pitchstone.
———2006. Killing in the Name of Identity: A Study of Bloody Conflicts. Charlottesville, VA: Pitchstone.
Vygotsky, L. S. 1978. *Mind in Society*. Cambridge, MA: Harvard University Press.
———1989. Thought and Language. Cambridge, MA: MIT Press.
Walker, I., and Pettigrew, T. F. 1984. Relative Deprivation Theory: An Overview and Conceptual Critique. *British Journal of Social Psychology* 23: 301–310.

Wann, D. L. and Branscombe, N. 1990. Die-Hard and Fair-Weather Fans: Effects of Identification on BIRGing and CORFing Tendencies. *Journal of Sport and Social Issues* 14: 103–117.

Wassem, M. 2007. Islam and the West: The Perspective from Pakistan. In *Identity Matter,* ed. J. L. Peacock, P. Thornton, and P. Inman, 307–332. Oxford: Berghahn.

Wetzel, C., and Walton, M. 1985. Developing Biased Social Judgments: The False-Consensus Effect. *Journal of Personality and Social Psychology* 49: 1352–1359.

Wheeler, N. J., and Booth, K. 1992. The Security Dilemma. In *Dilemmas of World Politics: International Issues in a Changing World,* ed. J. Baylis and N. J. Rengger, 29–60. Oxford: Clarendon Press.

Wilder, D. 1984. Perceptions of Belief Homogeneity and Similarity Following Social Categorisation. *British Journal of Social Psychology* 23: 323–333.

Worchel, S., Iuzzini, J., Coutant, D., and Ivaldi, M. 2000. A Multidimensional Model of Identity: Relating Individual and Group Identities to Intergroup Behavior. In *Social Identity Processes,* ed. D. Capozza and R. Brown. London: Sage.

Worchel, S., Morales, J. F., Paez, D., and Deschamps, J. C. 1998. *Social Identity.* London: Sage.

Wright, S. C. 1997. Ambiguity, Social Influence, and Collective Action: Generating Collective Protest in Response to Tokenism. *Personality and Social Psychology Bulletin* 23: 1277–1290.

Wright, S., Taylor, D., and Moghaddam, E. 1990. Responding to Membership in a Disadvantaged Group: From Acceptance to Collective Protest. *Journal of Personality and Social Psychology* 58: 994–1003.

Yadov V. A. 1995. *Social'nye I Social'no Psycologicheskie Mechanizmy Formirovaniya Social'noi Identichnisti.* [Social and social-psychological mechanisms of the formation of social identity]. *World of Russia* 3–4: 40–67.

Yadov. V. A. 1993. *Social'naya Identichnost'* [Social identity]. Moscow: Academic Press.

Young, I. M. 1997. *Interesting Voices: Dilemmas of Gender, Political Philosophy, and Policy.* Princeton, NJ: Princeton University Press.

Zanna, M. P., and Rempel, J. K. 1988. Attitudes: A New Look at an Old Concept. In *The Social Psychology of Knowledge,* ed. D. Bar-Tal and A. W. Kruglanski, 315–334. Cambridge: Cambridge University Press.

Zartman, W. I., ed. 1995. *Collapsed States: The Disintegration and Restoration of Legitimate Authority.* London and Boulder: Lynne Rienner.

Zürcher, E. J., and van Schendel, W., eds. 2001. *Opting Out of the Nation.* London: I. B. Tauris.

INDEX OF NAMES

INDEX OF SUBJECTS

LIST OF PREVIOUS PUBLICATIONS

BOOKS

(2006) (Co-ed. with D. Rothbart) *Identity, Morality and Threat*. Lexington, MA, Lexington Books, 409pp.

(2003) *Social'naya identichnost' i konflict* [Social identity and conflict]. Simferopol: Dolya, 360pp.

(2002) *Sistema social'nyh identichnostey: opyt analiza ethnicheskoi situachii v Krymu* [The system of social identities: the analysis of ethnic situation in Crimea]. Simferopol: Dolya, 255pp.

(2001) (Ed.) *Mezhethnicheskoe soglasie v Krymu: puti dostizeniya* [Interethnic coexistence in Crimea: the ways of achievement]. Simferopol: Dolya, 263pp.

(1998) *Psihodiagnostika mezhetnicheskih otnoshenii v Krymu* [Psychodiagnostic of interethnic relations in Crimea]. Simferopol: St. University, 135pp.

BOOK CHAPTERS AND ARTICLES

English

(2007) Interrelations between national and ethnic identity and the readiness for conflict behavior. In James Peacock (Ed.), *Identity Matters*. Berghahn.

(2006) Identity salience as a determinant of the perceptions of others. In Daniel Rothbart and Karina Korostelina (Eds.), *Identity, Morality, and Threat*. Lexington, MA: Lexington Books.

(2006) National identity formation and conflict intensions of ethnic minorities. In Mari Fitzduff and Chris E. Stout (Eds.), *The Psychology of Resolving Global Conflicts* (3 vols.) From War to Peace (Contemporary Psychology) 1. New York: Praeger.

(2005) The impact of national identity on conflict behavior: Comparative analysis of two ethnic minorities in Crimea. In E. A. Tiryakian (Ed.), *Ethnicity, Ethnic Conflicts, Peace Processes: Comparative Perspectives*. Whitby, ON: De Sitter.

(2004) The impact of national identity on conflict behavior: Comparative analysis of two ethnic minorities in Crimea. *International Journal of Comparative Sociology*, 3–4, pp. 213–230.

(2003) The multiethnic state-building dilemma: National and ethnic minorities' identities in the Crimea. *National Identities*, 5 (2), pp. 141–159.

(2002) Identity based training: Toward peacebuilding in multicultural societies (Report No. NCRTL-RR-143). East Lansing, MI: National Center for Research on Teaching Learning. (ERIC Document Reproduction Service No. ED 462 636)

(2001) Identity based training. *Nauka i Osvita* [Science and education], 6, Odessa, pp. 59–64.

(2000) Peace building in multiethnic Crimea. *Give & Take: A Journal on Civil Society in Eurasia*, *3* (1), pp. 26–27.

(2000) The social-psychological roots of the ethnic problems in Crimea. *Democratizatsiya*, *8* (2), pp. 219–231.

(2000) Crimean psychologists investigate –multi-ethnic conflict and social change. *Psychology International: Journal of American Psychological Association Office of International Affairs*, *11* (2), pp. 1–3.

Russian and Ukrainian (Selected Publications)

(2003) Problema vzaemozvyazku miz social'noyu identichnostuy, attitudami I gotovnost'uy do konflictnoyu povedinki [Problems of interrelations among social identity, attitudes and readiness for conflict behavior]. *Aktual'ni problemu psyhologii* [Topical problems of psychology], *1*, Kiev, pp. 25–28.

(2002) Problemy formuvanya nacional'noyi identichnosti yak osnova byhovanya osobystosti [Problems of national identity formation as basis for personal development]. *Aktual'ni problemu psyhologii* [Topical problems of psychology], *8*, Kiev, pp. 85–88.

(2002) Formuvanya nacional'noyi identichnosti yak zavdanya gumanizatsii osvity [Formation of national identity as task of humanisation of education]. *Aktual'ni problemu psyhologii* [Topical problems of psychology], *7*, Kiev, pp. 106–111.

(2002) Ethnicheskaya identicnost' I ostenka situactiy: opyt exsperimental'nogo issledovaniya [Ethnic identity and estimation of situations: The experimental study]. *Zhurnal practicheskogo psihologa* [Journal of the practicing psychologist], *8*, Kiev, pp. 118–134.

(2002) Social'na identichnist' ak determinanta spriinyatay I ocinki inshih grup [Social identity as determinant of perception and estimation of outgroups]. *Aktual'ni problemu psyhologii* [Topical problems of psychology], *4*, Kiev, pp. 35–40.

(2002) Osobistisna I etnichna identichnosti kryms'kyh tatar irossiyan [Personal and ethnic identity among Crimean Tatars and Russians]. *Problemy zagal'noi ta pedagogichnoi psihologii* [The problems of general and pedagogic psychology], *1*, Kiev, pp. 117–121.

(2002) Funkstii I vyrazennost'soctial'noi identichnosti: problemy vzaemozvyazku [Functions and salience of social identity: Problems of interrelations]. *Aktual'ni problemu psyhologii* [Topical problems of psychology], *3*, Kiev, pp. 87–91.

(2001) Identichnost' yak systema: struktura I smuslovoi zmist elementiv [Identity as a system: Structure and meaning of elements]. *Problemy zagal'noi ta pedagogichnoi psihologii* [The problem of general and pedagogic psychology], *7*, Kiev, pp. 118–124.

(2001) Kross-culturnaya adaptastiya [Cross-cultural adaptation]. Material for training, Simferopol, 72pp.

(2001) Identichnost' i tolerantnost' [Identity and tolerance]. Material for training, Simferopol, 44pp.

(2001) Mezhethniccheskaya adaptacia I ethnichaskie stereotypy: problemy vzaimosvyazi [Interethnic adaptation and ethnic stereotypes: The problems of interconnection]. *Nauka i Osvita* [Science and education], *3*, Odessa, pp. 59–64.

(2001) Identichnost' i tolerantnost': na putyah formirovaniya kul'tury mira v Krymu [Identity and tolerance: On the ways of peace building in Crimea]. In K. V. Korostelina, O. A. Gabrielyan, and A. D. Shorkin (Eds.), *Mezhethnicheskoe soglasie v Krymu: puti dostizeniya* [Interethnic coexistence in Crimea: The ways of achievement], pp. 248–259. Simferopol: Dolya.

(2001) Problemy mezhethnicheskoi adaptatsii [The problems of ethnic adaptation]. C. V. Korostelina, O. A. Gabrielyan, and A. D. Shorkin (Eds.), *Mezhethnicheskoe soglasie v Krymu: puti dostizeniya* [Interethnic coexistence in Crimea: The ways of achievement], pp. 74–95. Simferopol: Dolya.

(2001) Problema vyvchennya struktury identichnostey yak chinika u prognozyvanni cochial'nogo rozvitku syspilstva [Problem of research of identities' structure as index in prognosis of social development]. *Problemy zagal'noi ta pedagogichnoi psihologii* [The problem of general and pedagogic psychology], *1*, Kiev, pp. 60–65.

(2001) Osobennosti motivastiono-potrebnostnoi sfery kak determinanta mezhetnicheskogo vzaimodeistviya [The peculiarities of motives and need as a determinant of interethnic relations]. *Sbirnik naukovih prast' institutu im. Dragomanova: psyhologiya* [Scientific paper of Dragomanov's Institute: Psychology], *12*, Kiev, pp.70–76.

(2001) Ethnicheskie stereotypy kak determinanta otsenki ethicheskih konflictov (vzglyad iz Kryma na Kosovo) [Ethnic stereotypes as a determinant of estimation of ethnic conflict (the view from the Crimea to Kosovo)]. *Practychna psyhologiya ta social'na robota* [Applied psychology and social work], *2*, Kiev, pp.32–37.

(2001) Kulturnye razmernosti i kross-kul'turnaya adaptachiya [Cultural dimensions and cross-cultural adaptation]. *Zhurnal practicheskogo psihologa* [Journal of the practicing psychologist], *7*, Kiev, pp.118–138.

(2000) Vyrachennost' social'noy identichnosti [The problems of social identity salience]. *Problemy zagal'noi ta pedagogichnoi psihologii* [The problem of general and pedagogic psychology], *6*, Kiev, pp. 59–67.

(2000) Mezethnicheskaya adaptaciya i ethnicheskie stereotypy: problema vsaimosvyazi [Interethnic adaptation and stereotypes: The problem of interrelations]. *Nauka i Osvita* [Science and education], *6*, Odessa, pp. 56–74.

(2000) Processy stereotipzatsii u krumsko-tatarskogo i slavyanskogo naseleniya [The processes of stereotypization of Crimean Tatars and Slavs]. *Problemy zagal'noi ta pedagogichnoi psihologii* [The problem of general and pedagogic psychology), *5*, Kiev, pp. 112–119.

(2000) Ethnicheskoe vsaimodeistvie v Krymu: analis modelei situachiy [Ethnic relations in Crimea: The analyses of models of situations]. *Nauka i Osvita* [Science and education], *5*, Odessa, pp. 31–35.

(1999) Etnicheskie osobennosti vospriayatiya studentov [The ethnic peculiarities of a student's perception]. *Psihologicheskie i pedagogicheskie aspecti prepodavaniya v VUZe* [Psychological and pedagogical aspects of reading in universities], *4*, Simferopol, pp. 27–29.

(1999) Problemy issledovaniya etnicheskih osobennostey formirivaniya lichnosti pebenka. [The problems of researches of ethnical peculiarities of firming of a child]. Material for the scientific conference "Kostukovskie chteniya" [The Kostuk's reading], Kiev, pp.161–167.

(1999) Etnicheskie osobennosti potrebitel'skogo povedeniya [The ethnical peculiarities of consumer behavior]. Material for the scientific conference "Kostukovskie chteniya" [The Kostuk's reading], Kiev, pp.168–173.

(1999) Social'no-psihologicheskie korni ethniceskih problem [The social-psychological roots of ethnic problems]. *Zhurnal practicheskogo psihologa* [Journal of the practical psychologist], *5*, Kiev, pp. 109–133.

(1999) Social'no psihologicheskie osnovy ethnicheskih konflictov [The social-psychological reasons of ethnical conflict]. *Cul'tura narodov Prichernomor'ya* [Culture of the peoples of Black Sea area], *1*, Simferopol, pp. 67–91.

(1999) Modeli etniceskih situaciy i osobennosti activnosti [The models of ethnic situations and peculiarities of activity]. *Uchenye zapiski SGU* (The scientific notes of Simferopol State University), *4*, Simferopol, pp. 43–54.

(1999) Culturnye determinanty mezhetnicheskih otnosheniy [The cultural determinants of interethnic relations]. *Uchenye zapiski SGU* [The scientific notes of Simferopol State University], *5*, Simferopol, pp. 104–116.

(1999) Problemy social'no-psyhologiceskogo issledovaniya conflictov (The social-psychological problem of conflict]. *Region*, *4*, pp. 32–46.

(1999) Ethnicheskaya identichnost' i affilyatsiya [Ethnic identity and affiliation]. *Uchenye zapiski TEI* [The scientific notes of Tavrichesky Ecological Institute], Simferopol, 1999, pp. 84–96.

CPSIA information can be obtained at www.ICGtesting.com
Printed in the USA
LVOW132251270812

296223LV00004B/23/P